AF380613

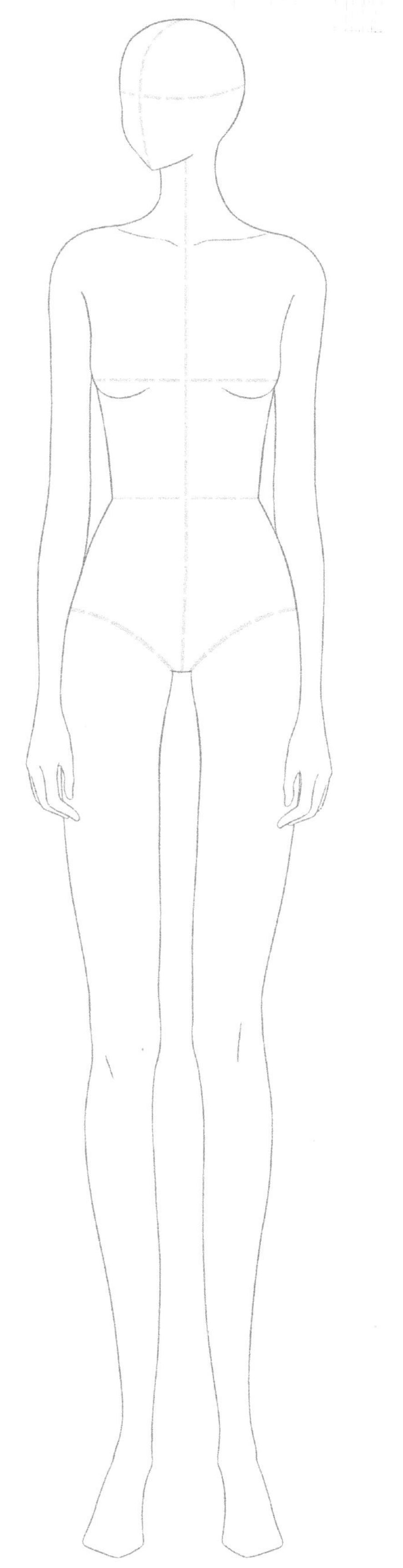

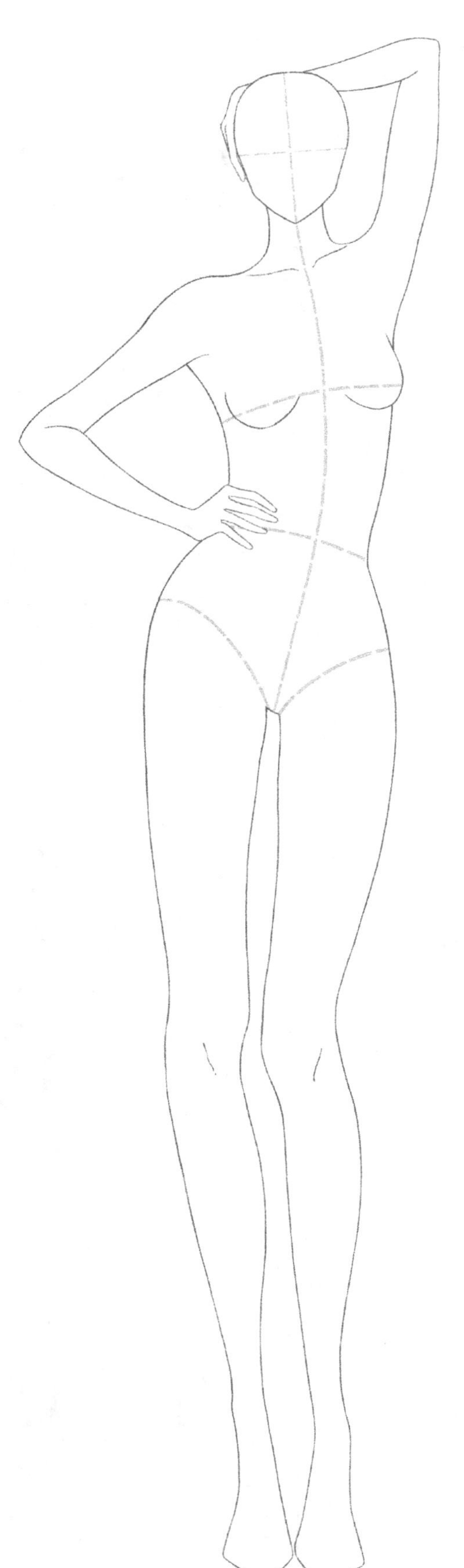
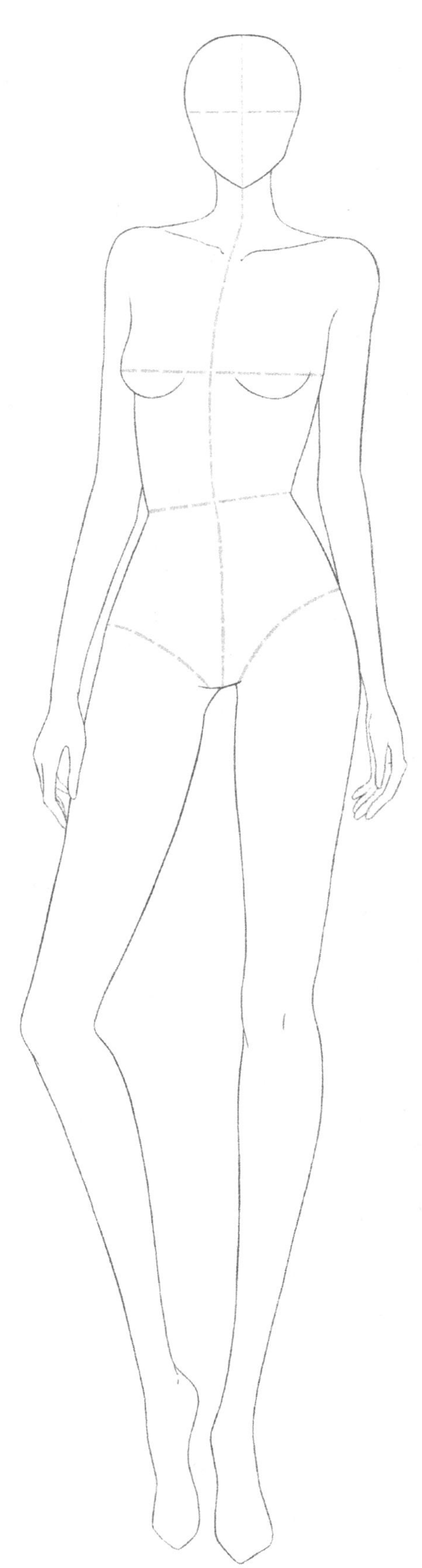

BYE
BYE
PAPER

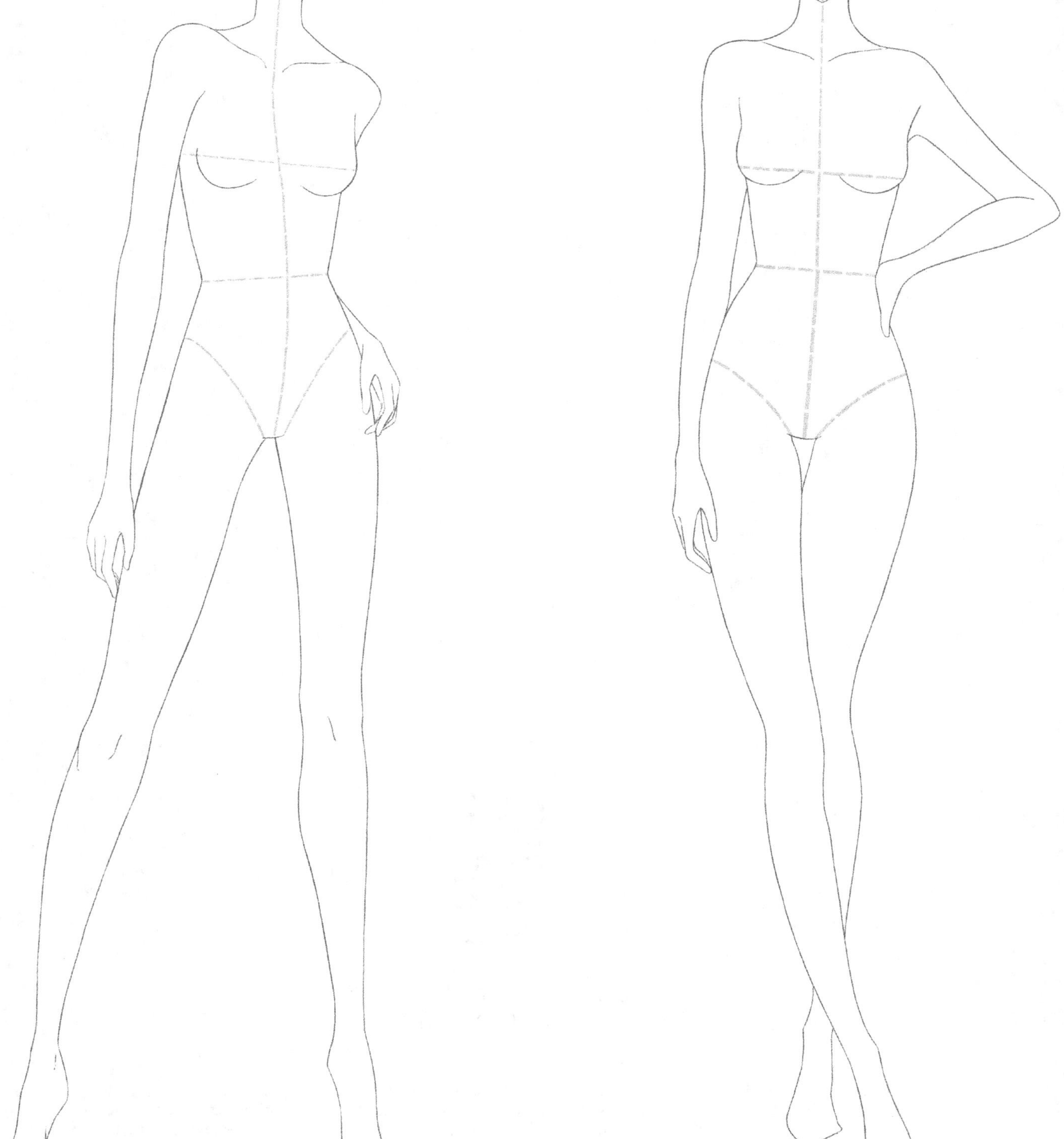

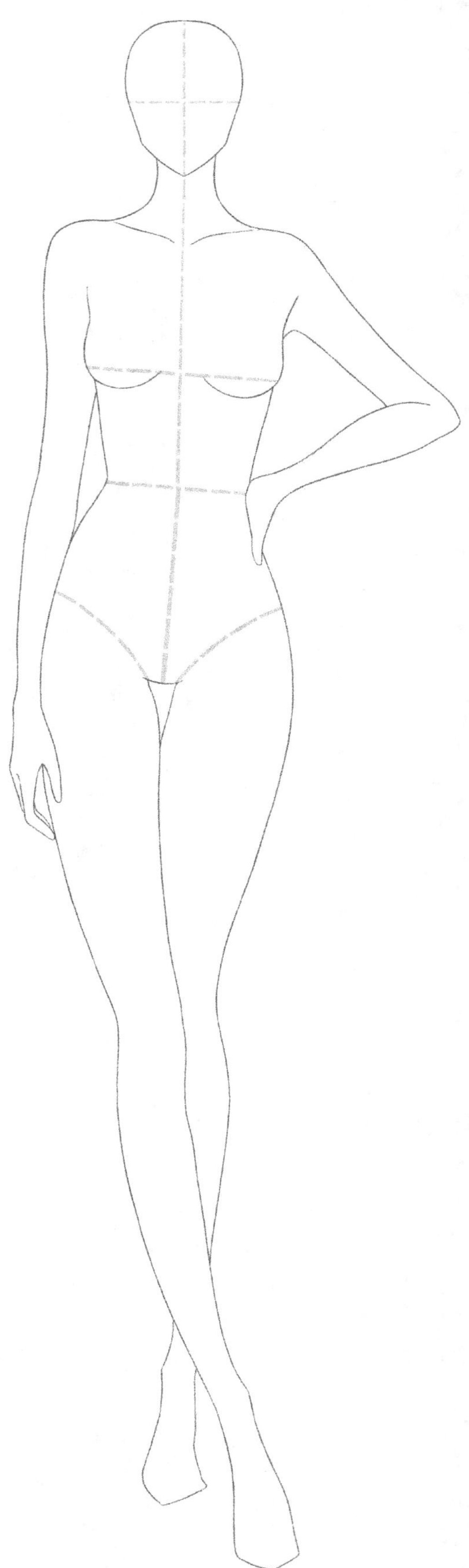

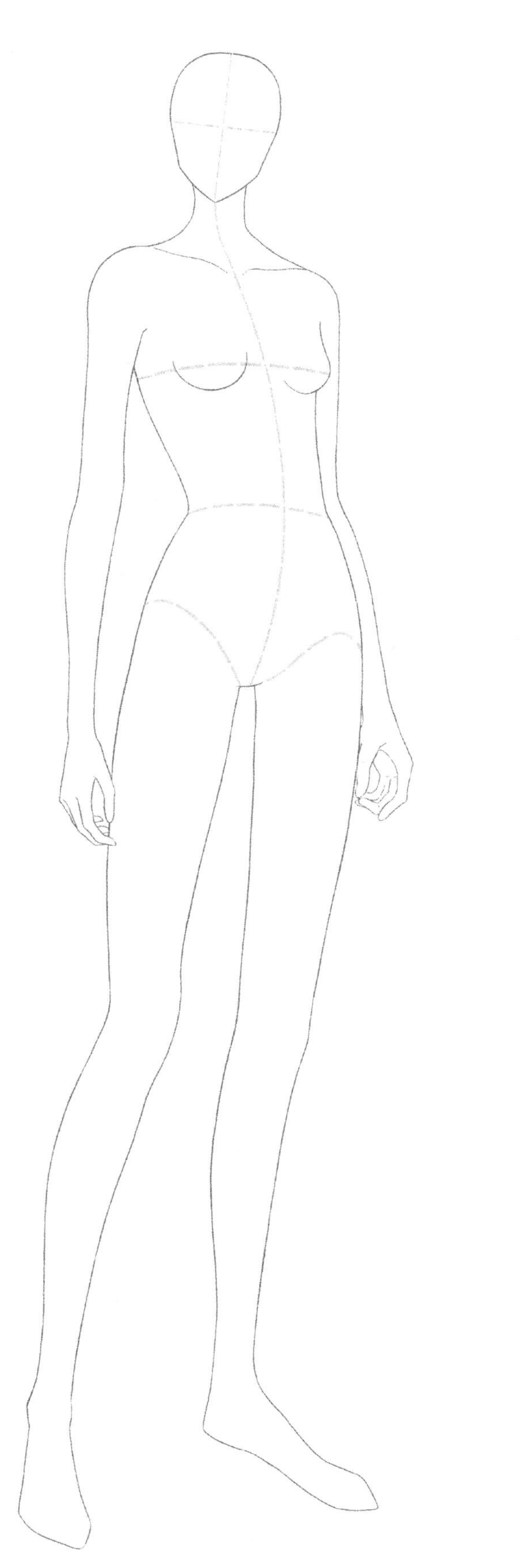
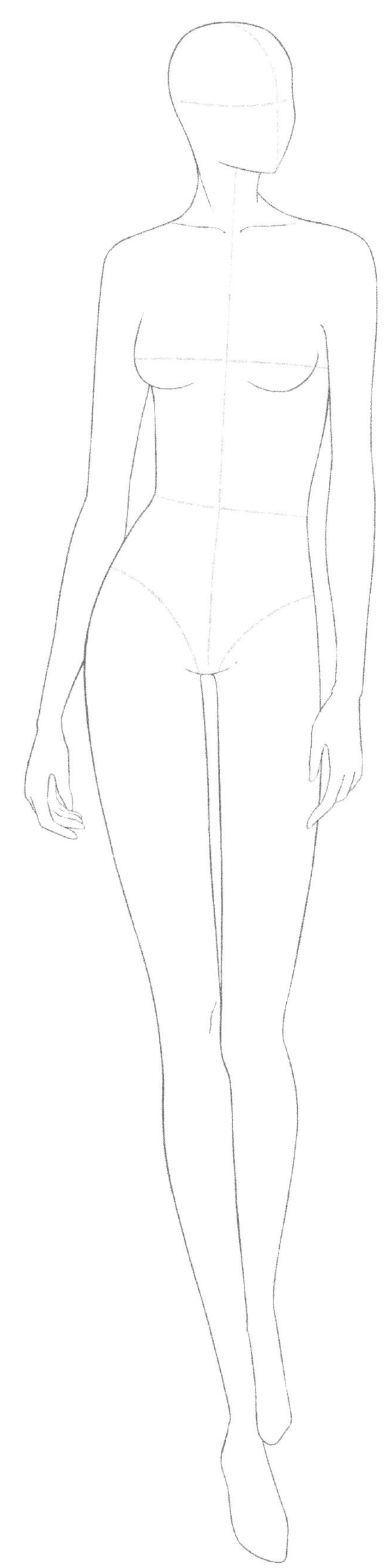

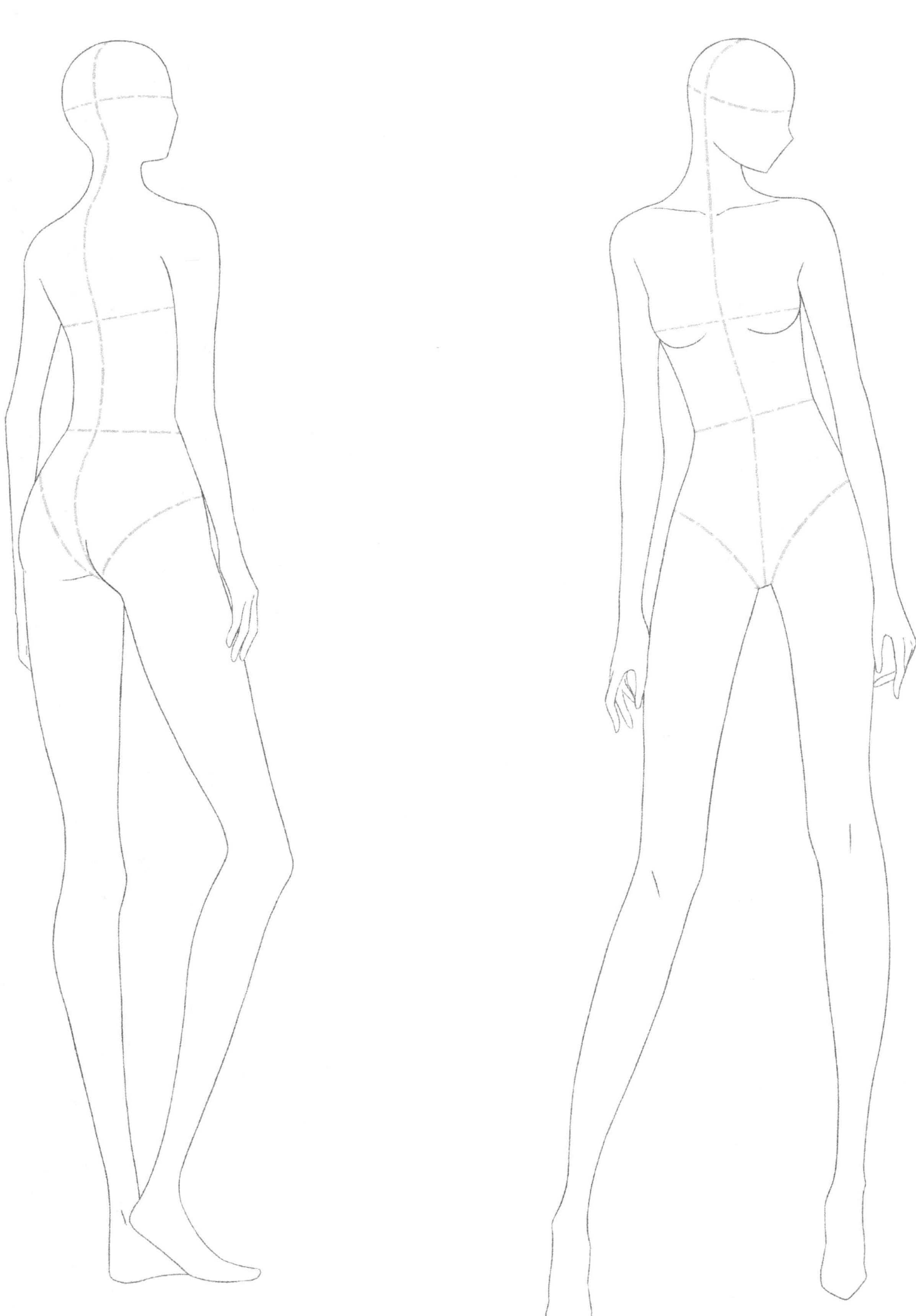

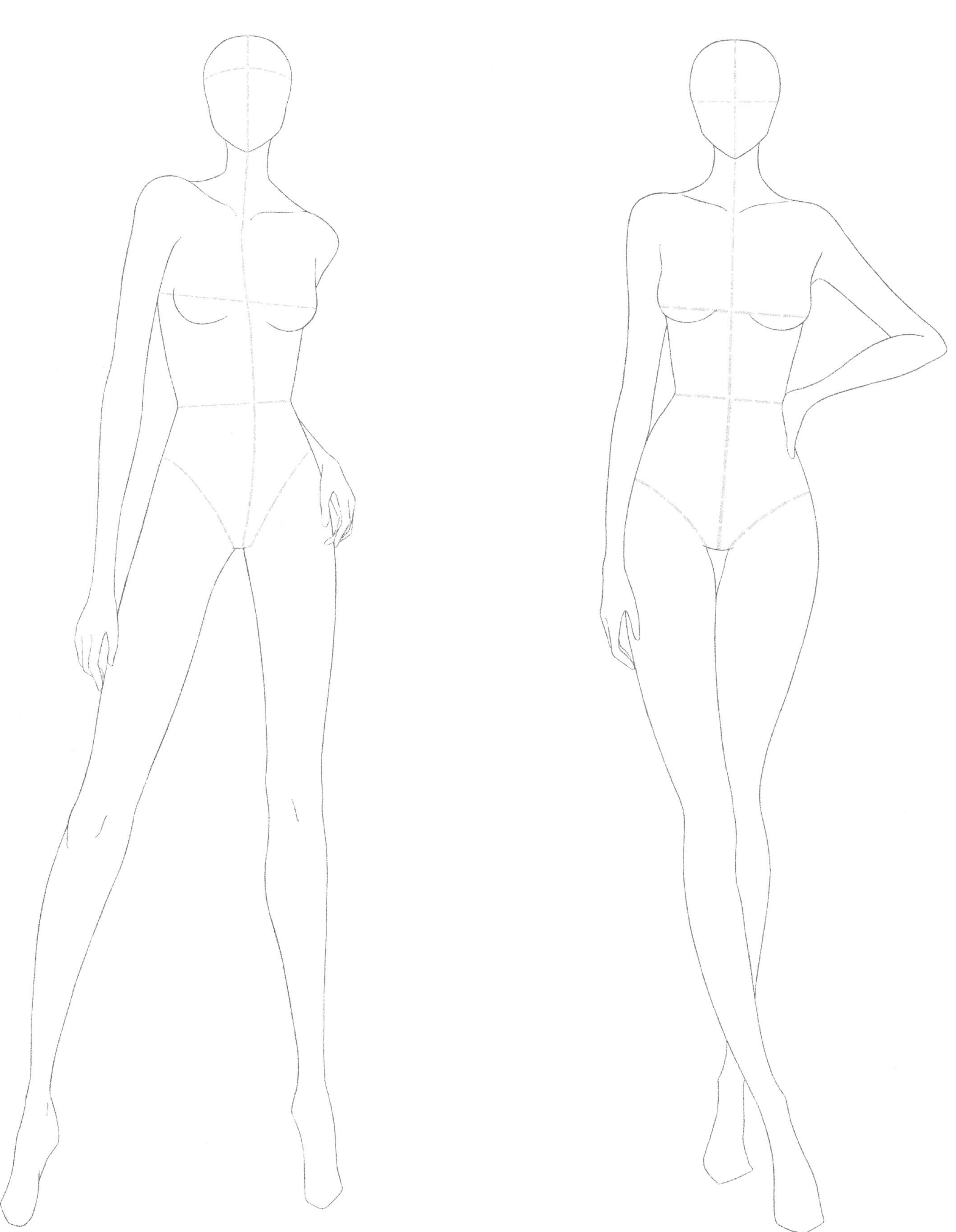

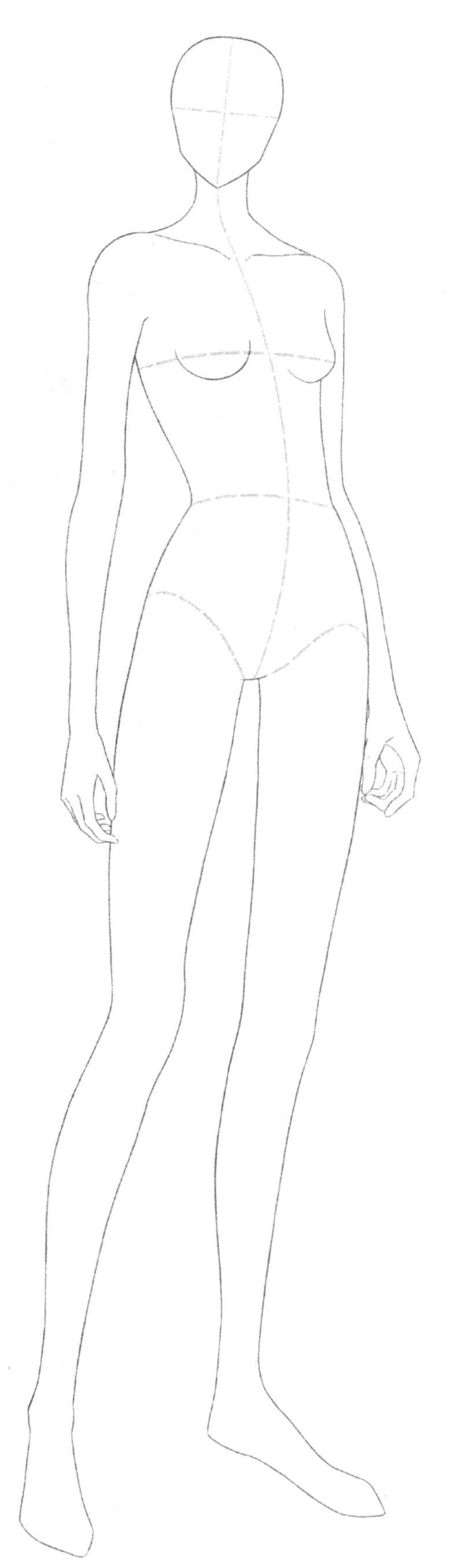
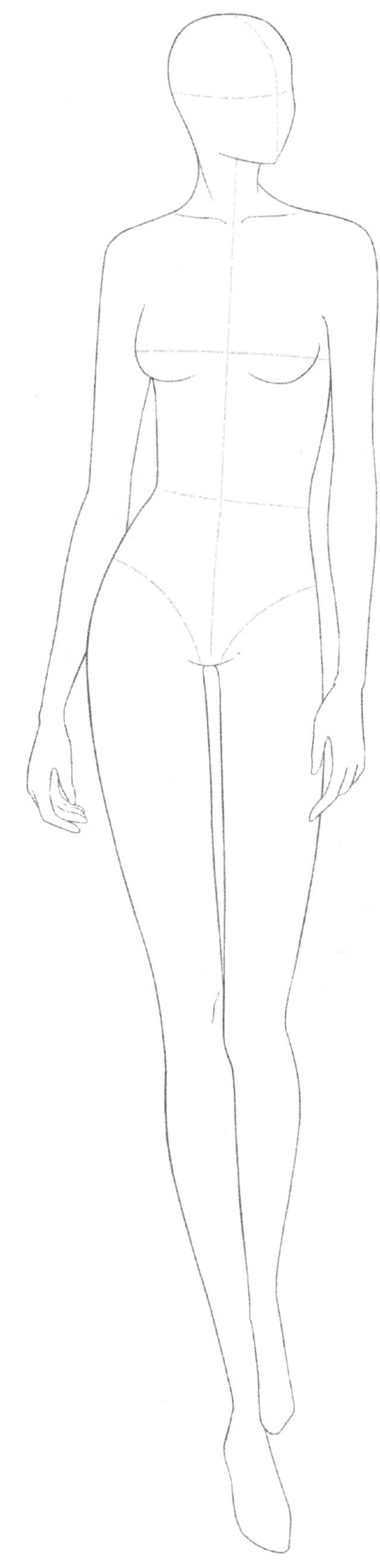

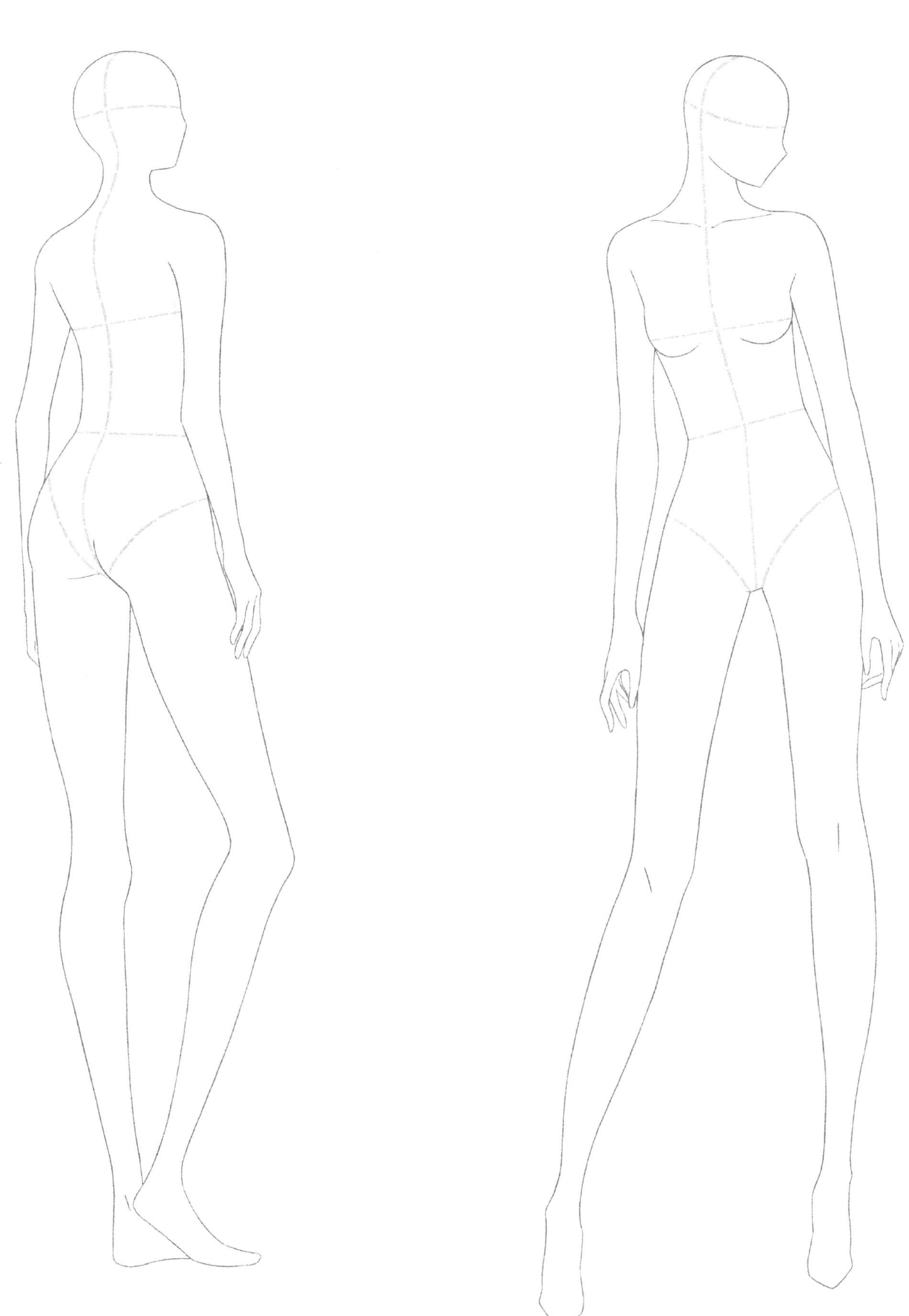

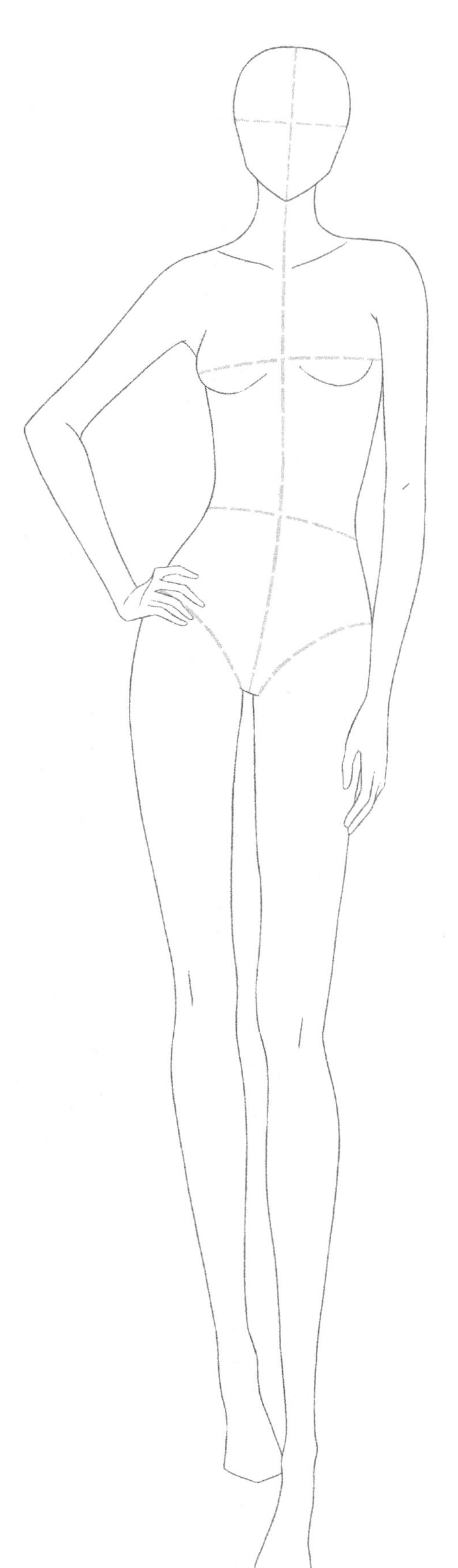
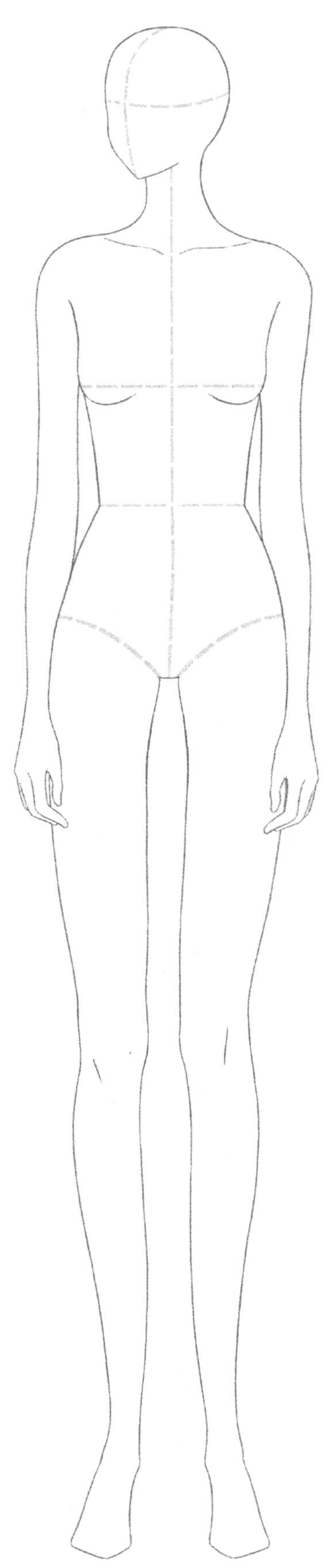

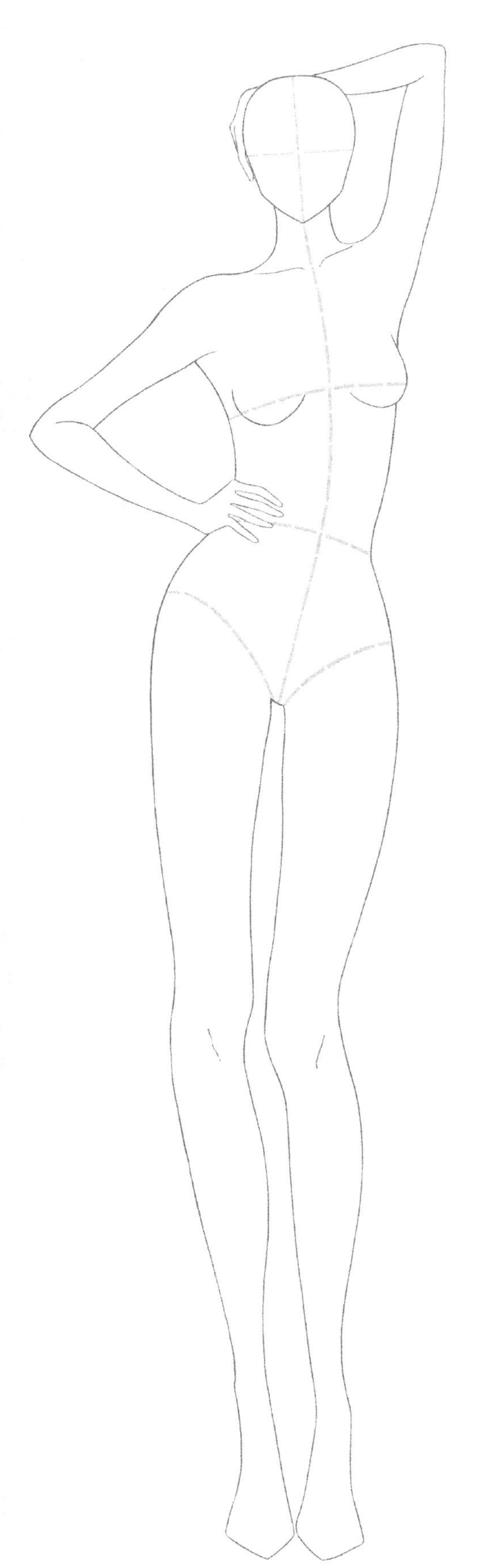
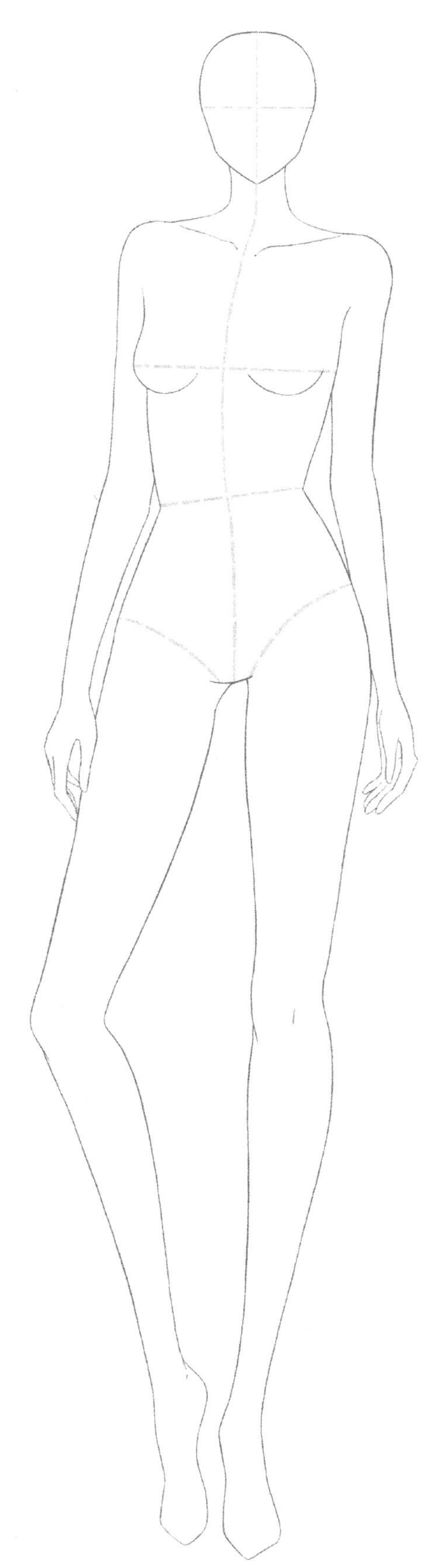

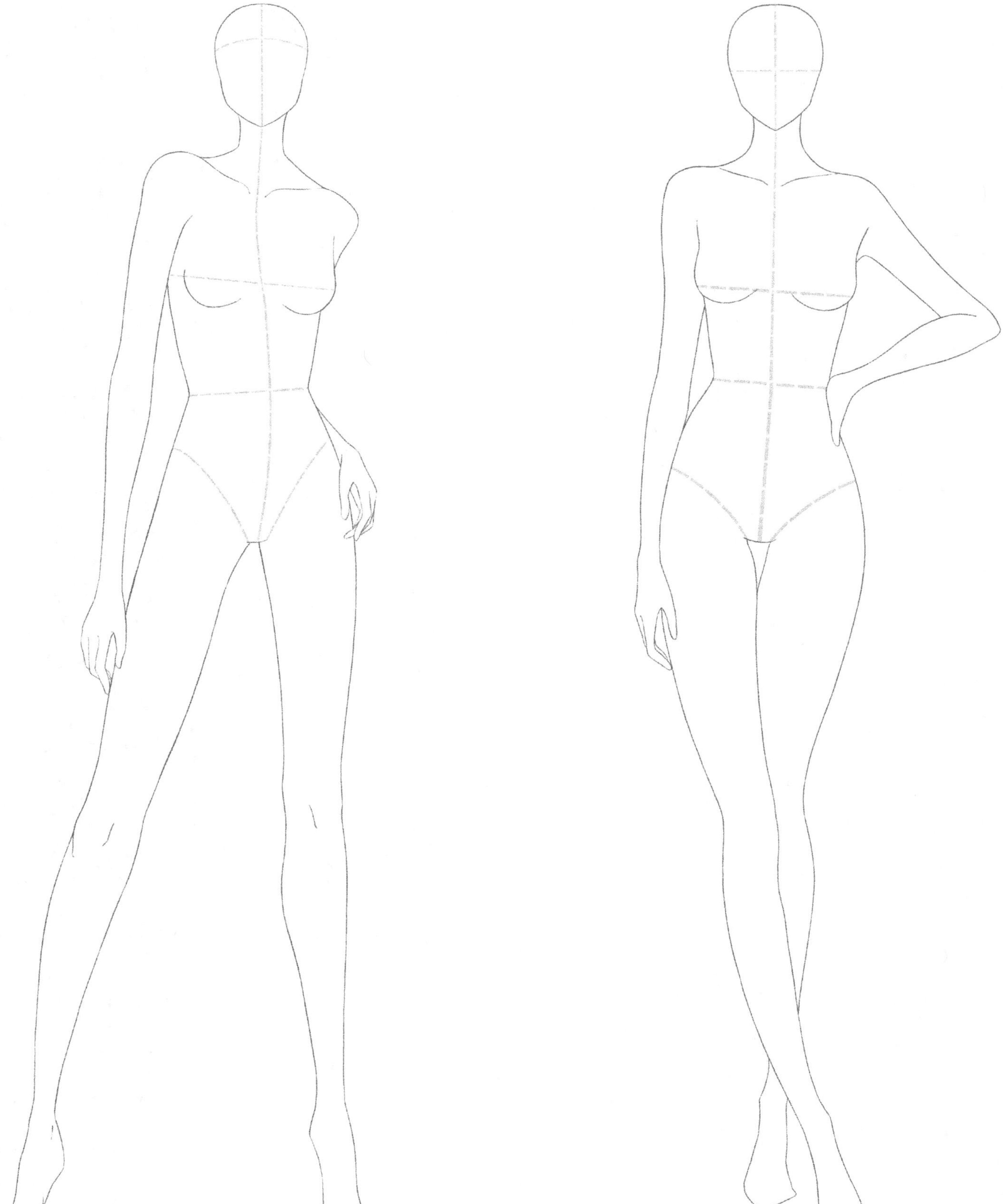

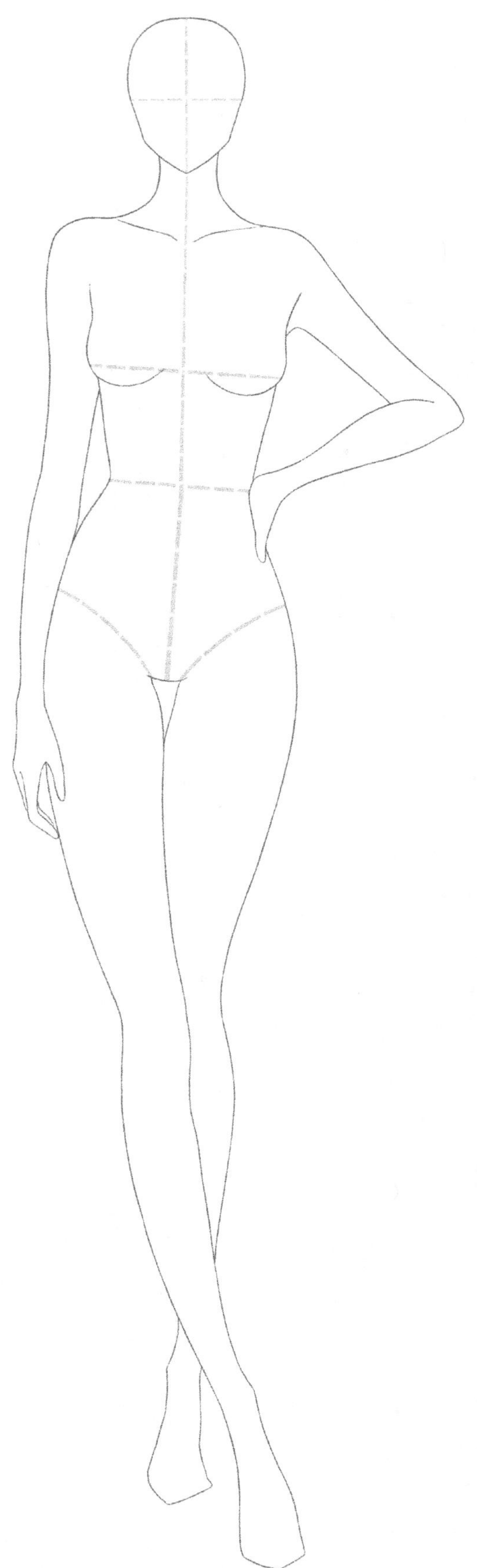

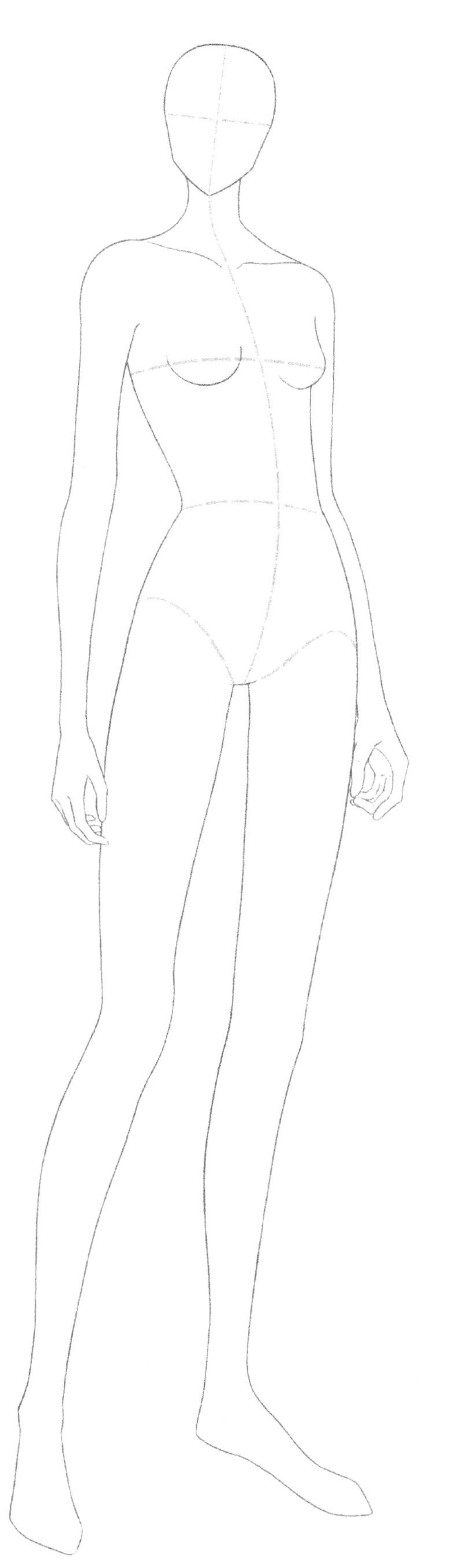
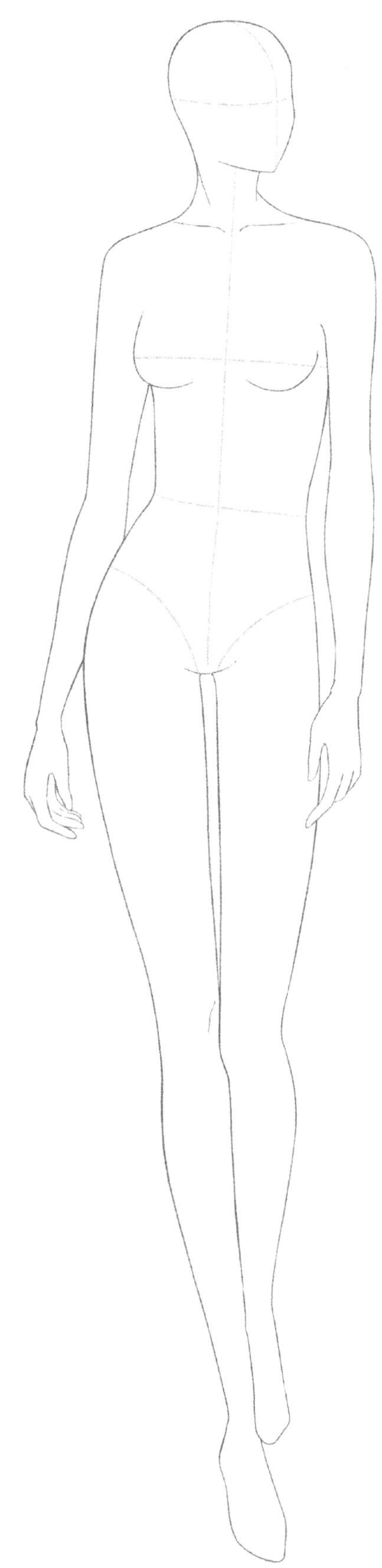

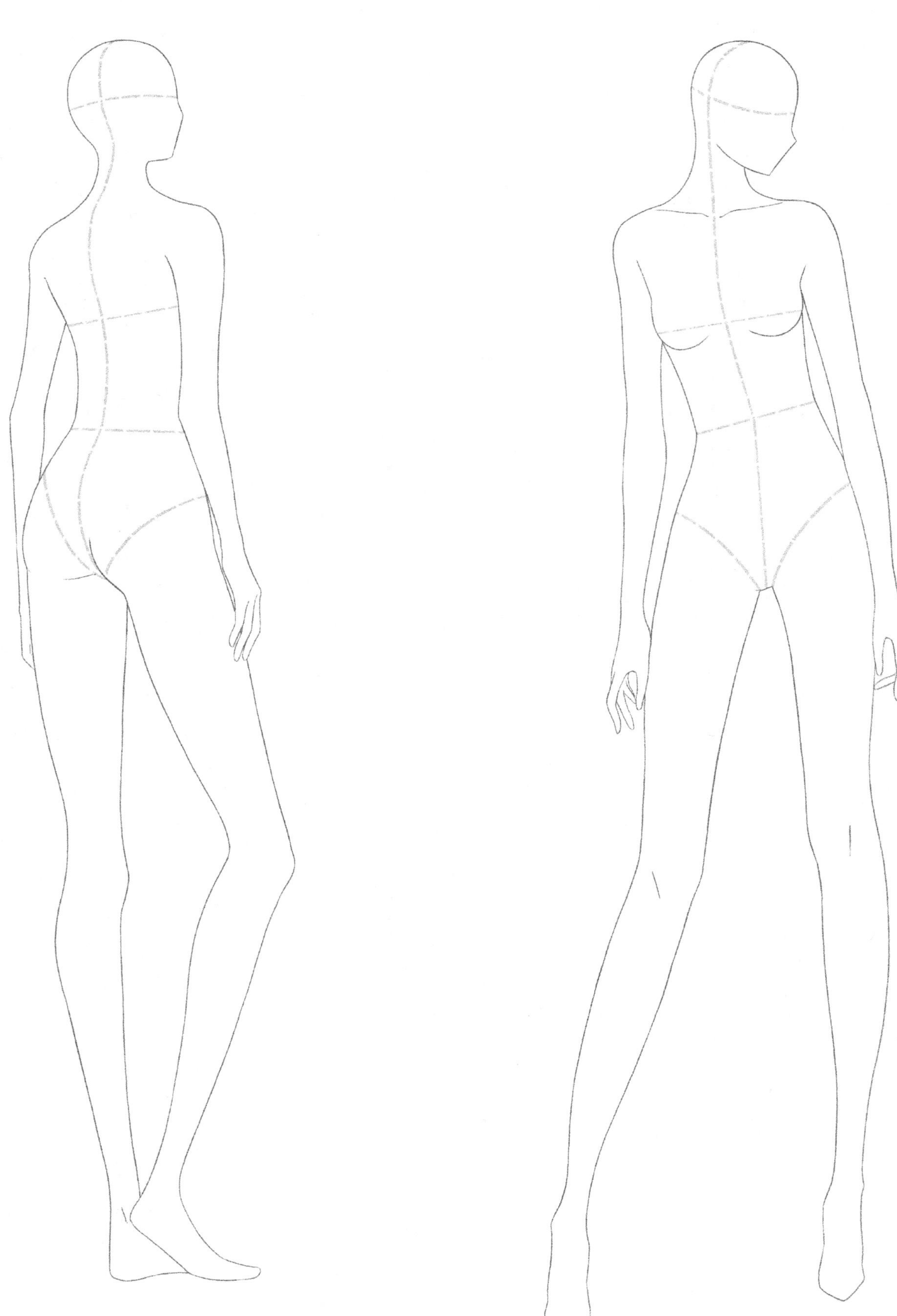

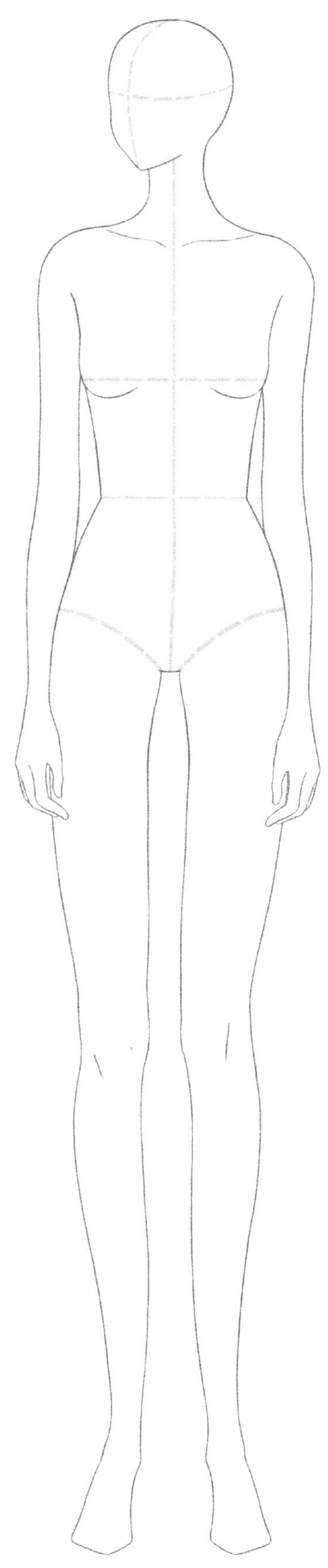

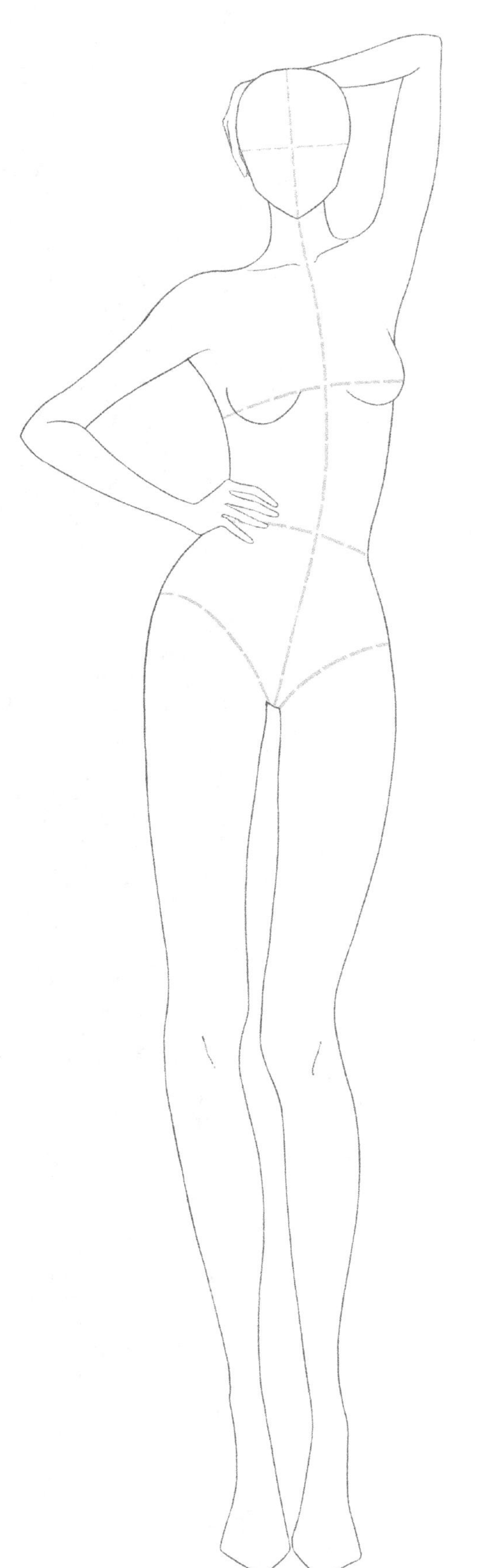
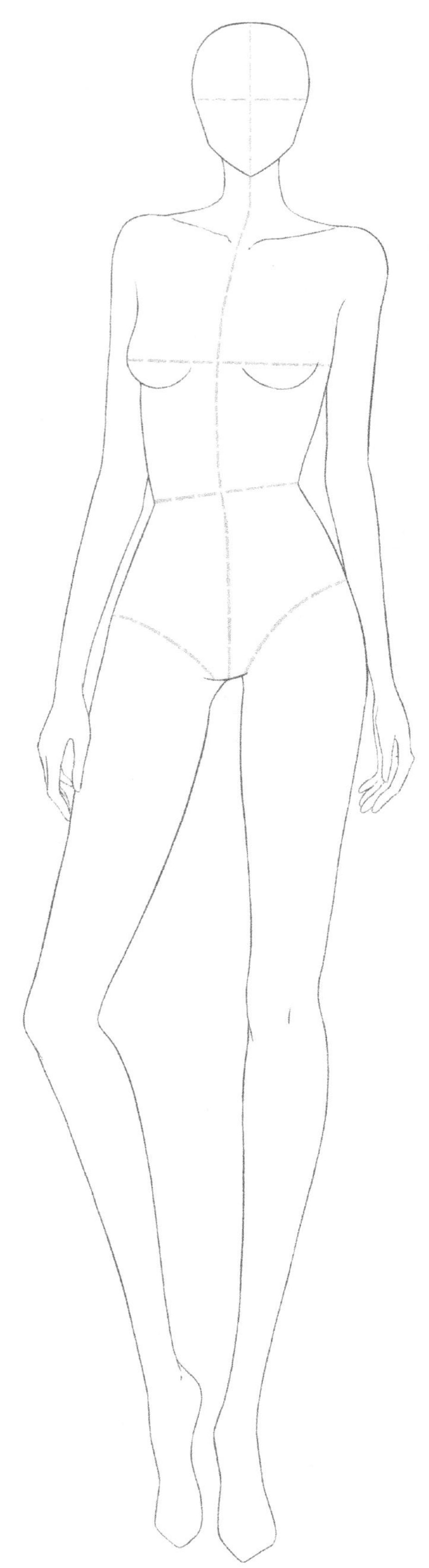

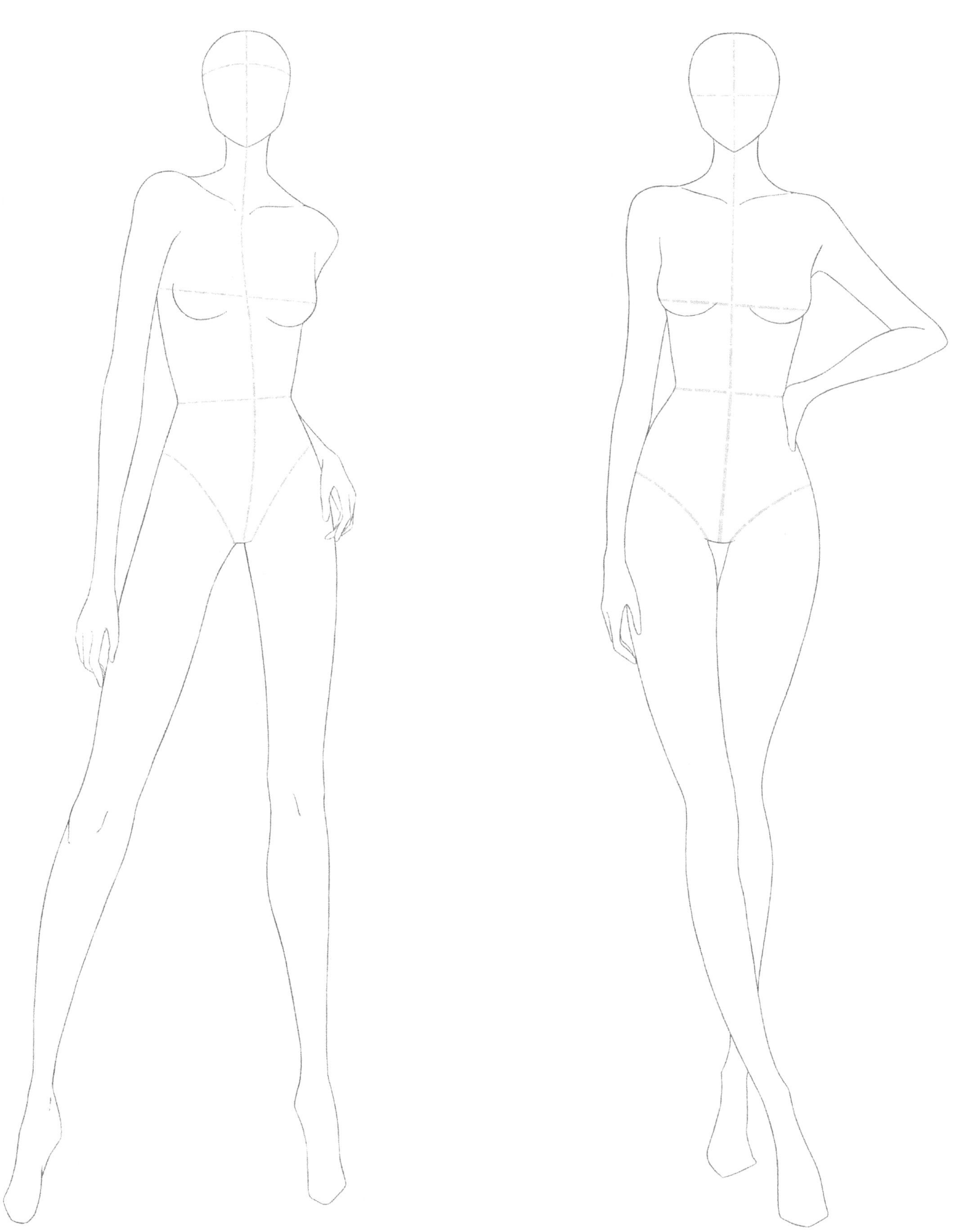

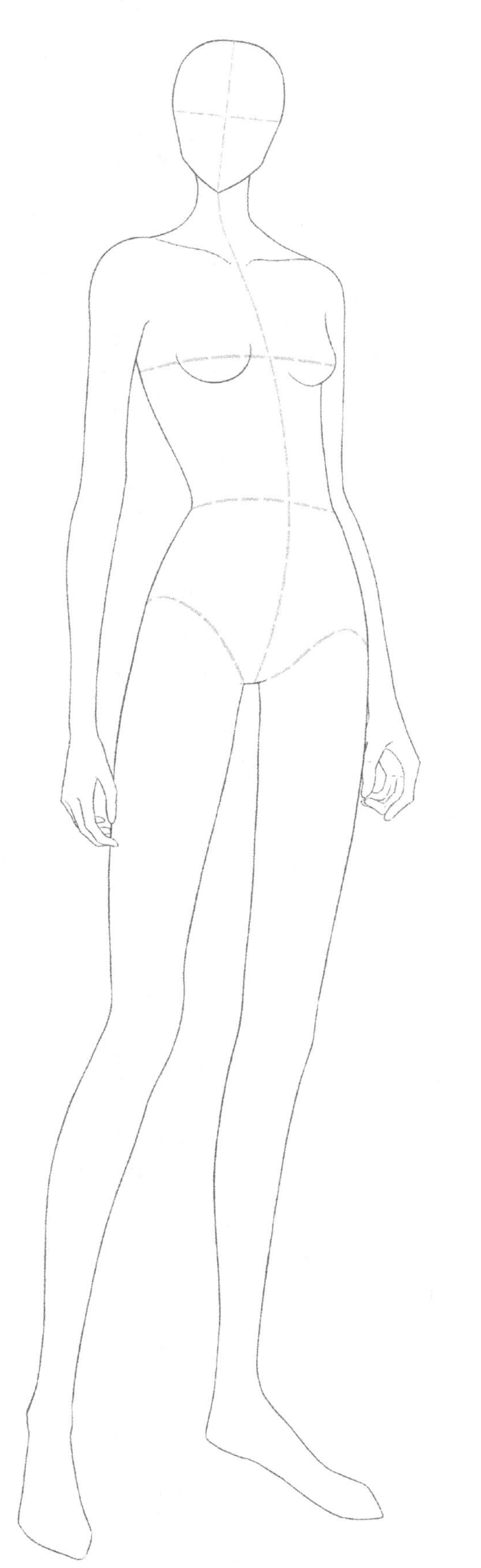
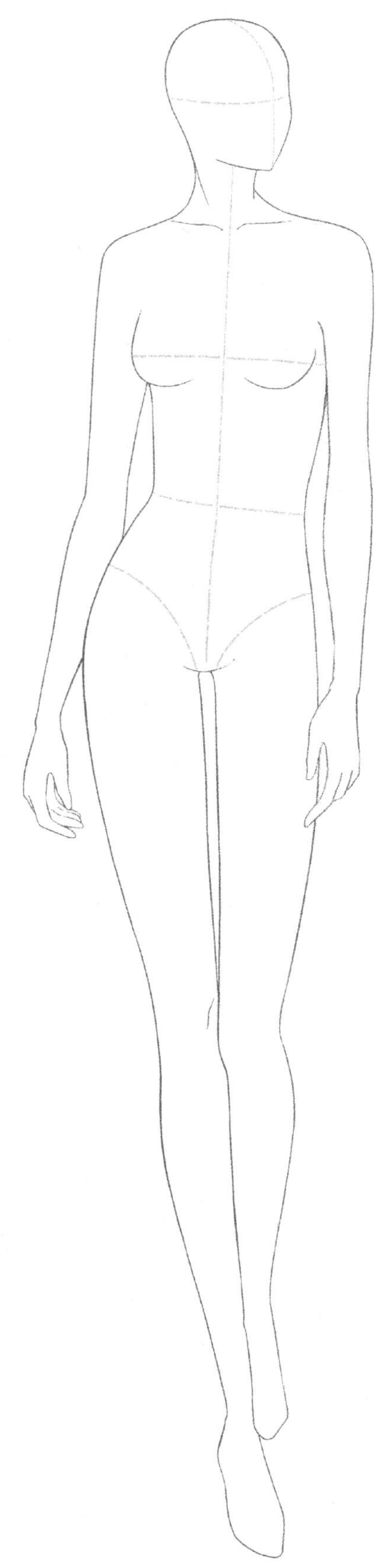

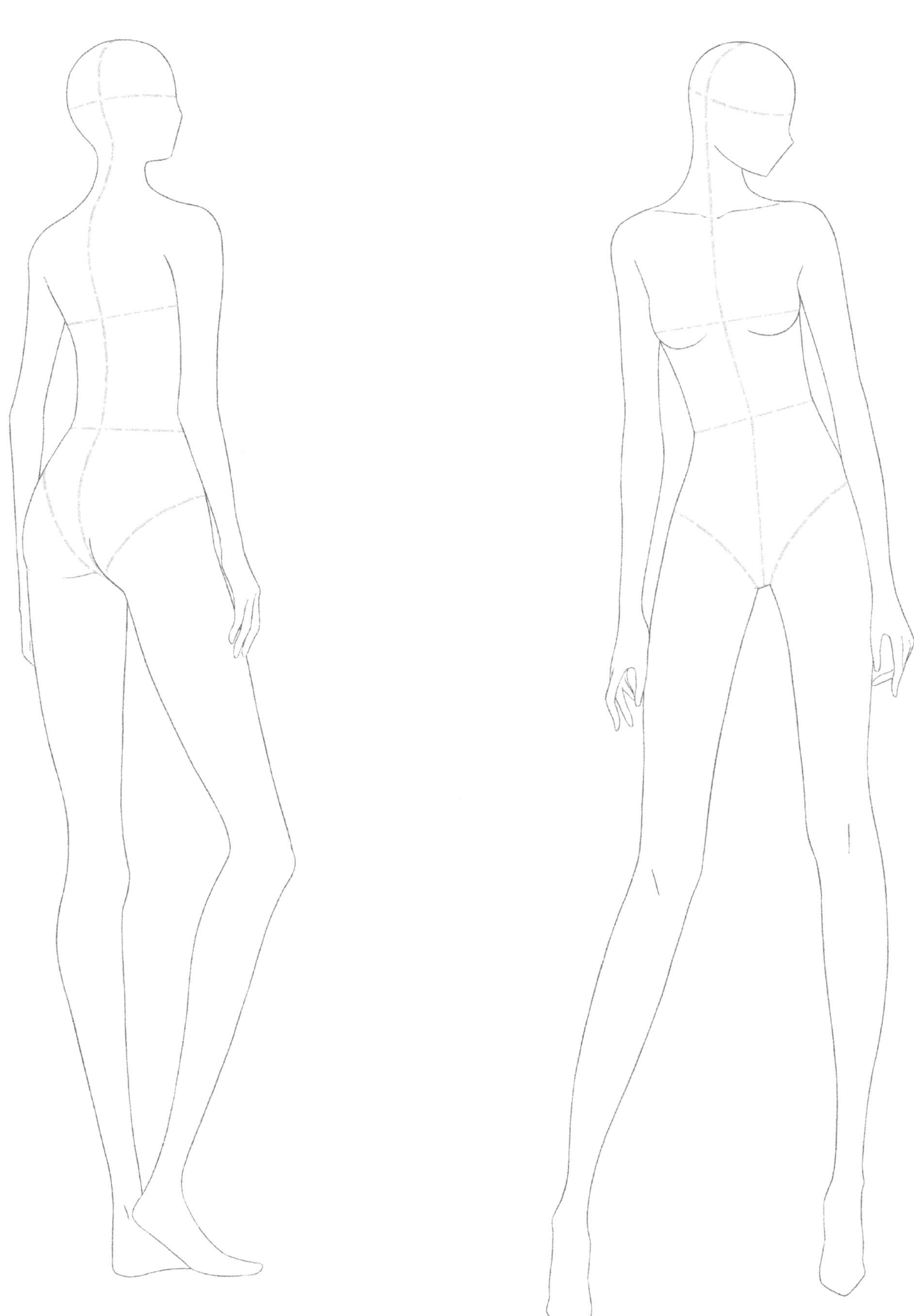

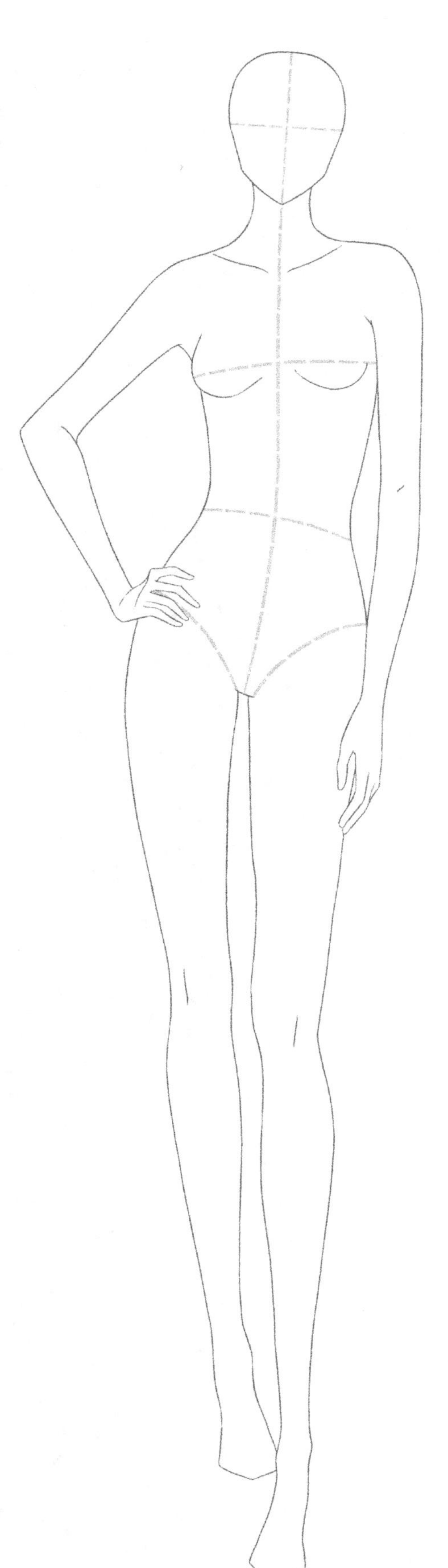
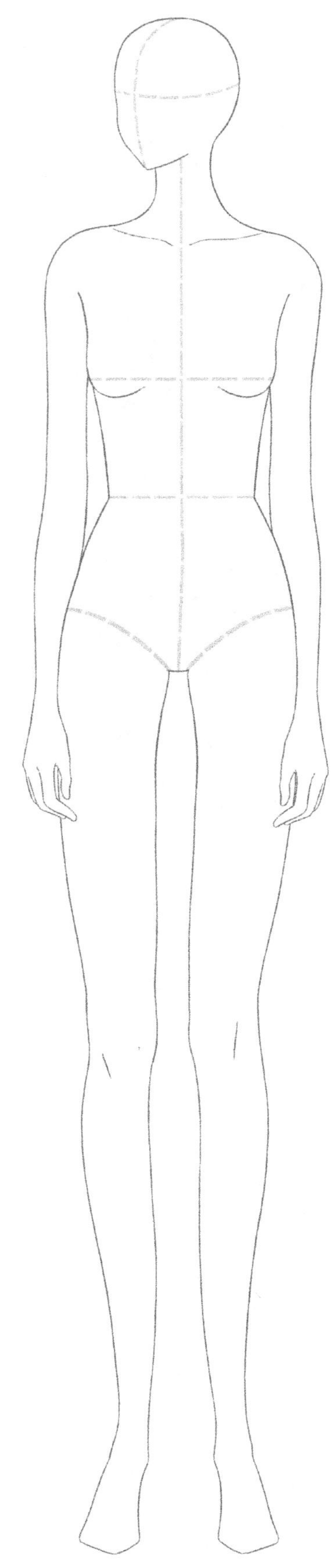

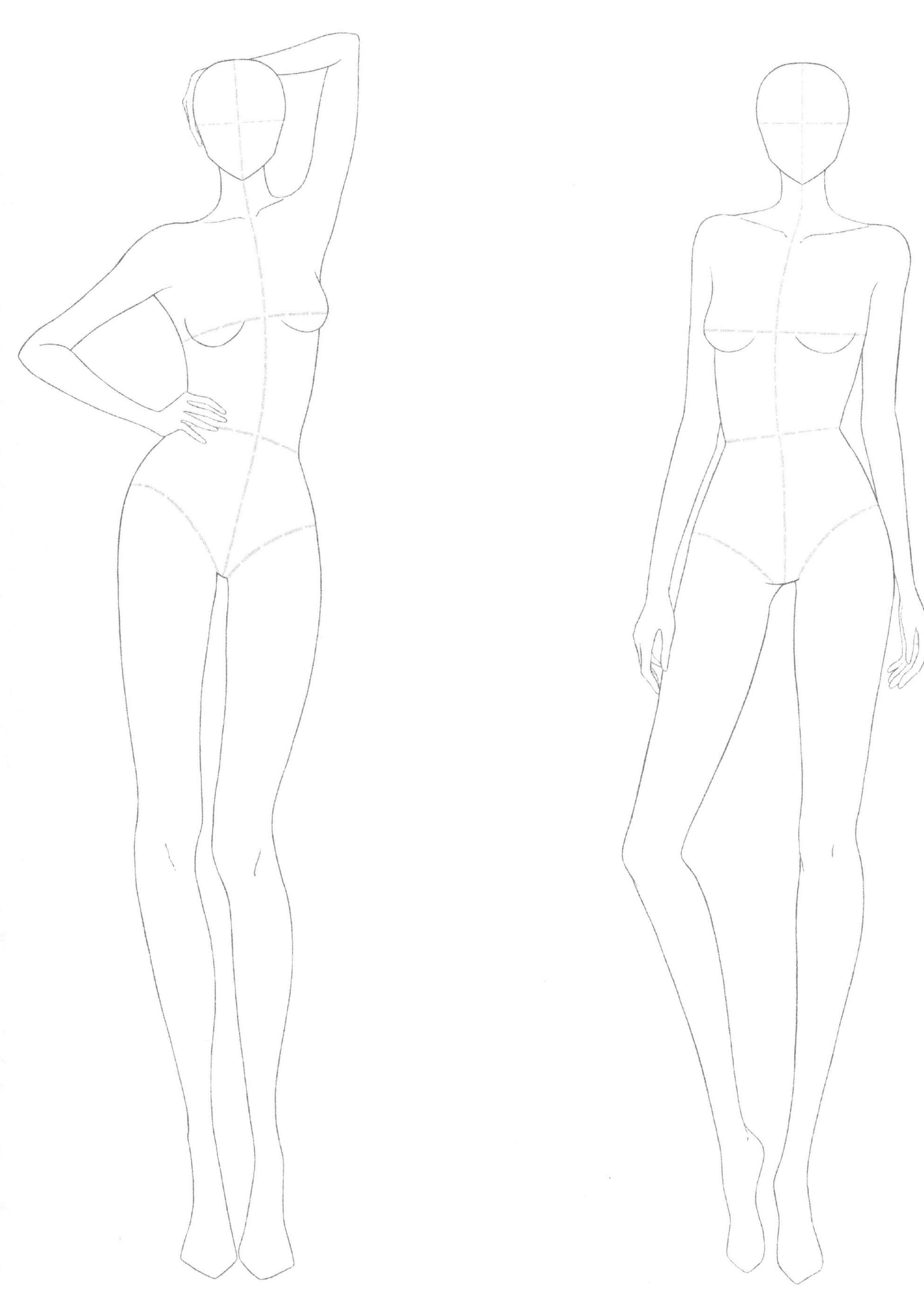

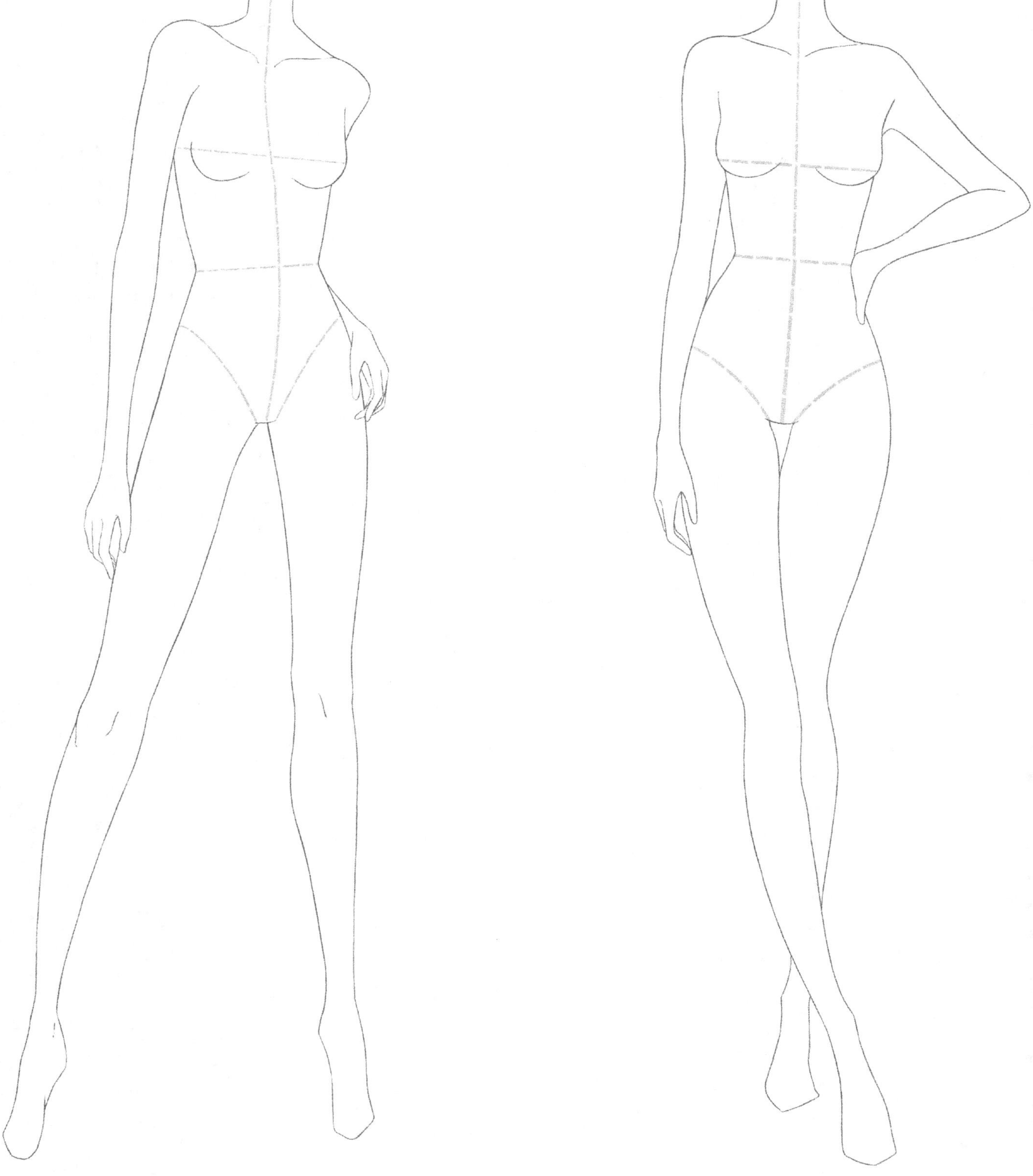

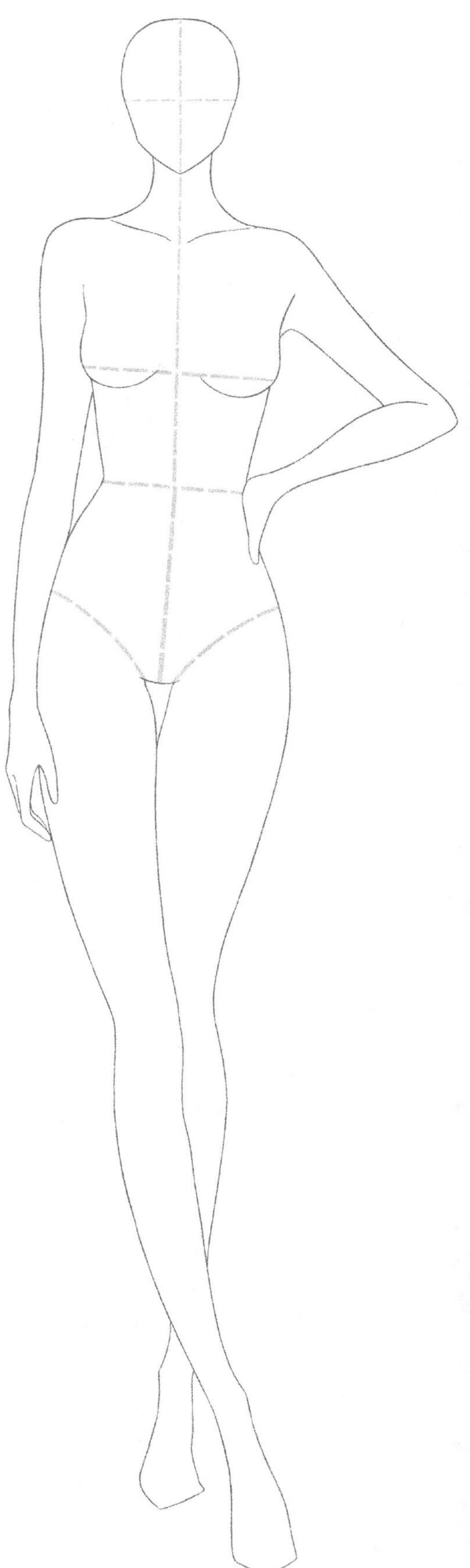

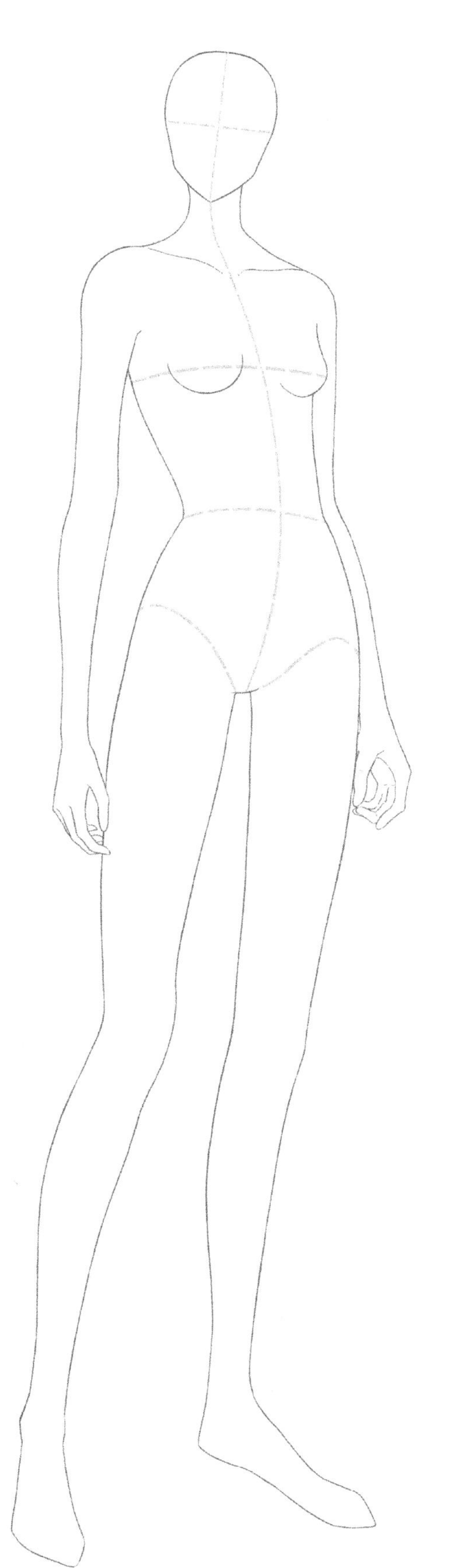
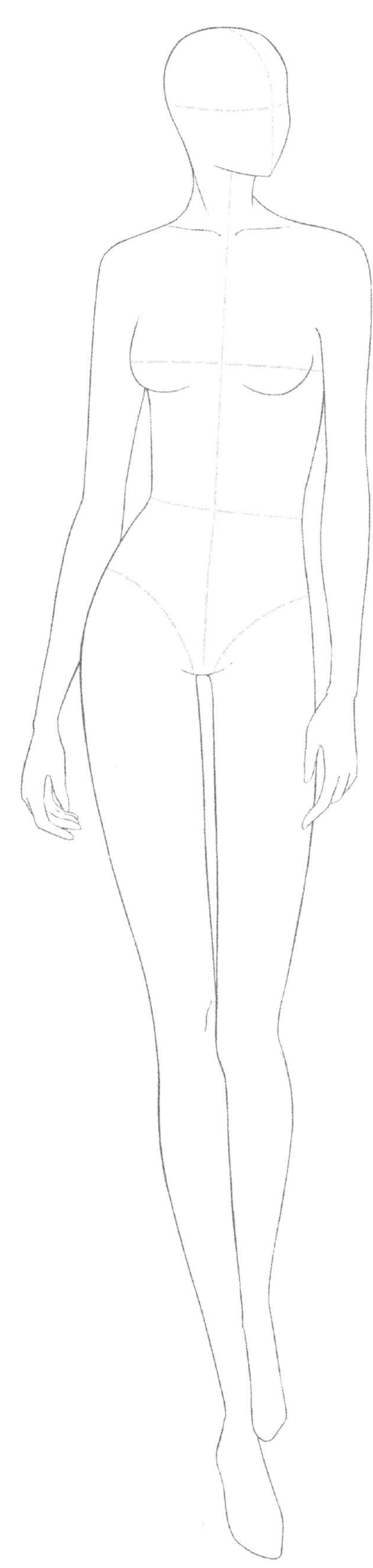

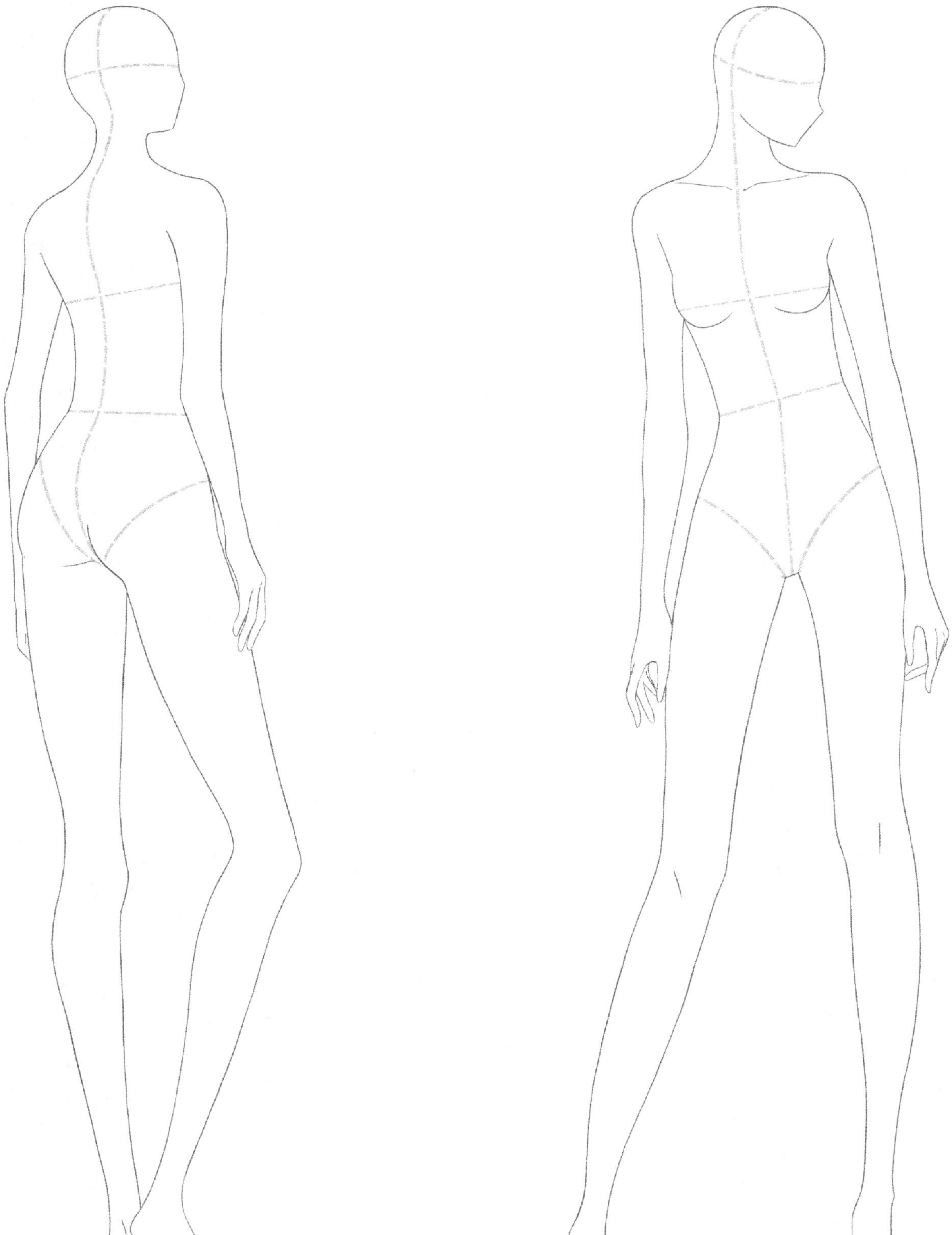

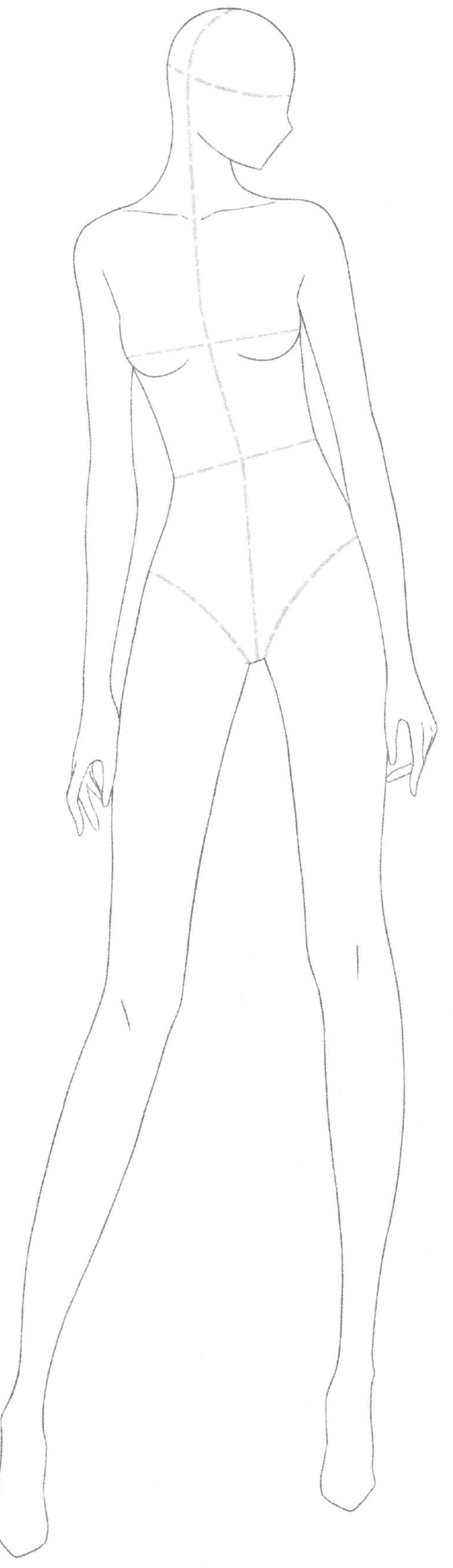

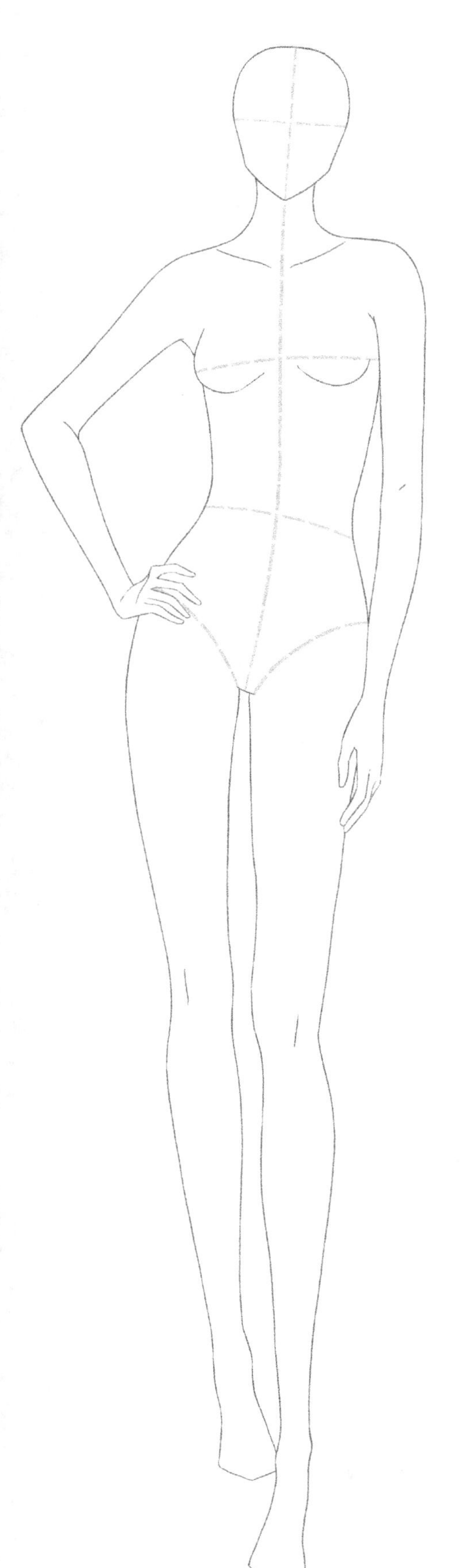
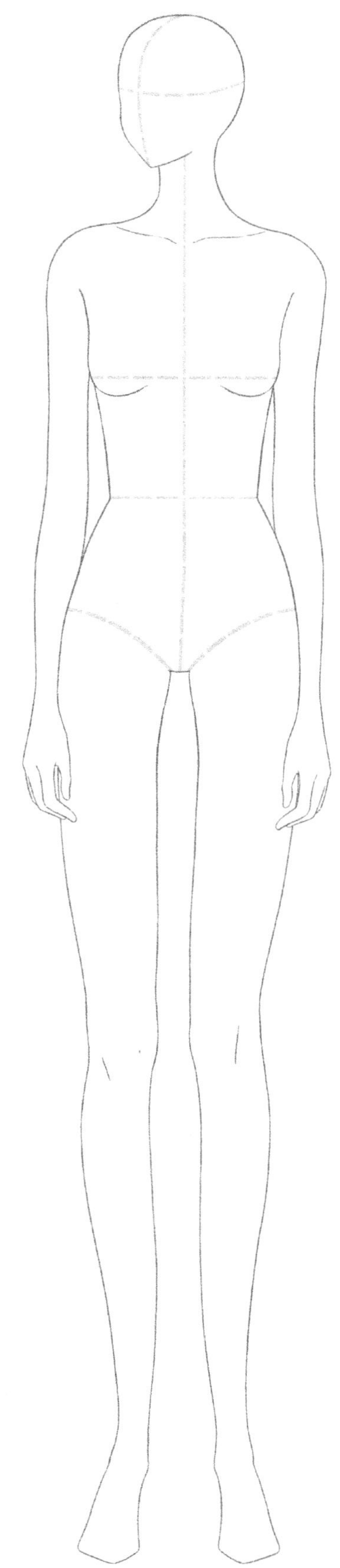

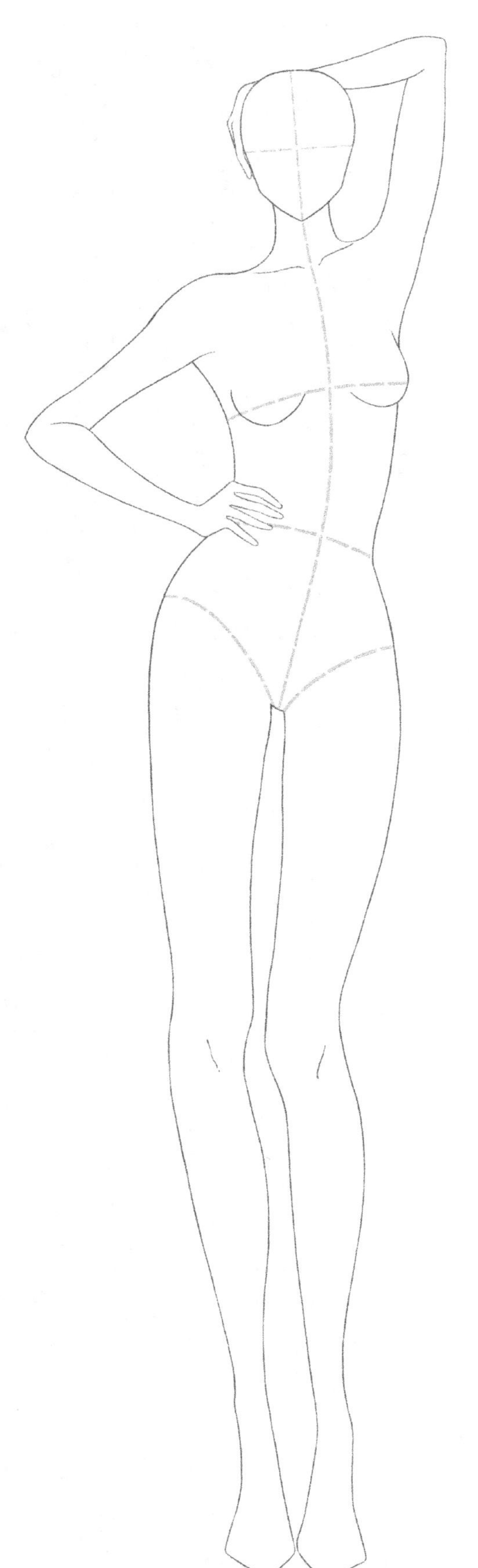
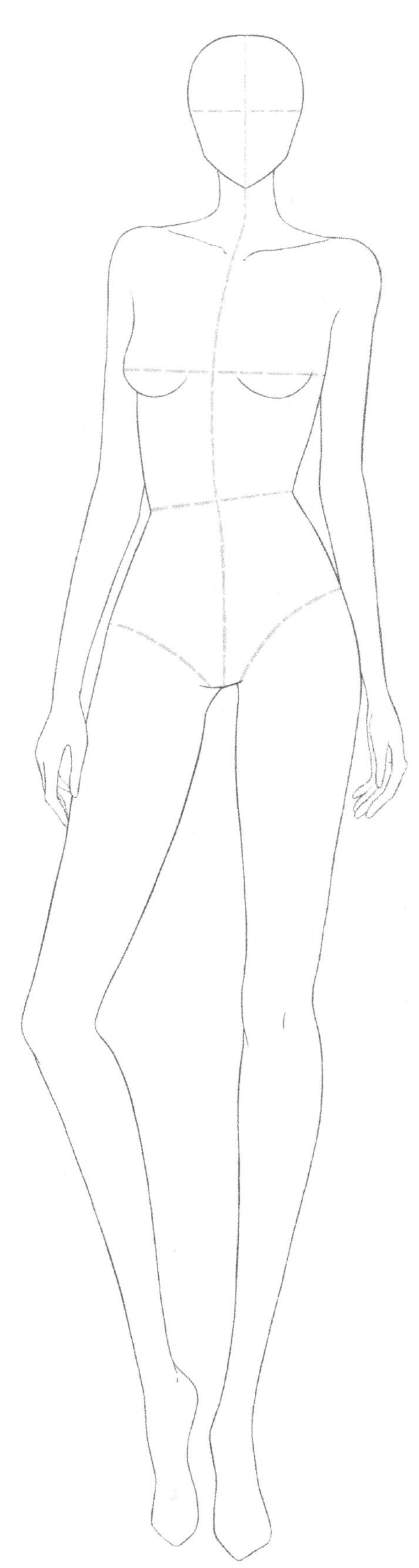

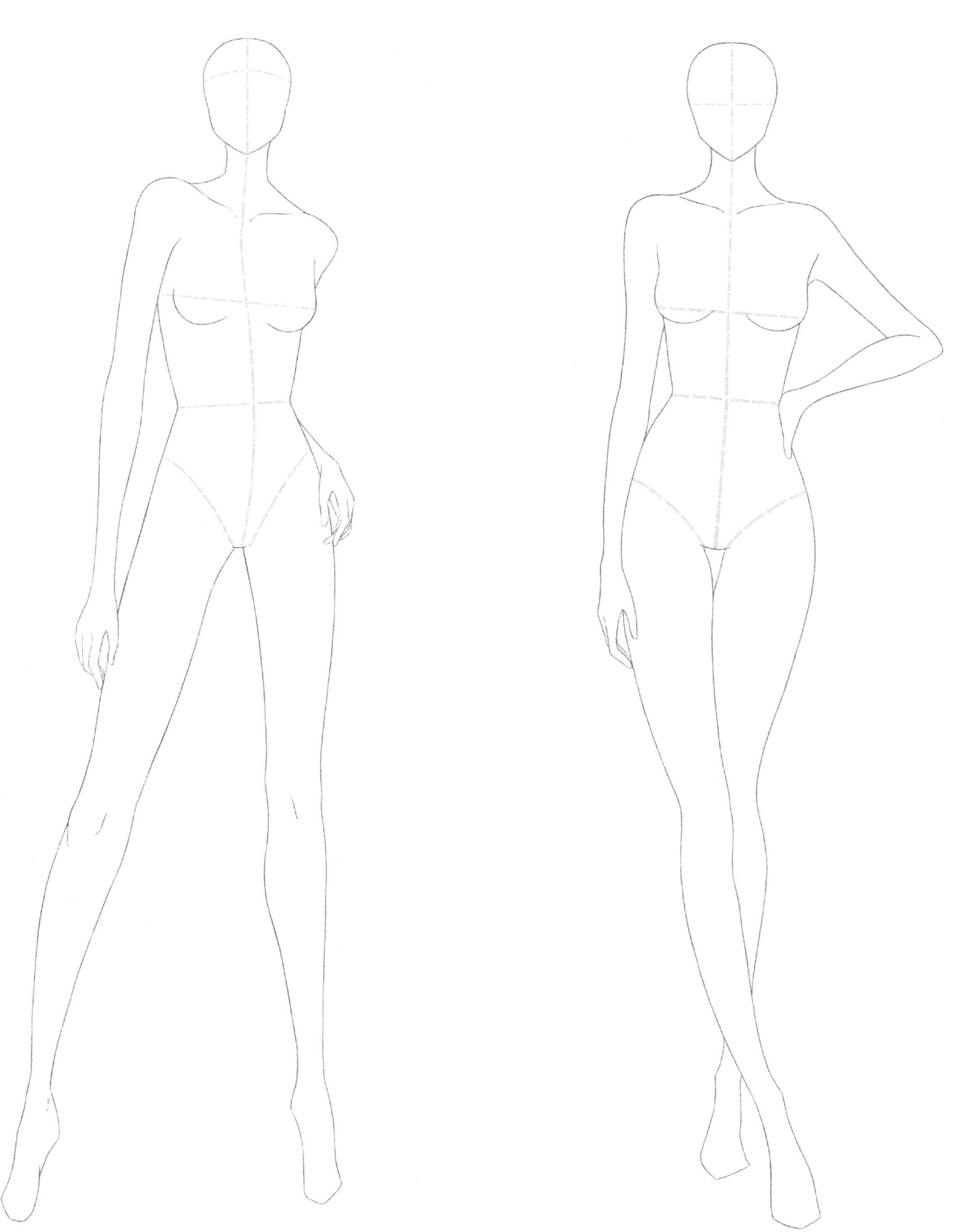

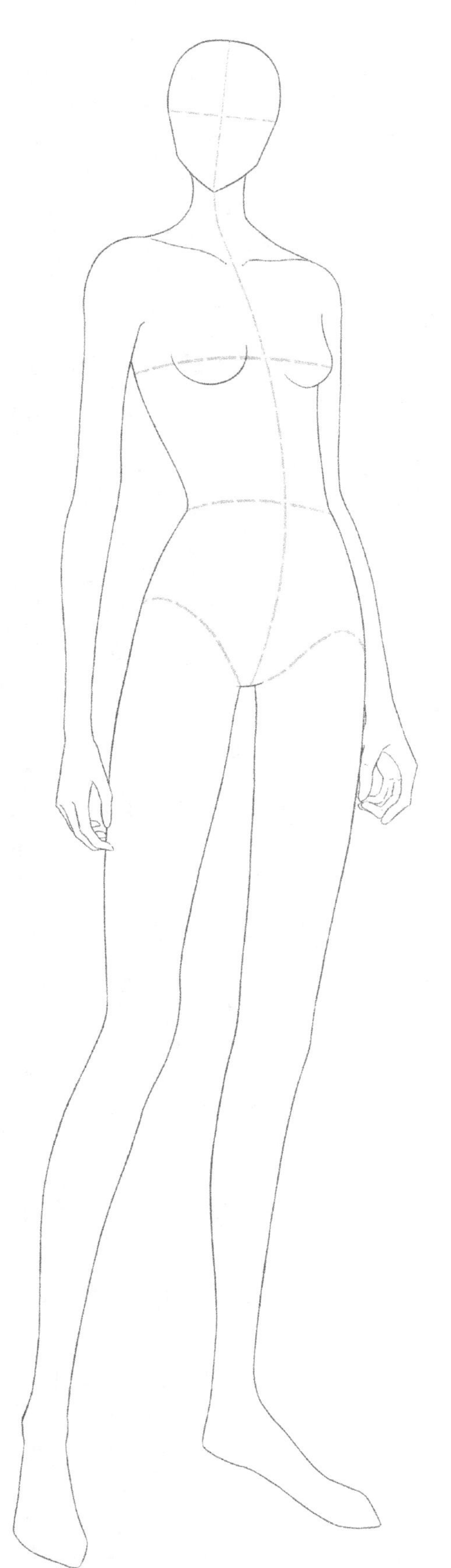
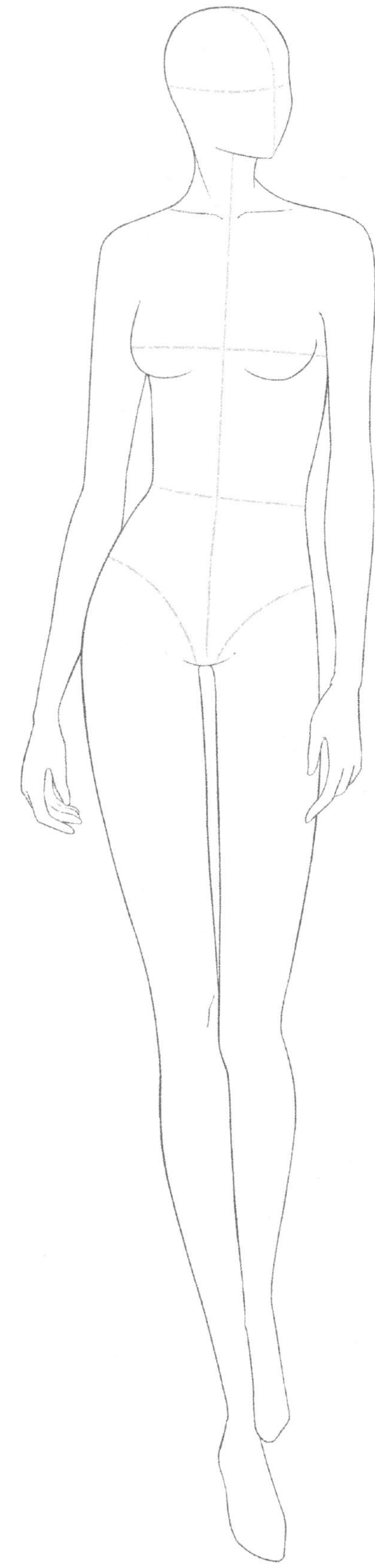

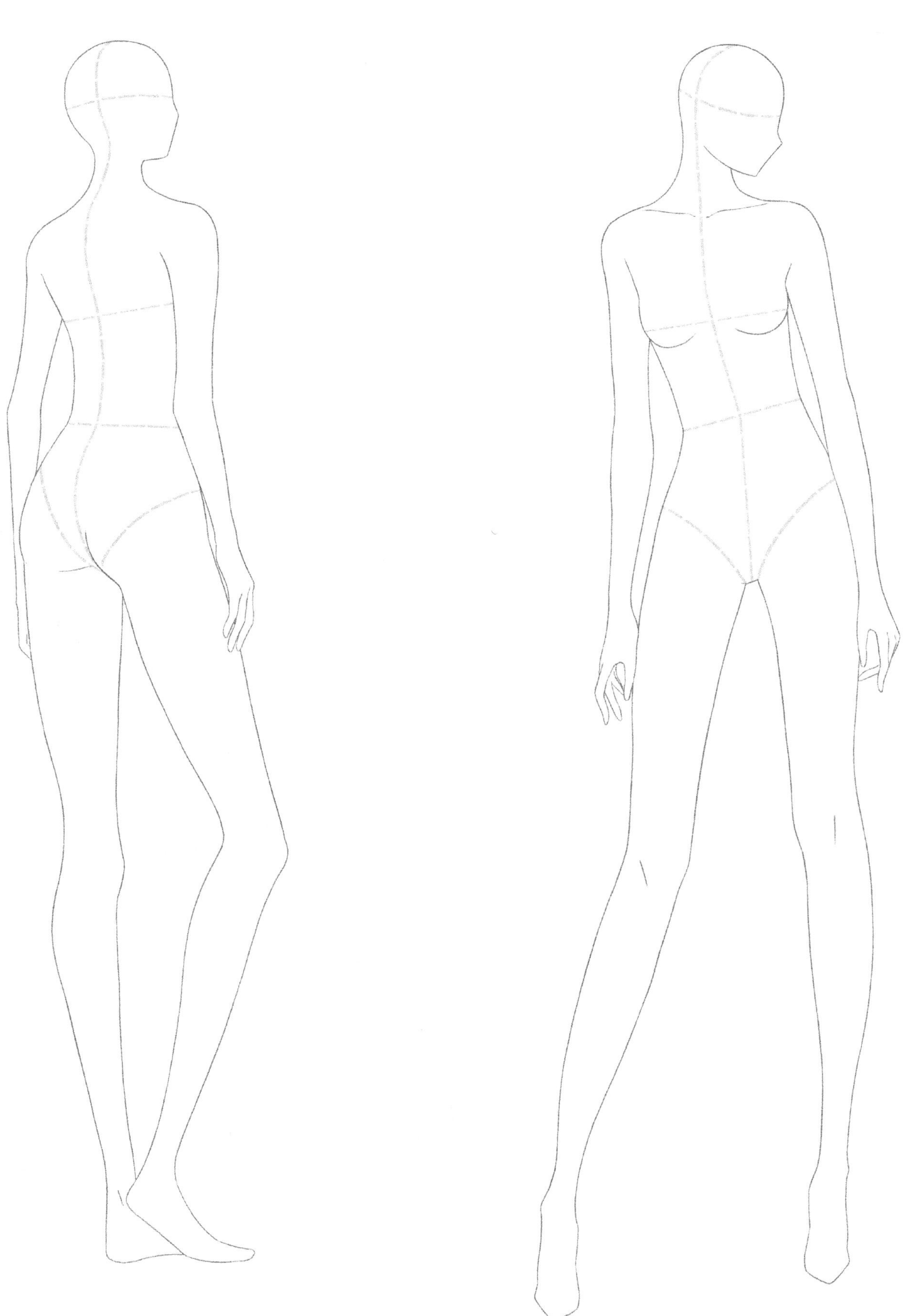

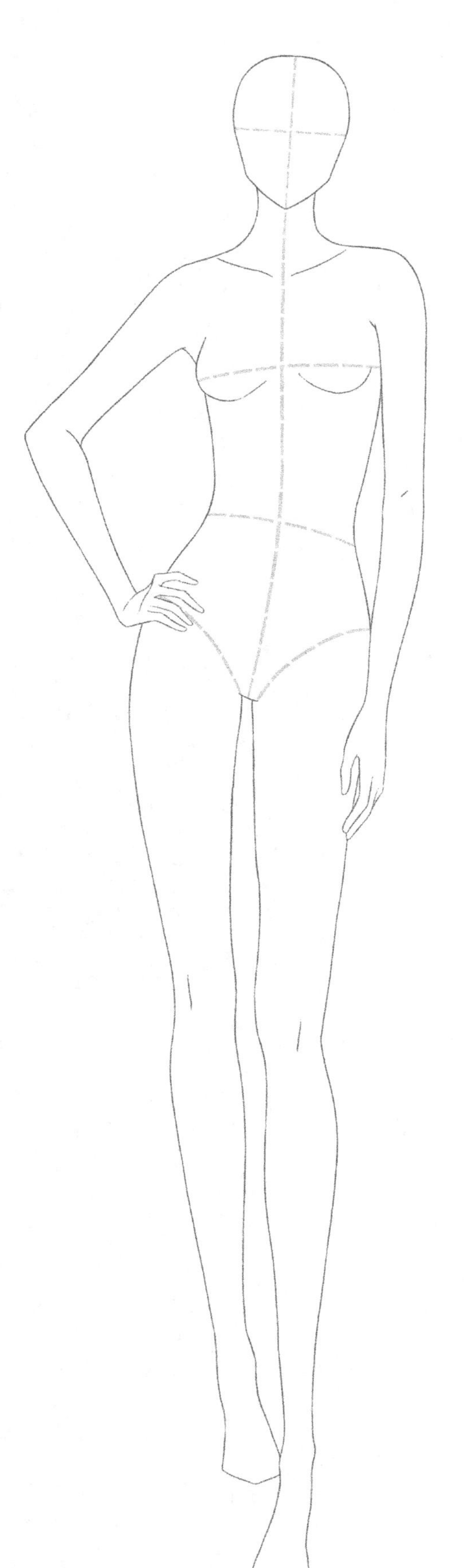
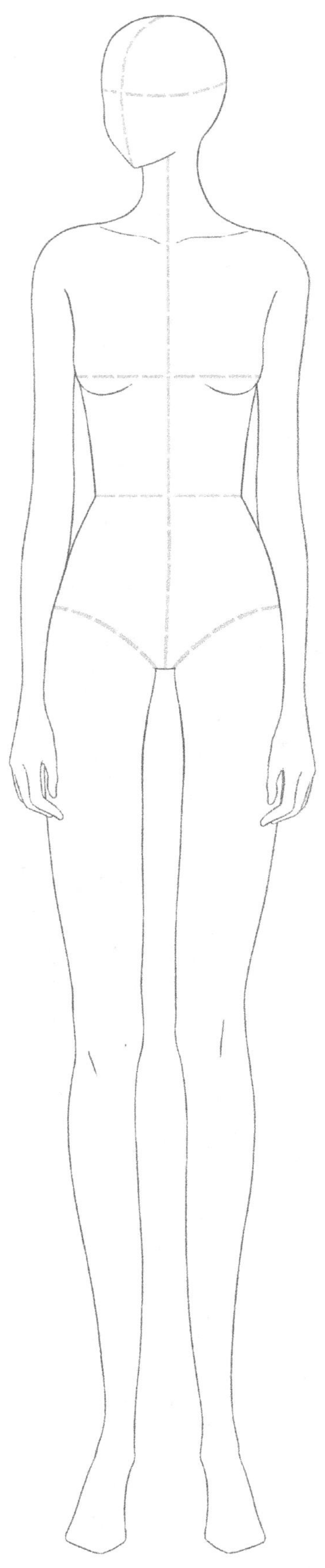

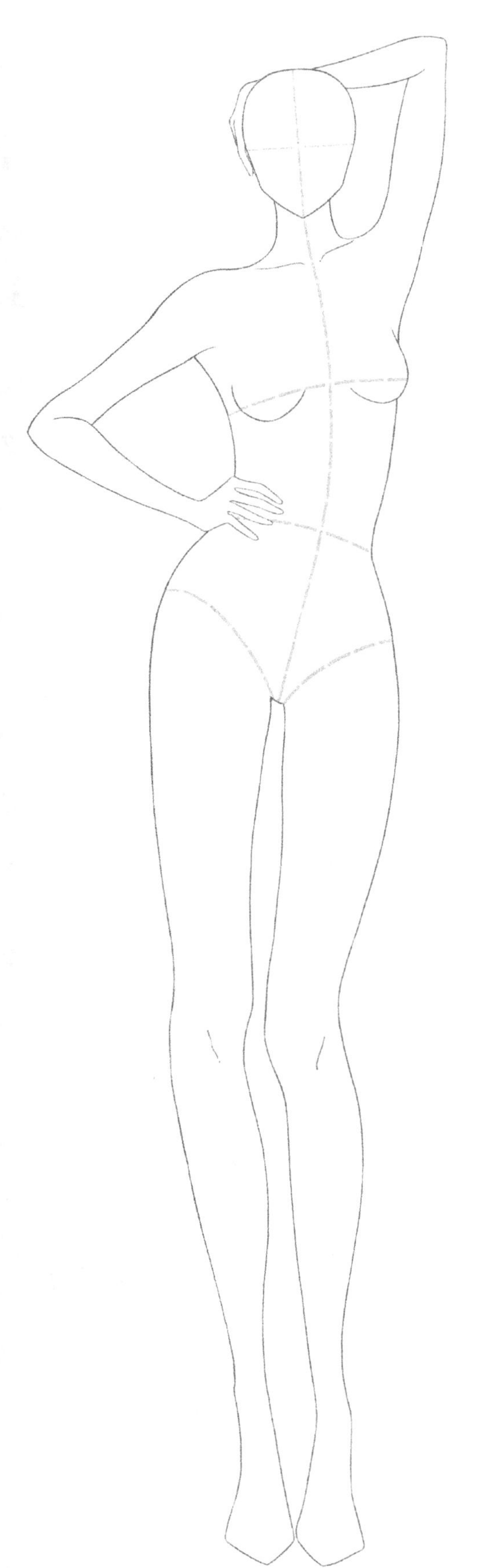
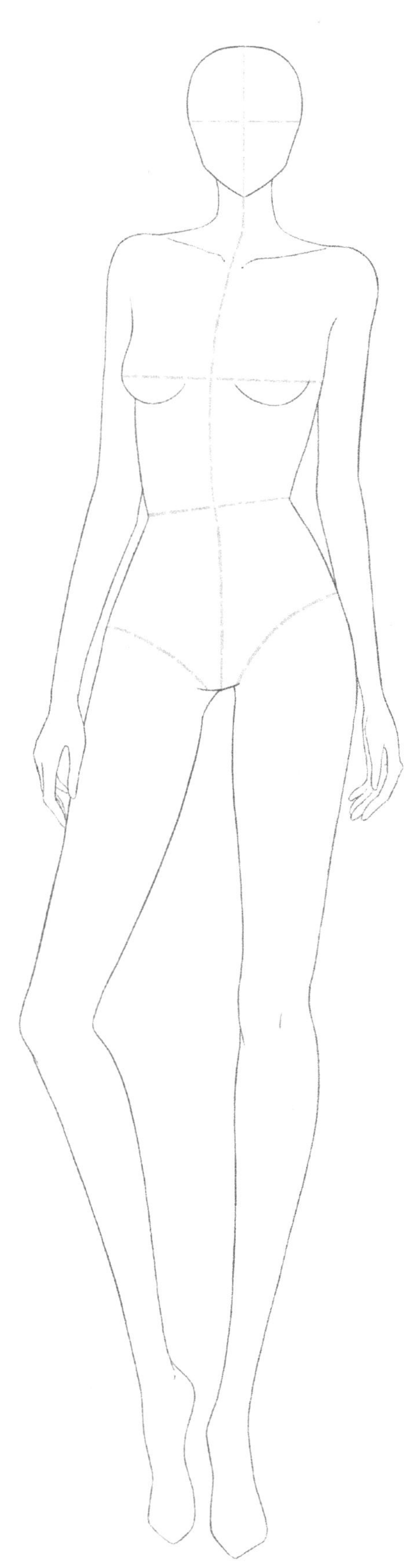

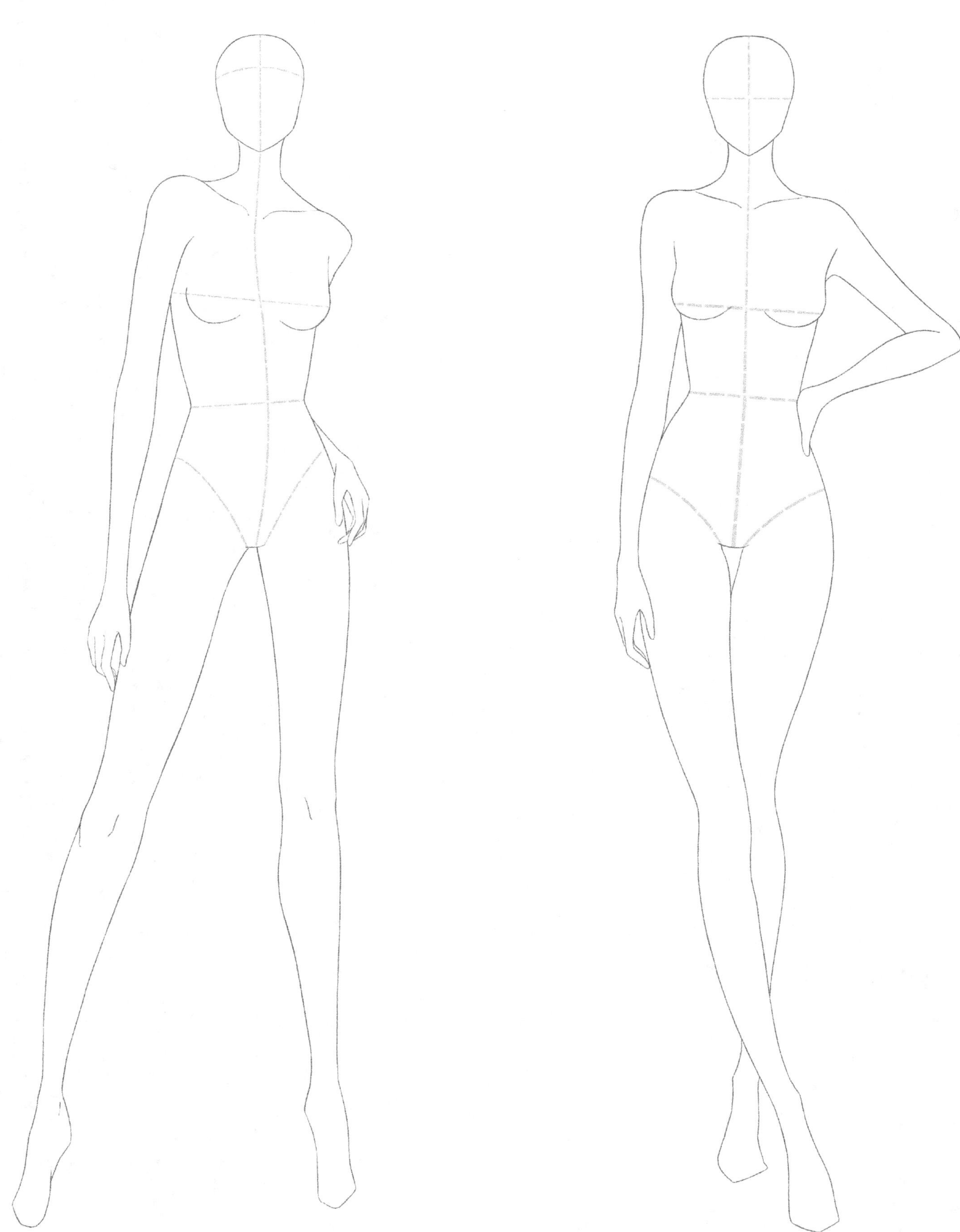

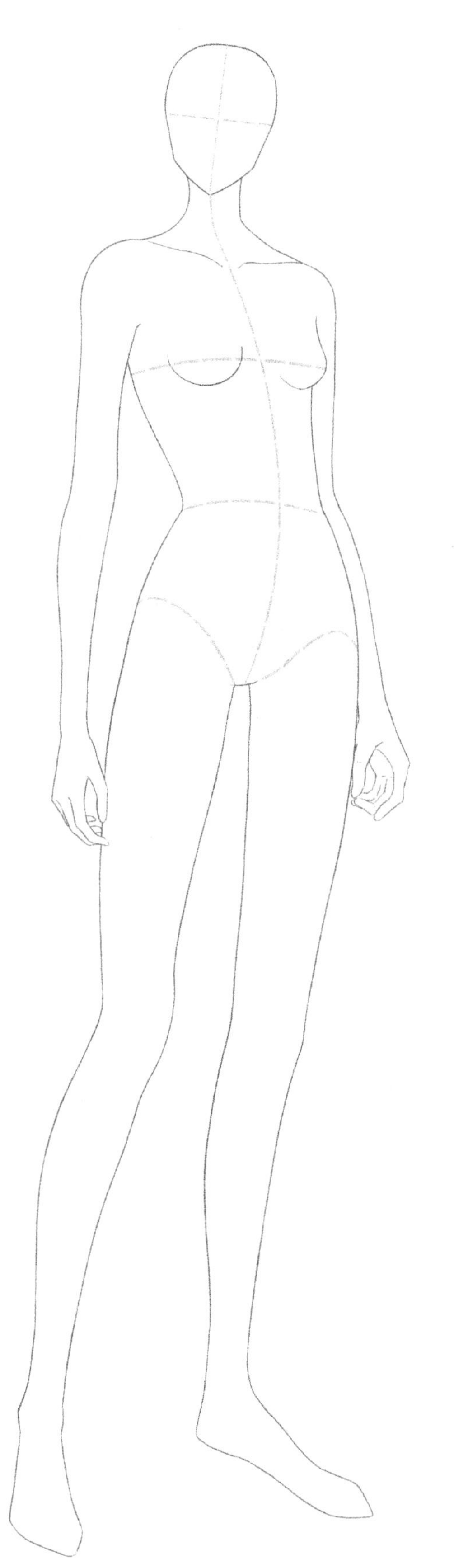
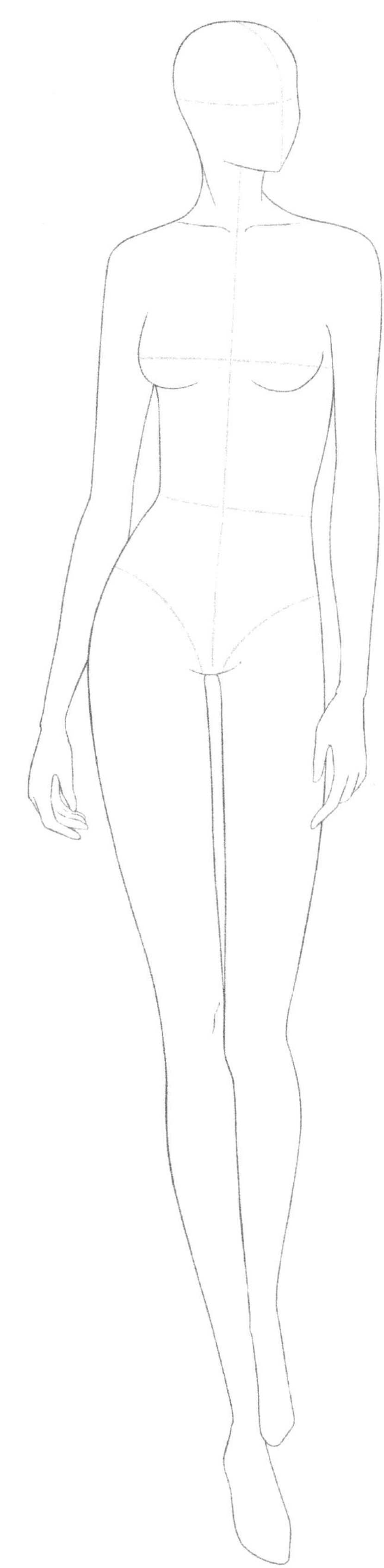

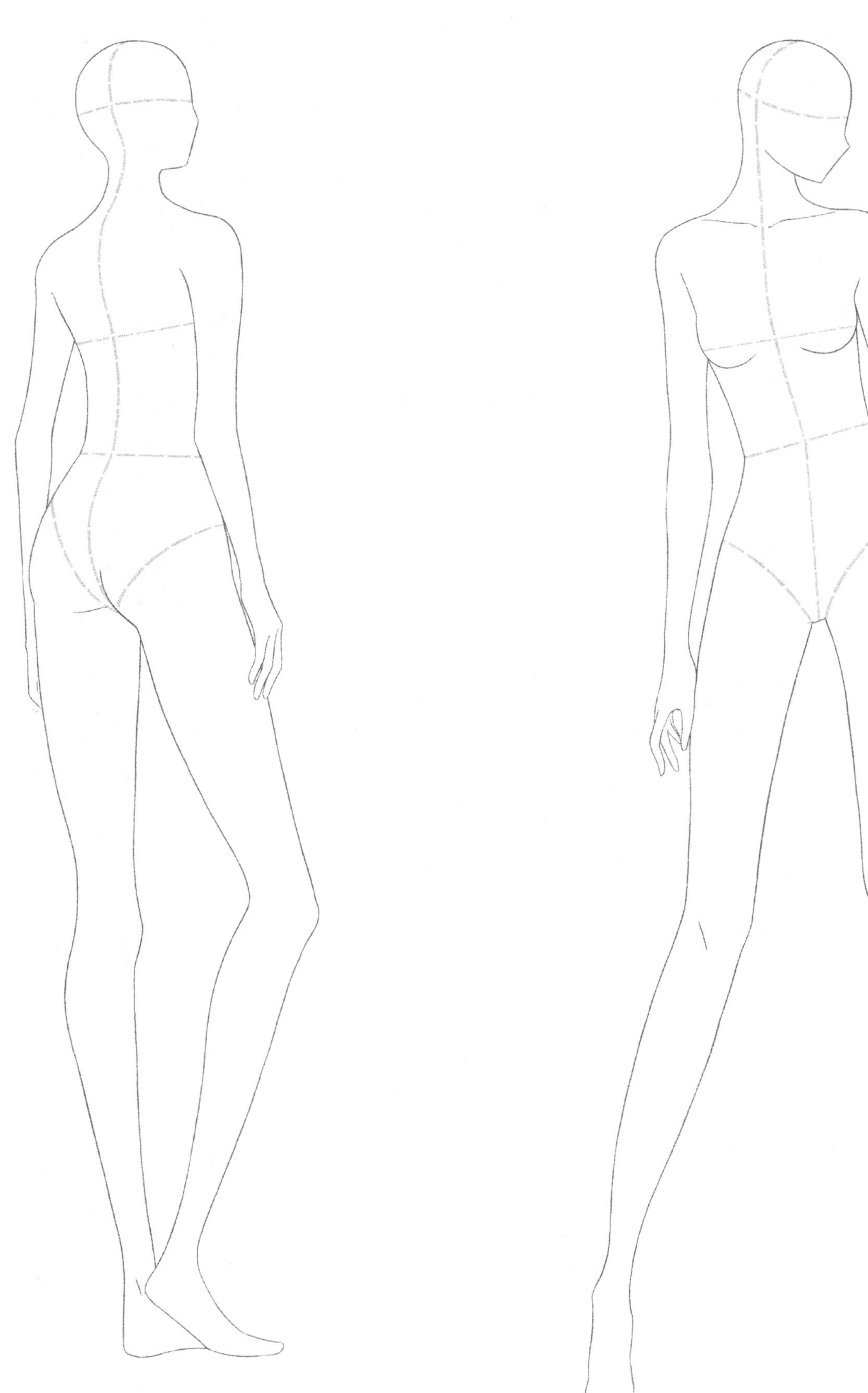

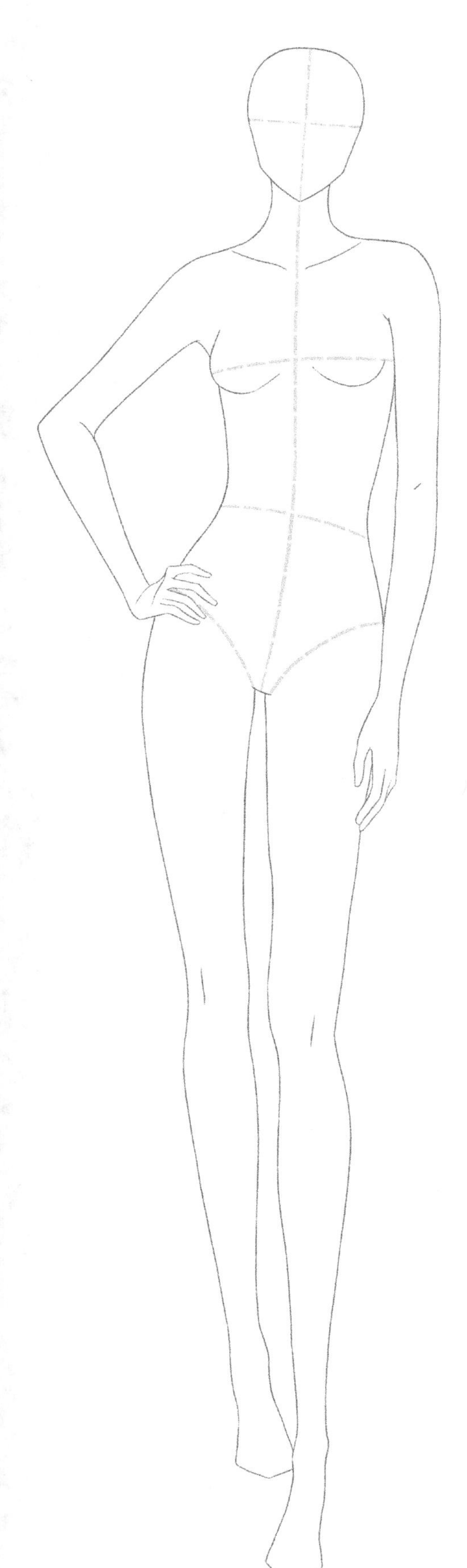
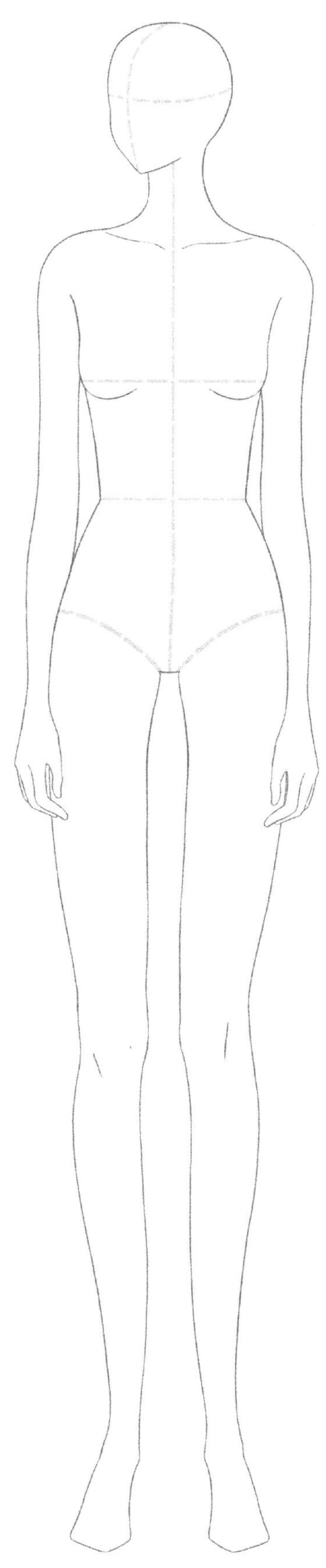

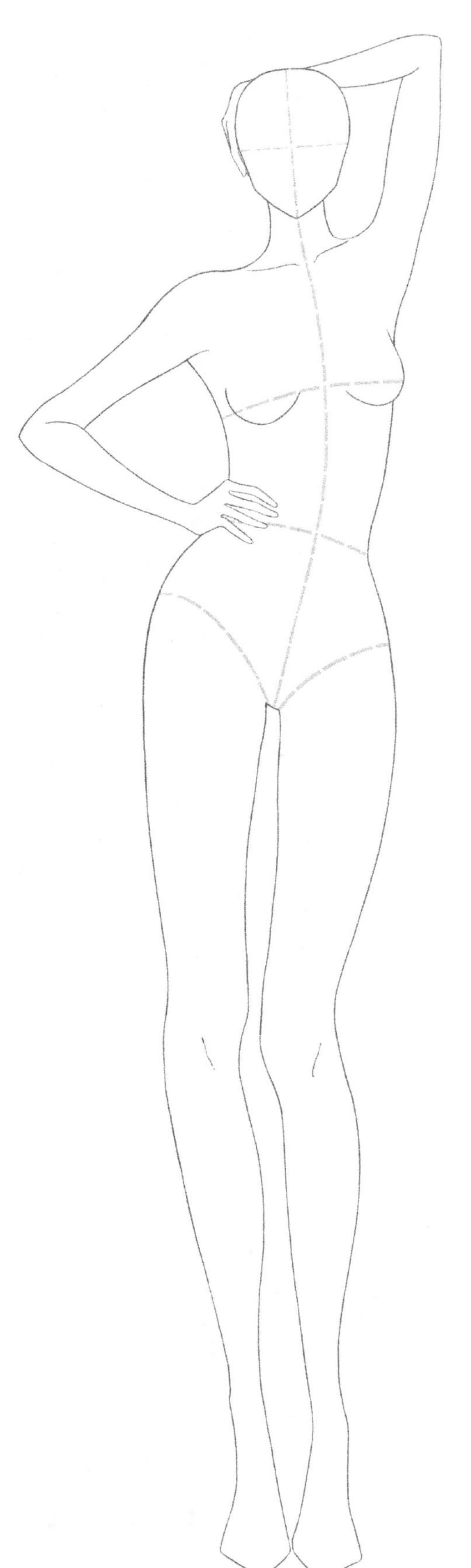
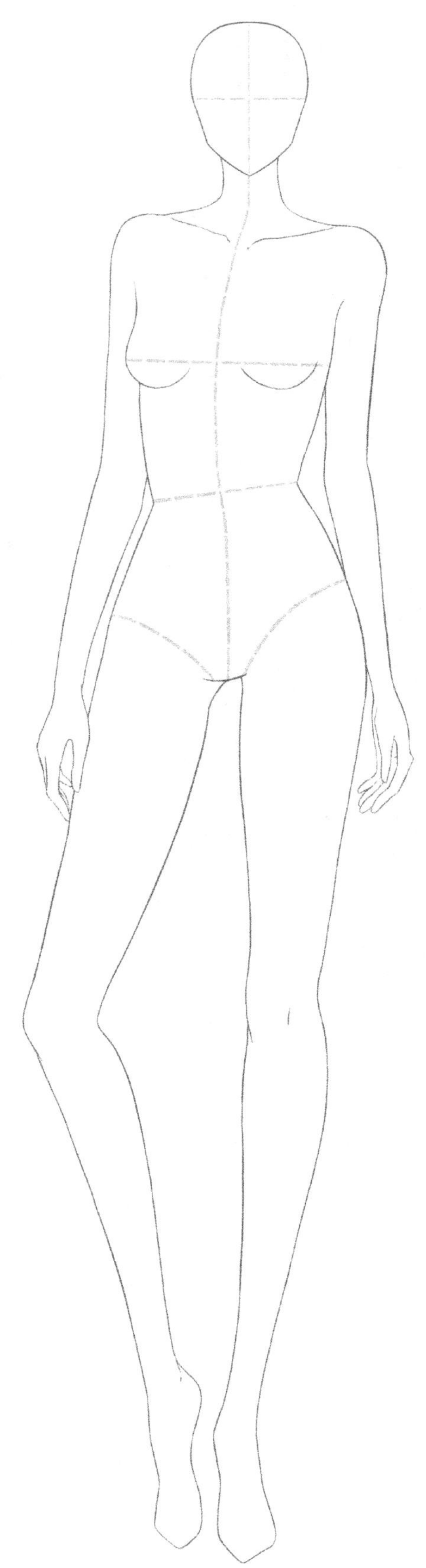

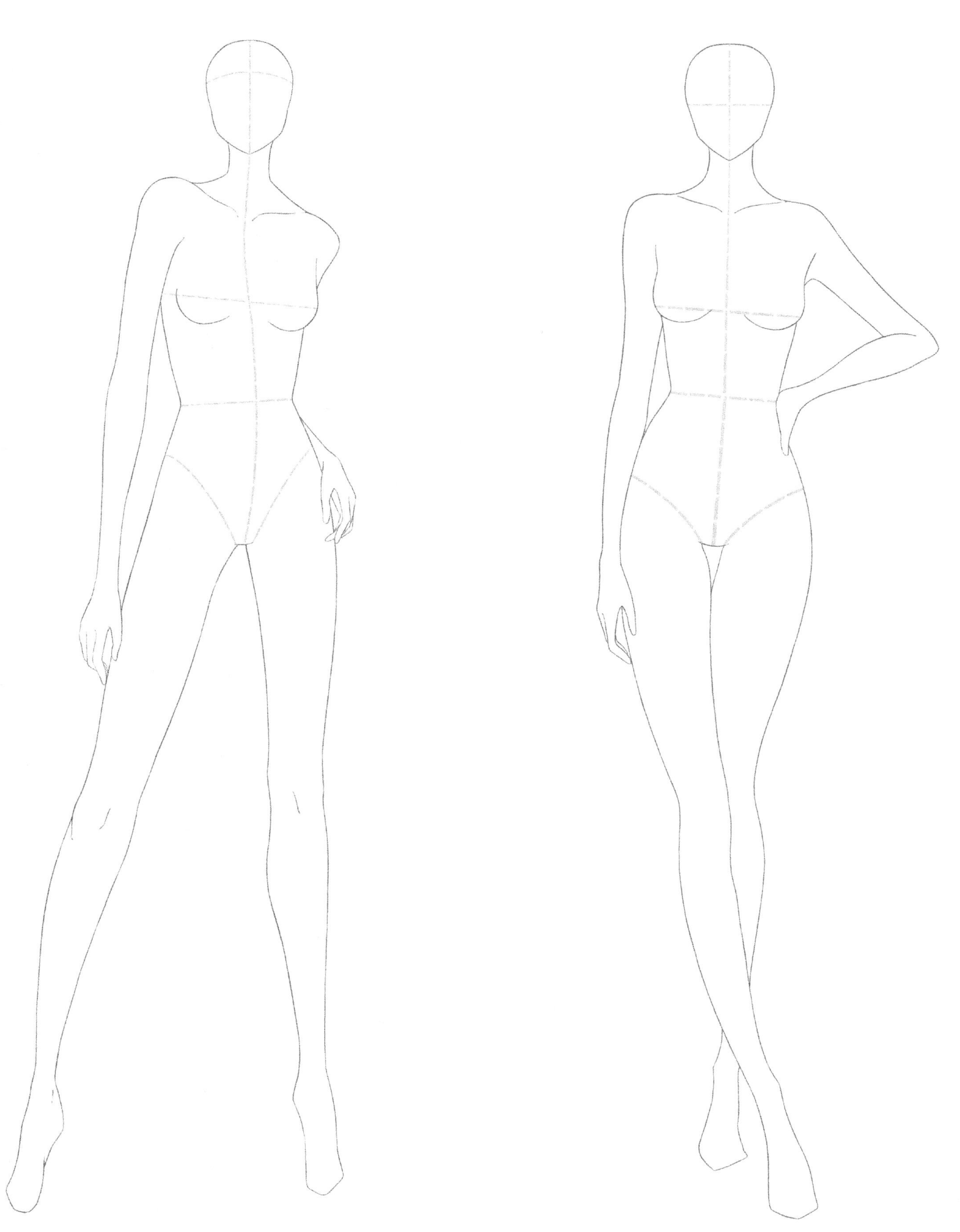

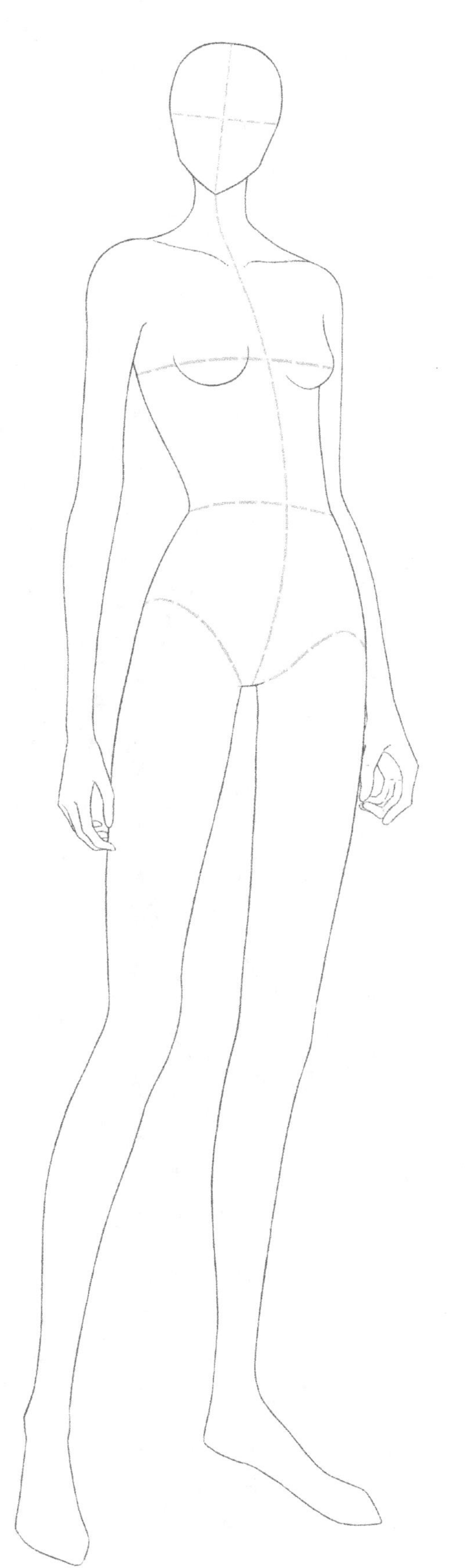
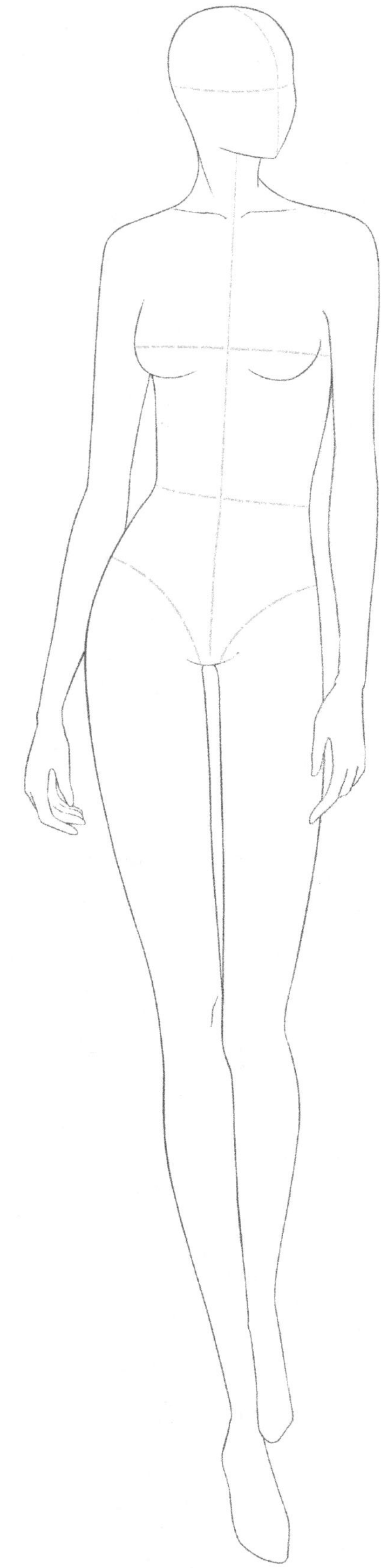

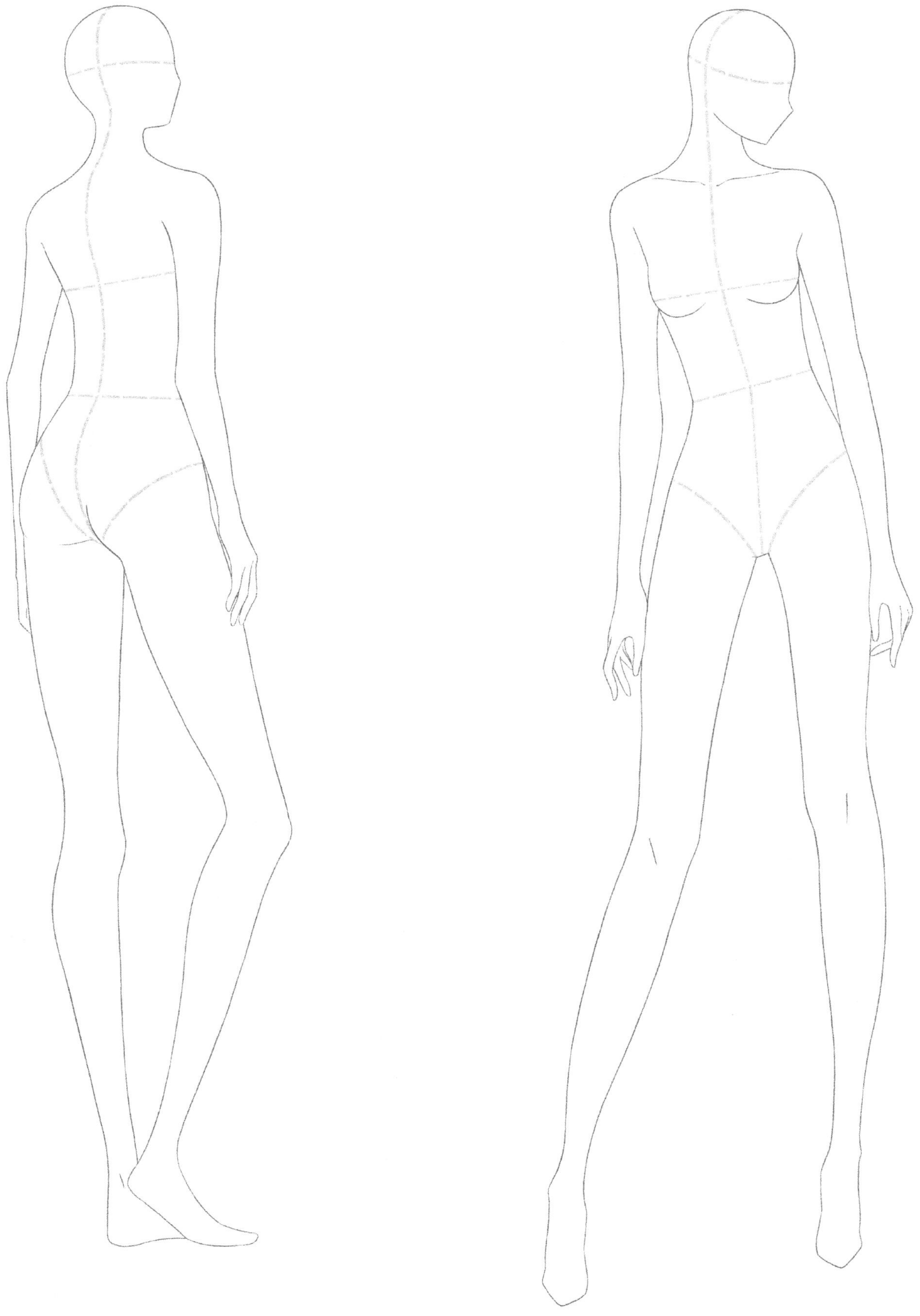

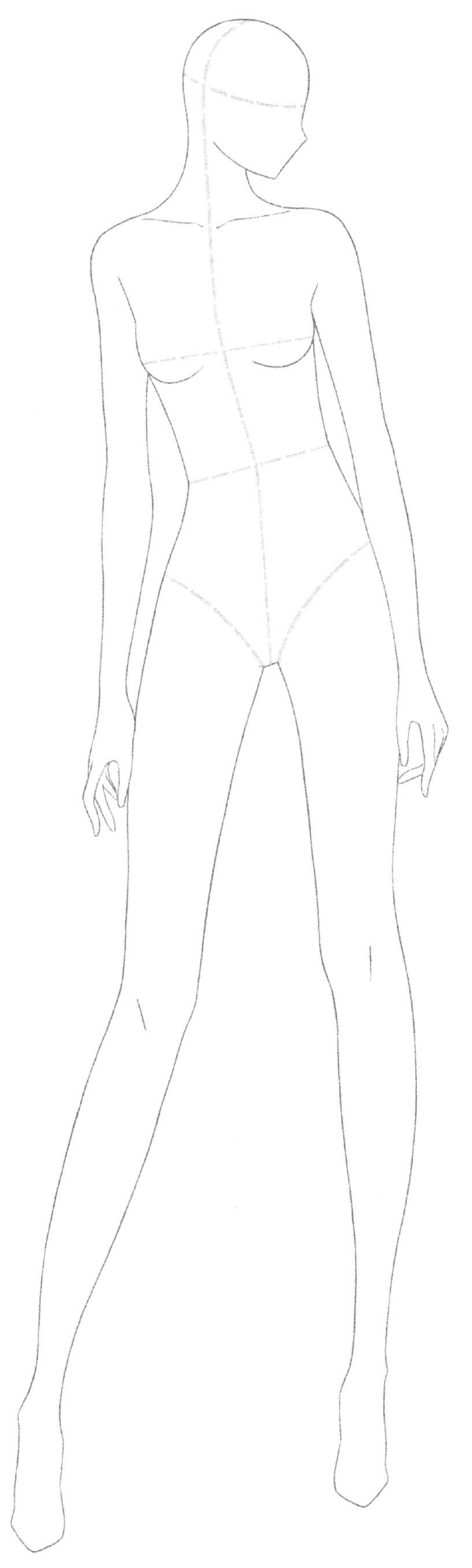

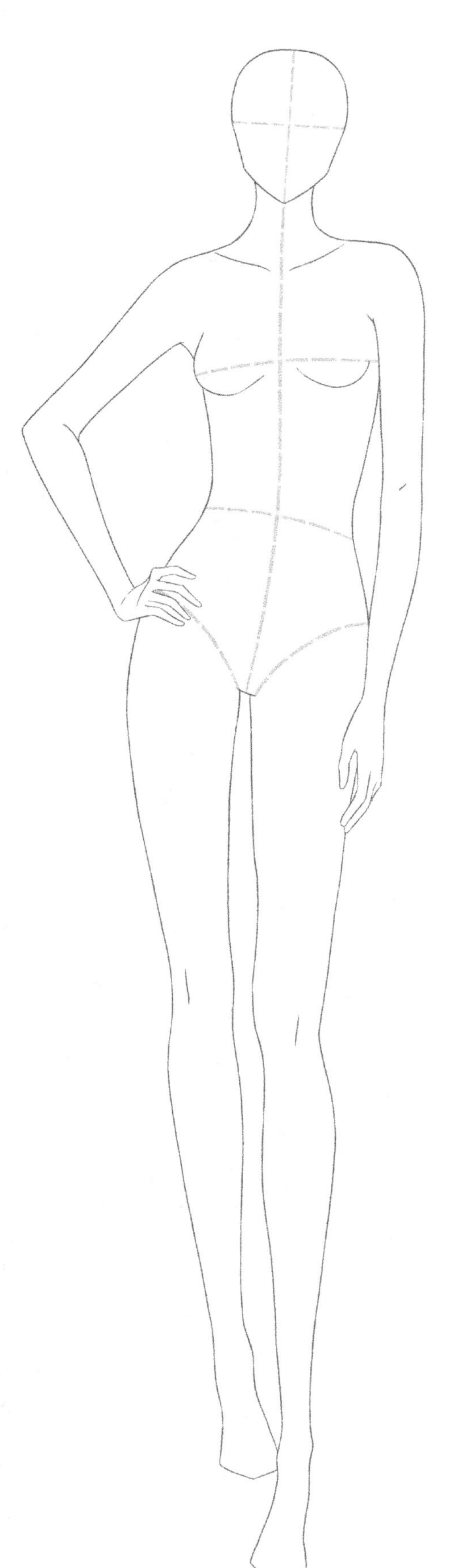
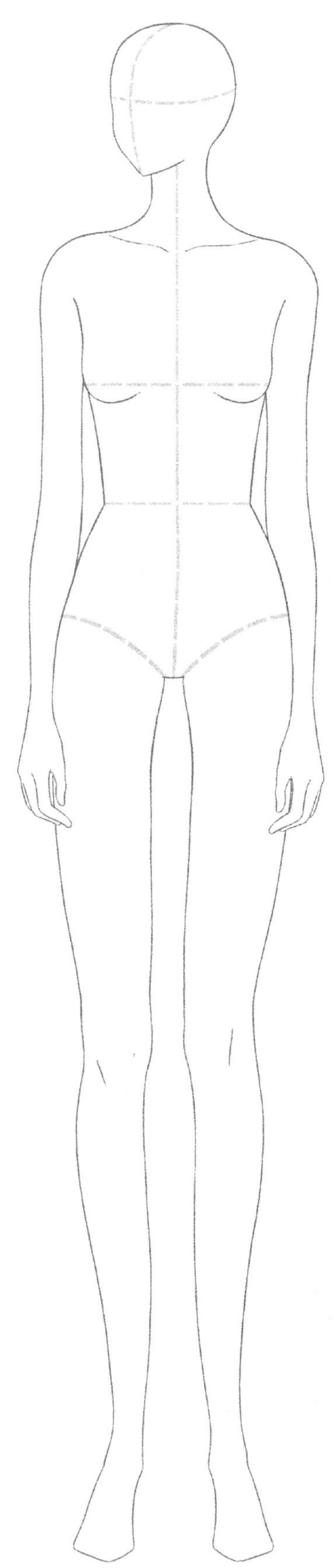

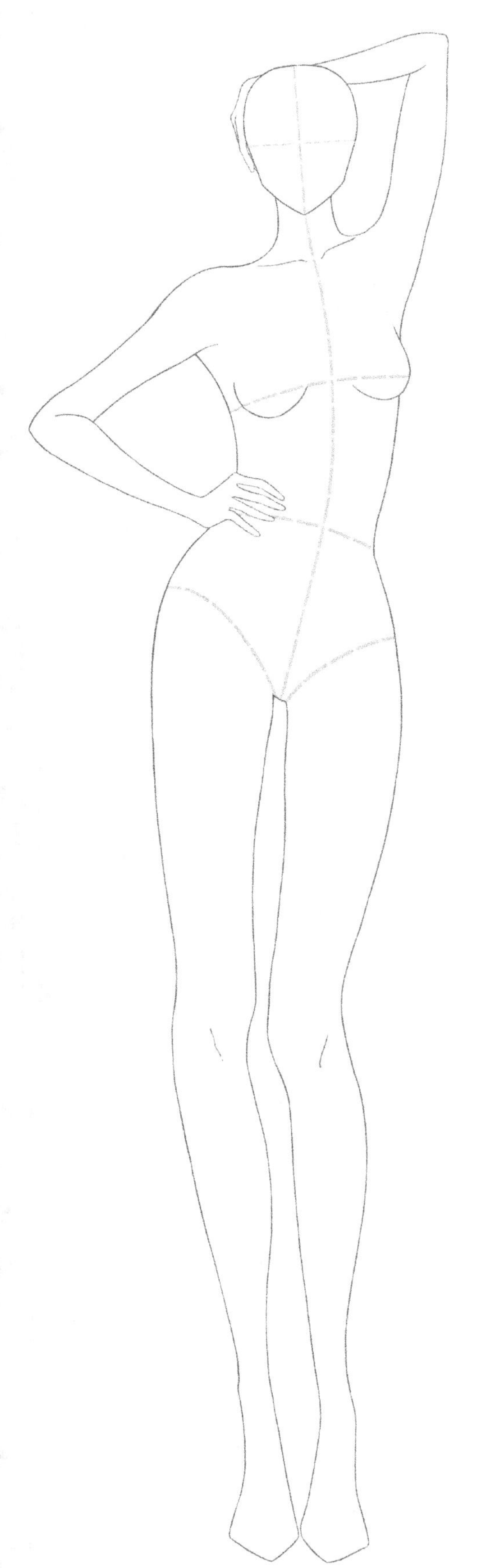
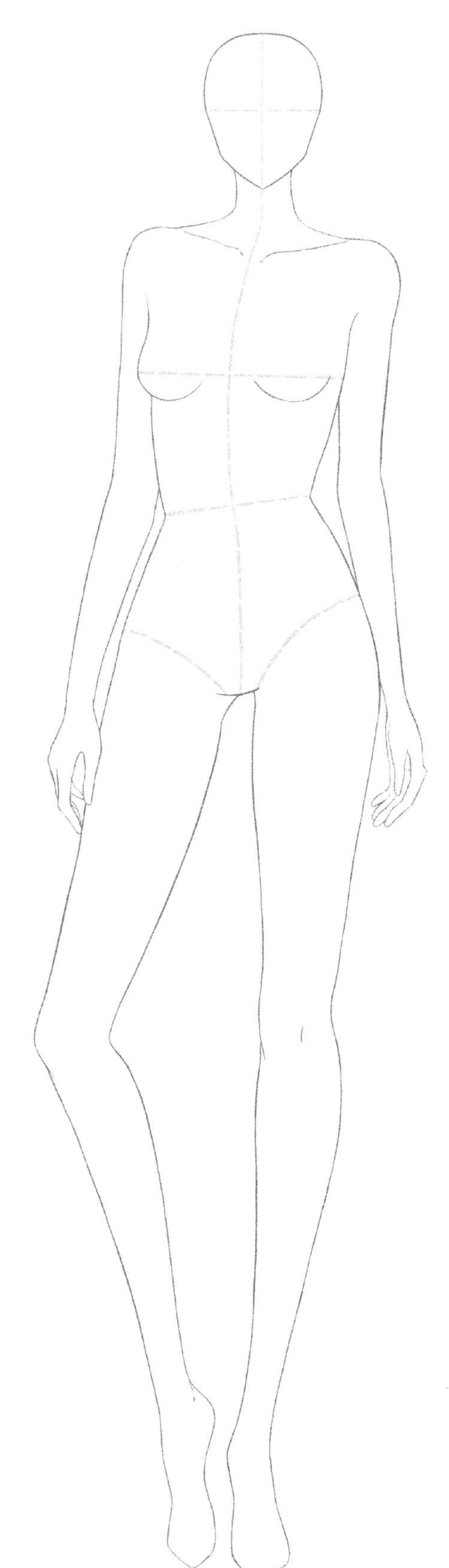

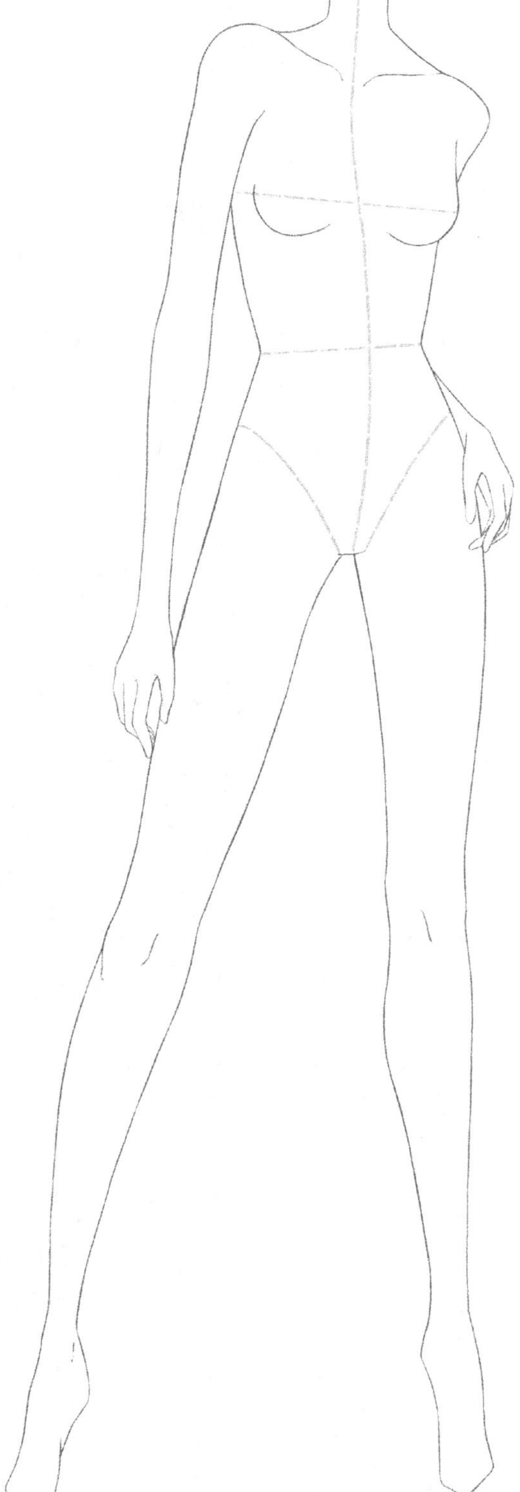

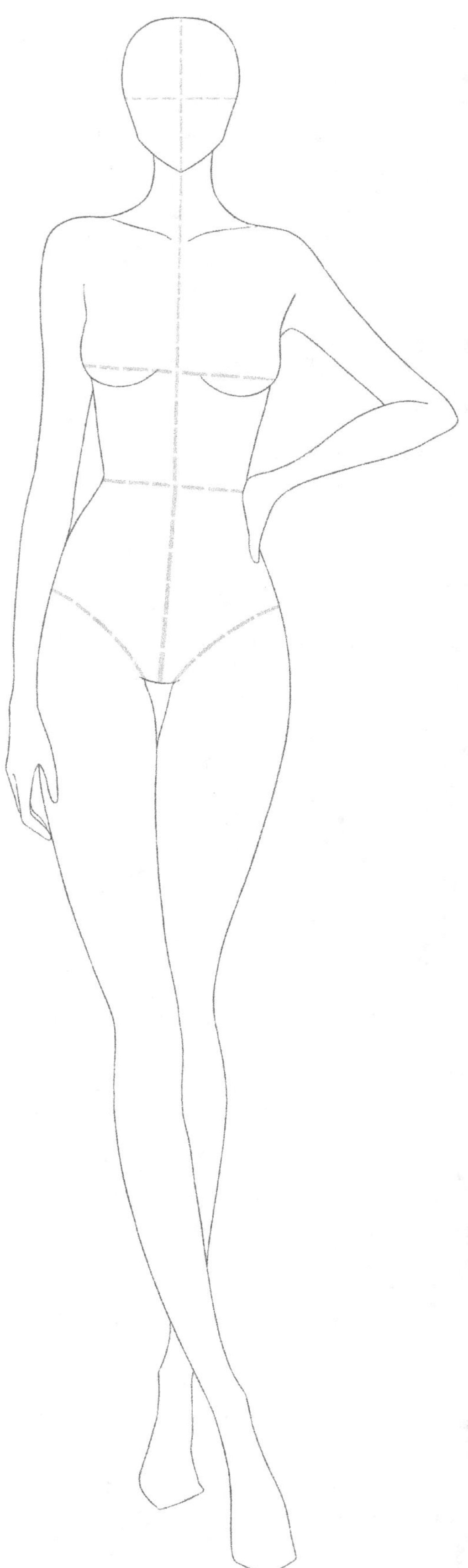

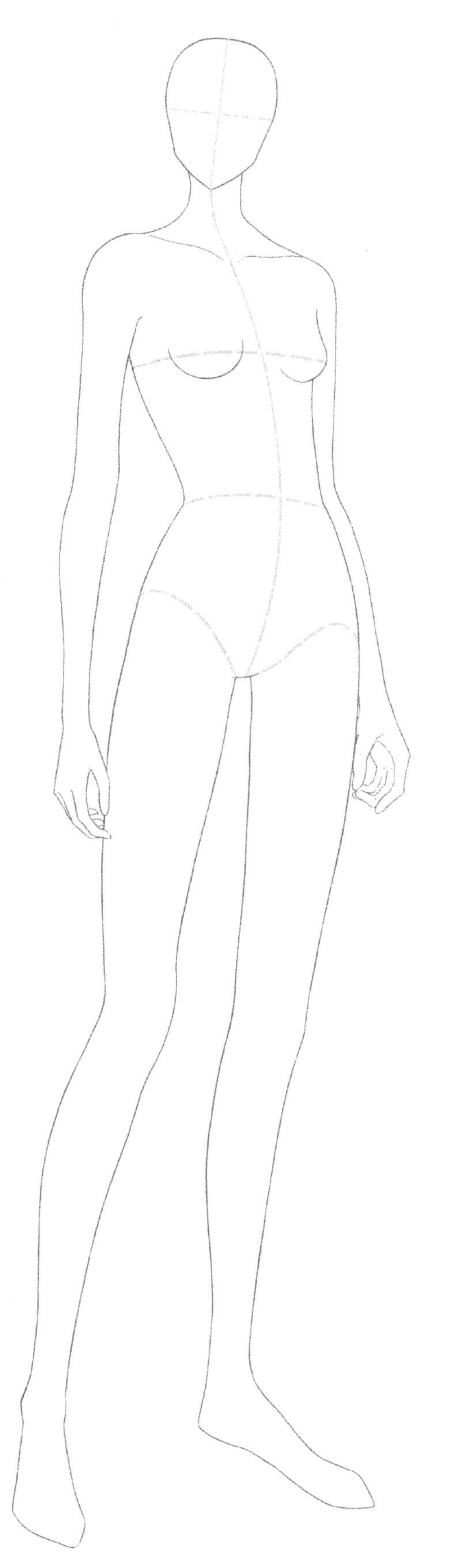
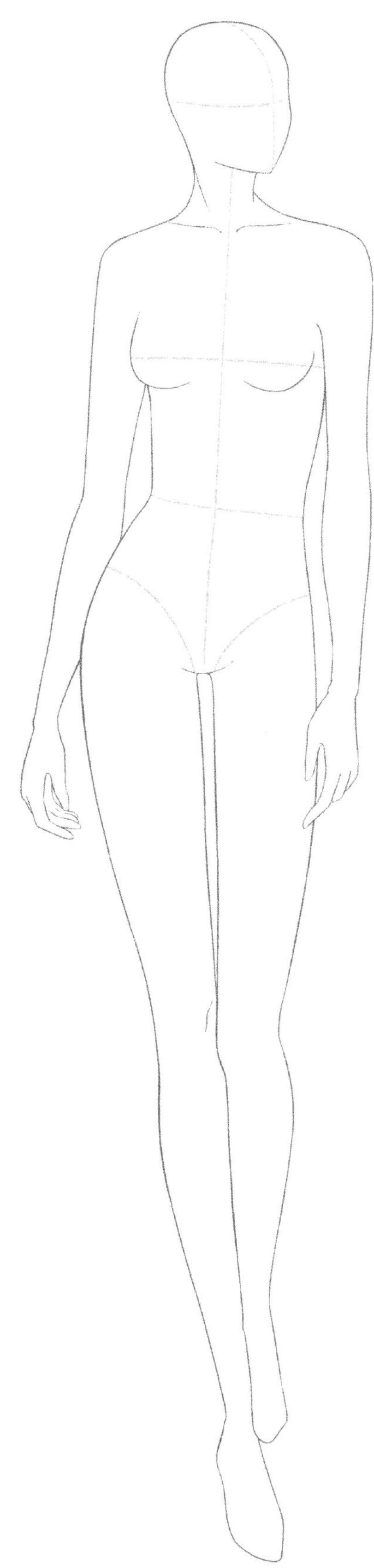

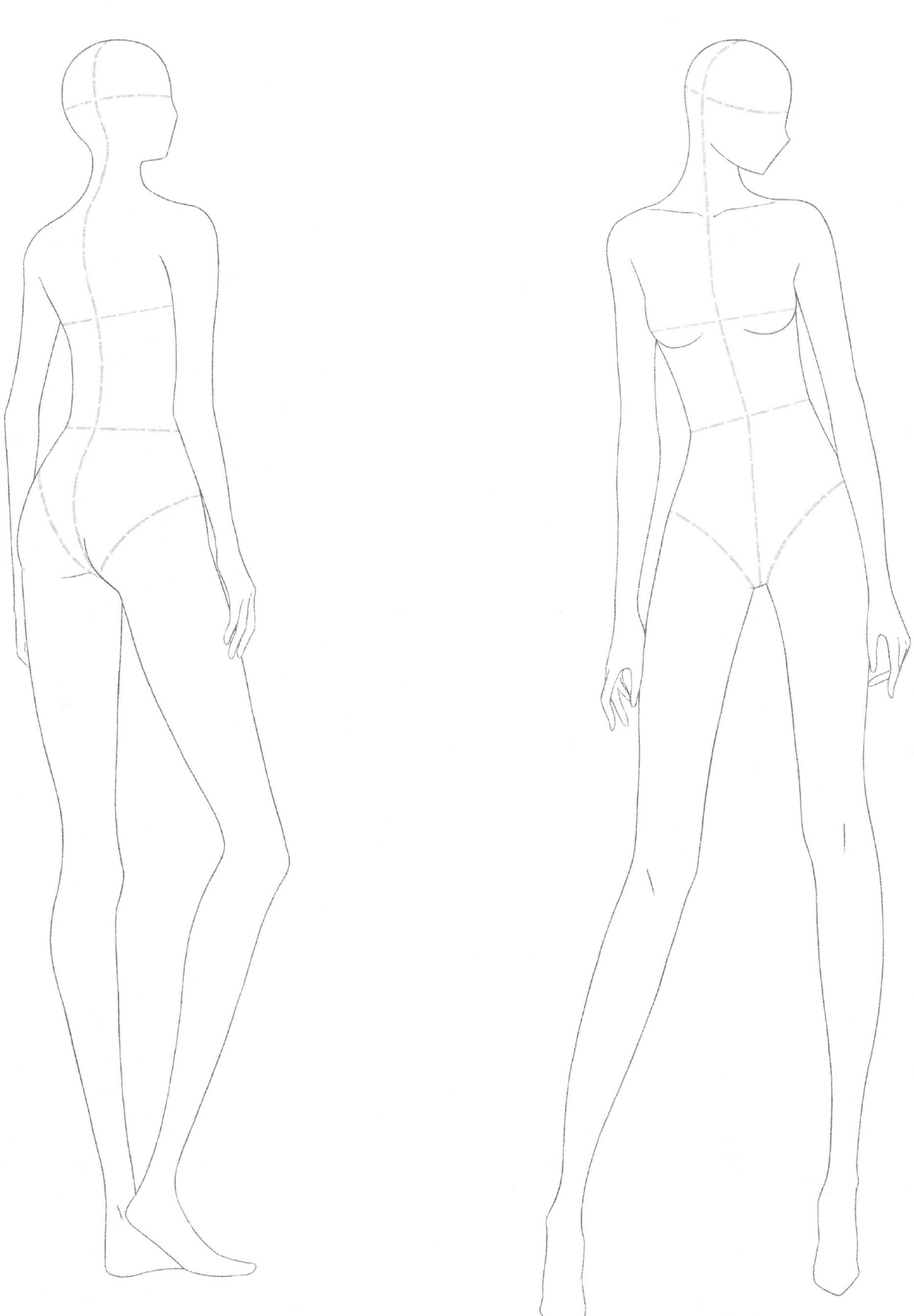

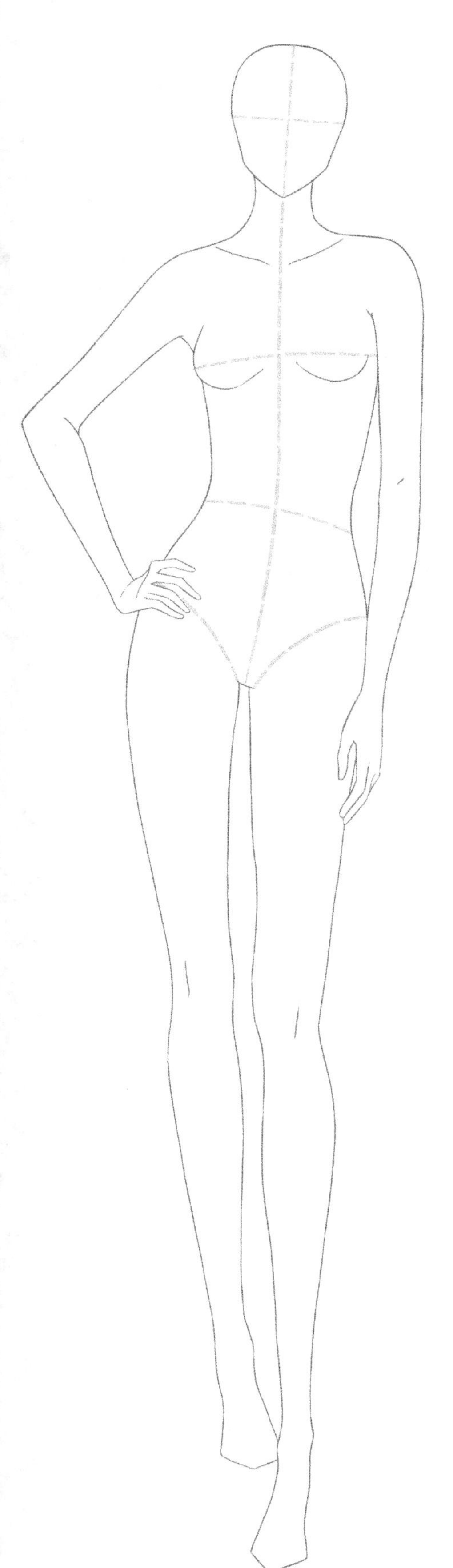
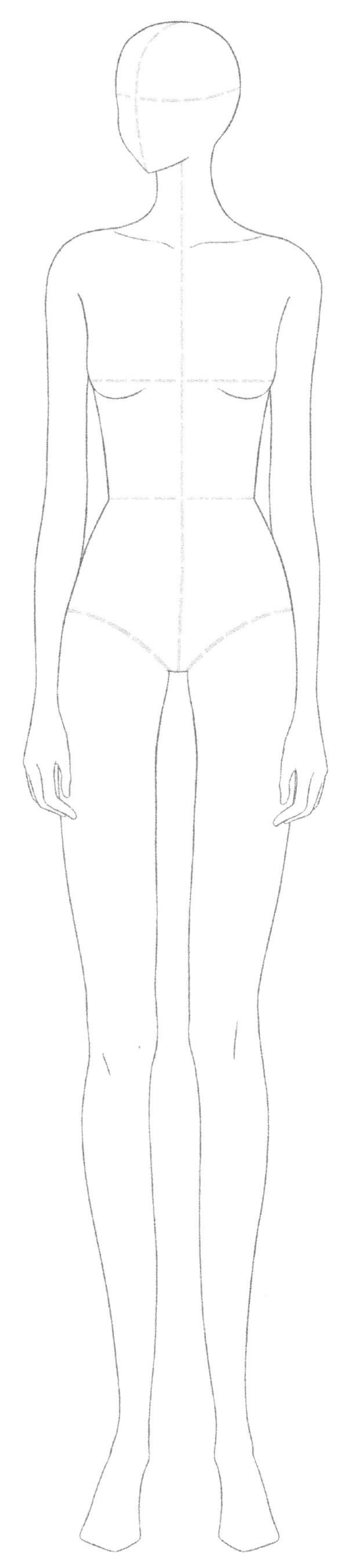

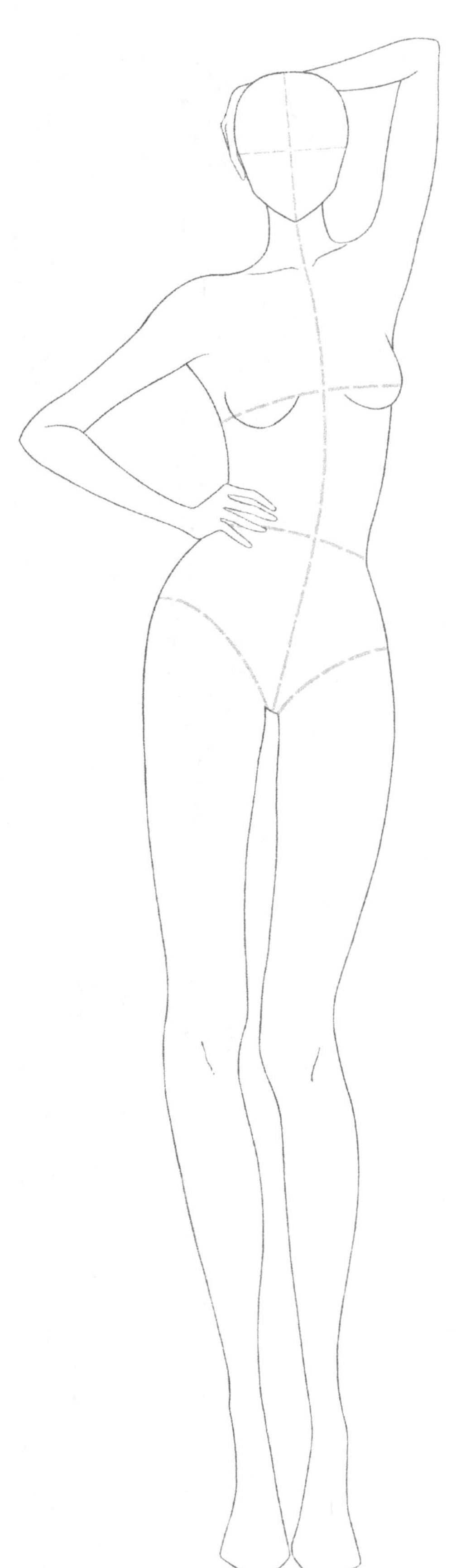
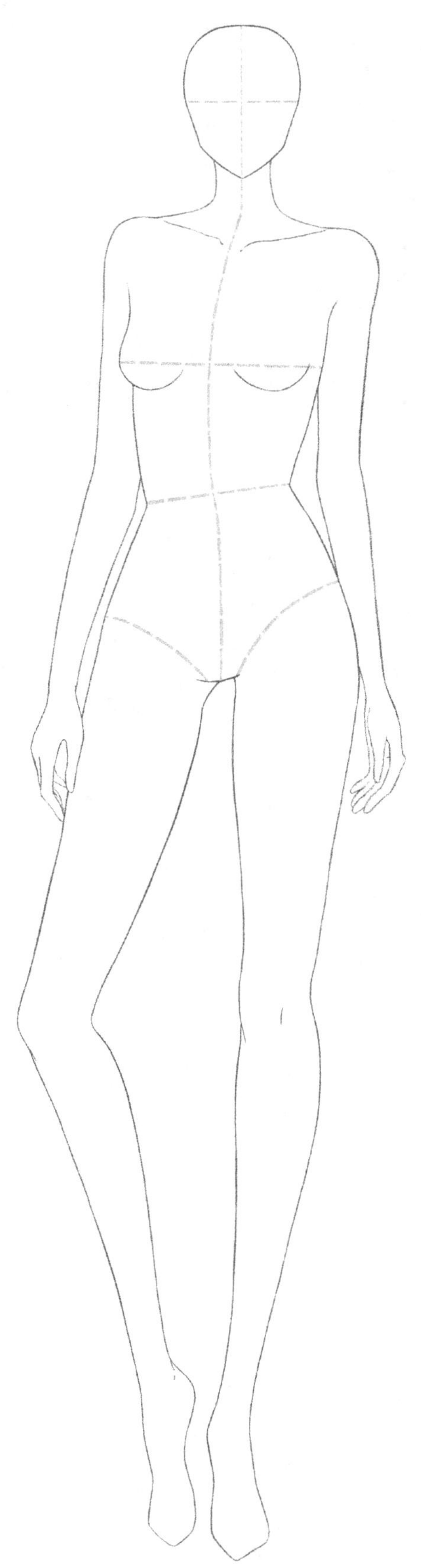

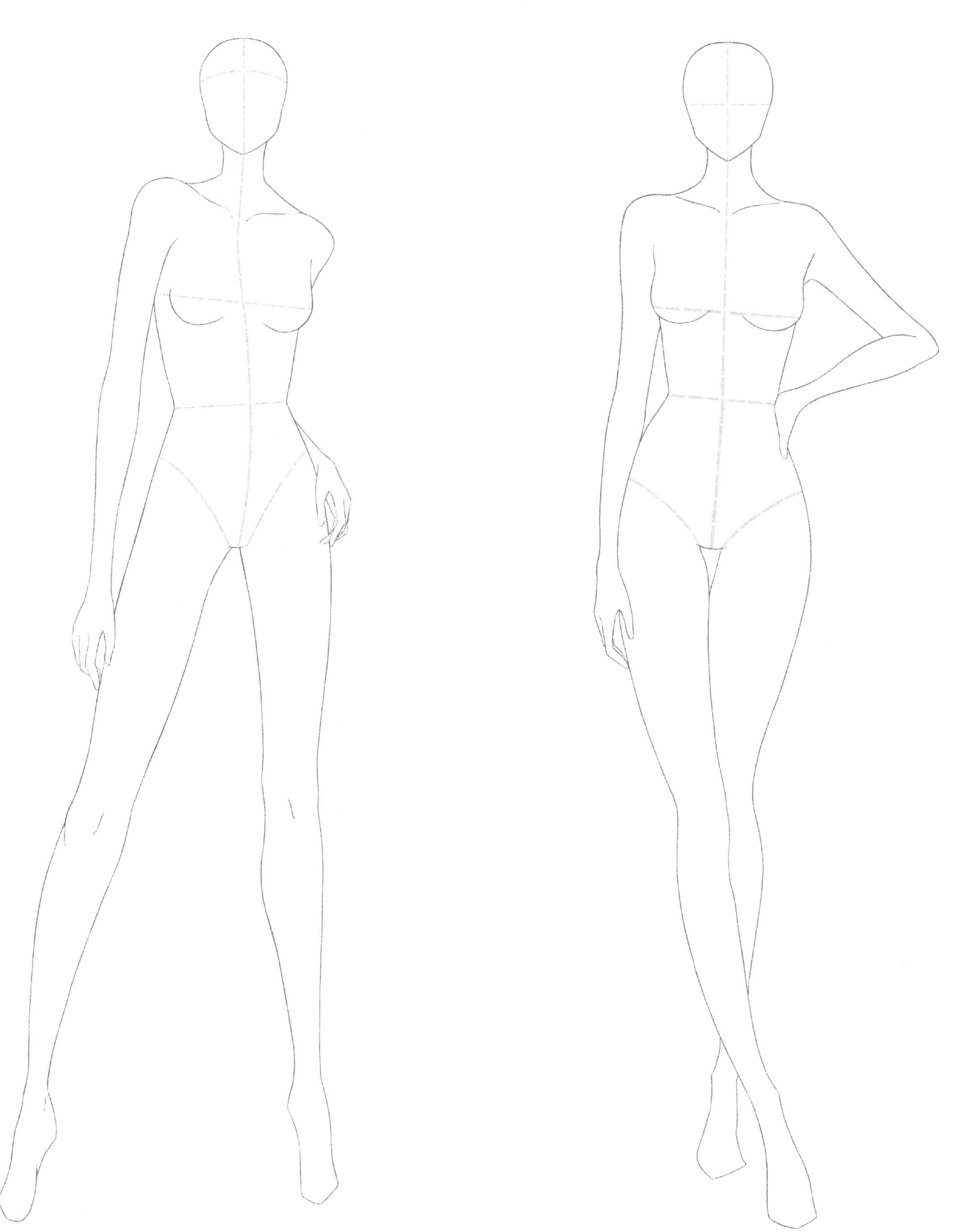

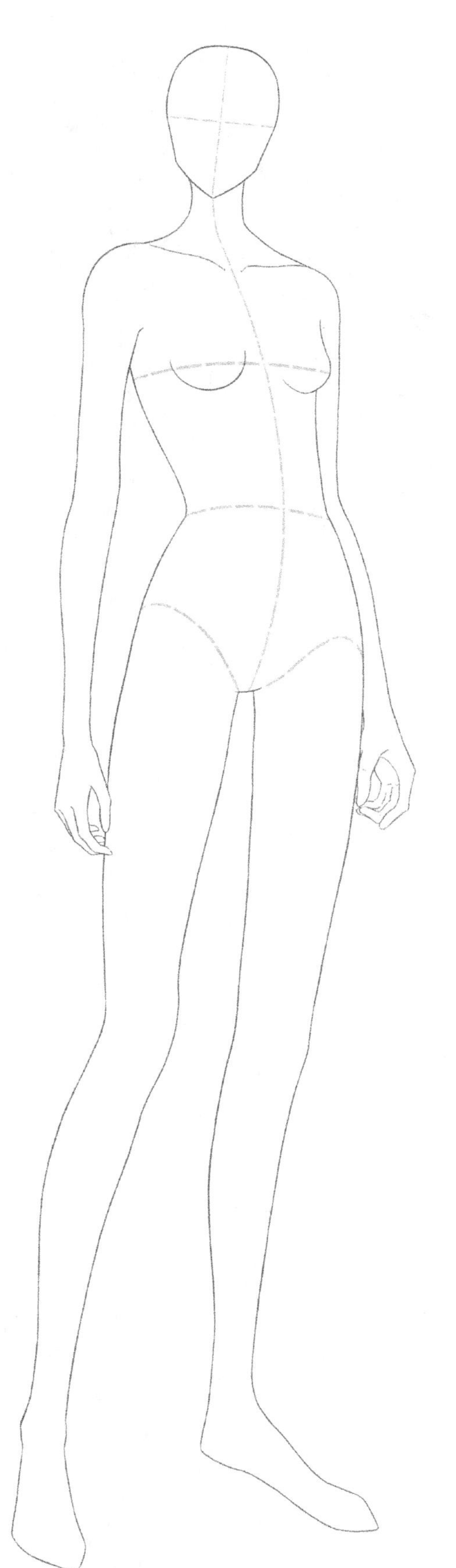
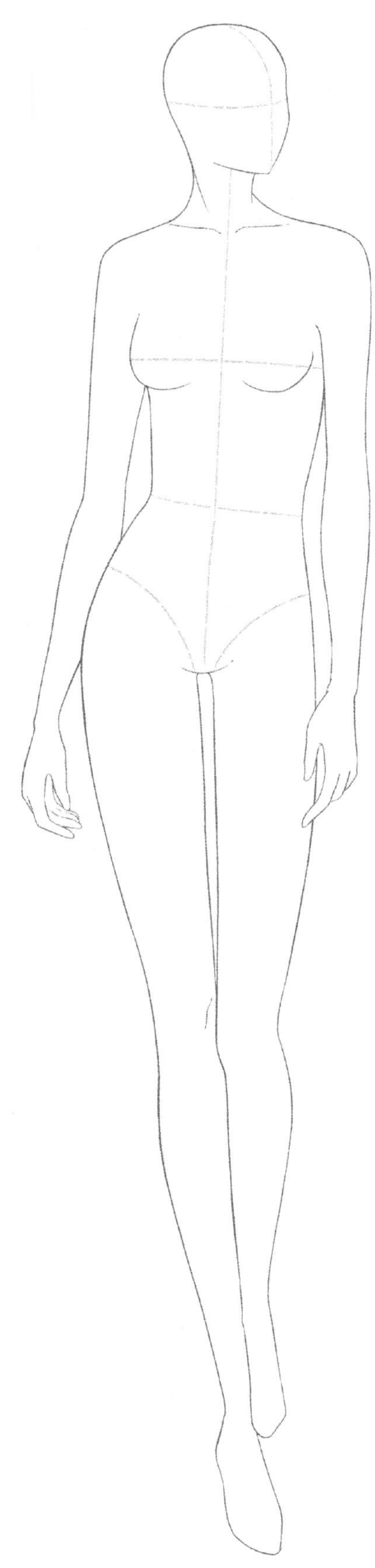

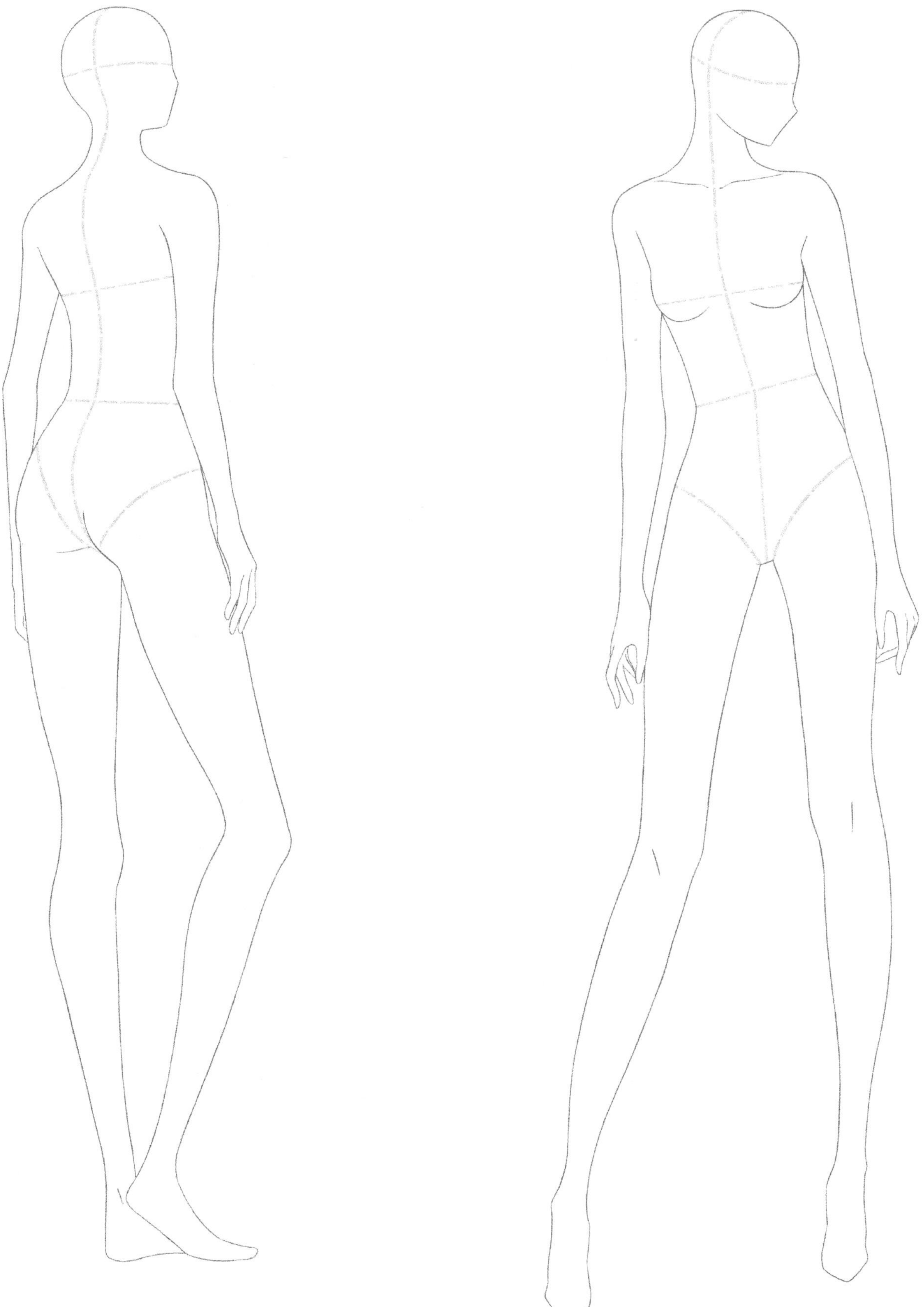

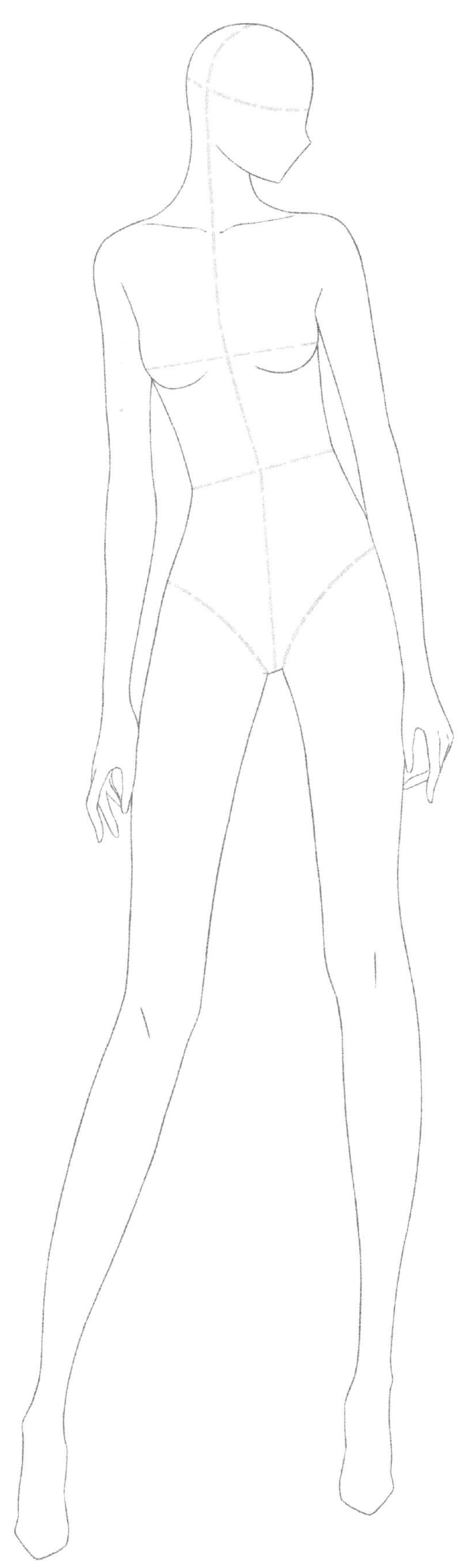

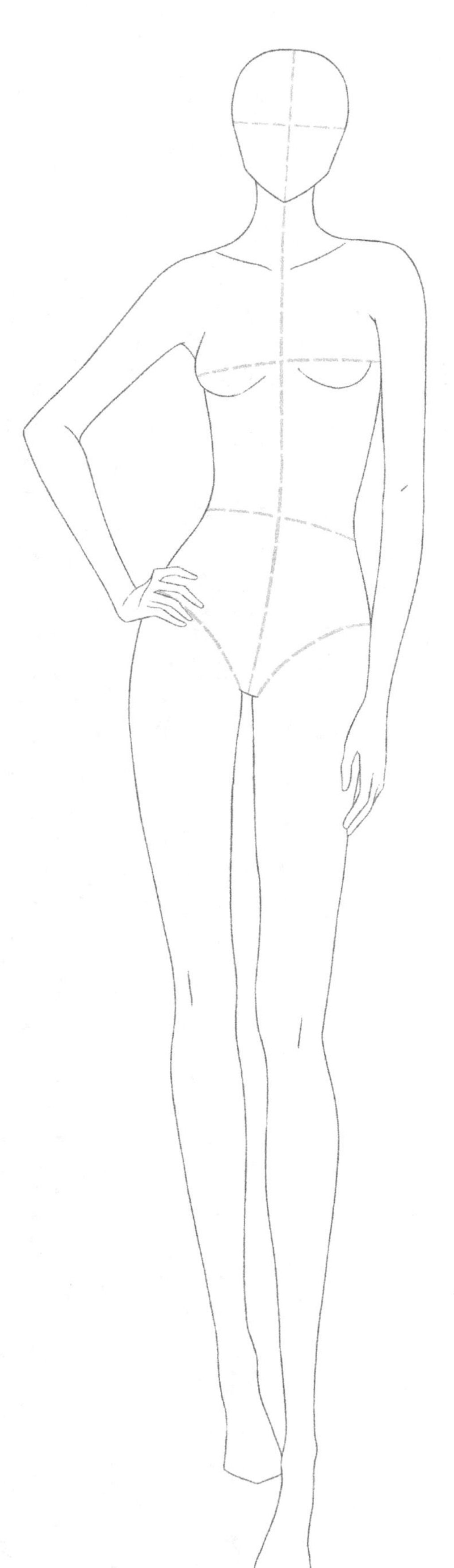
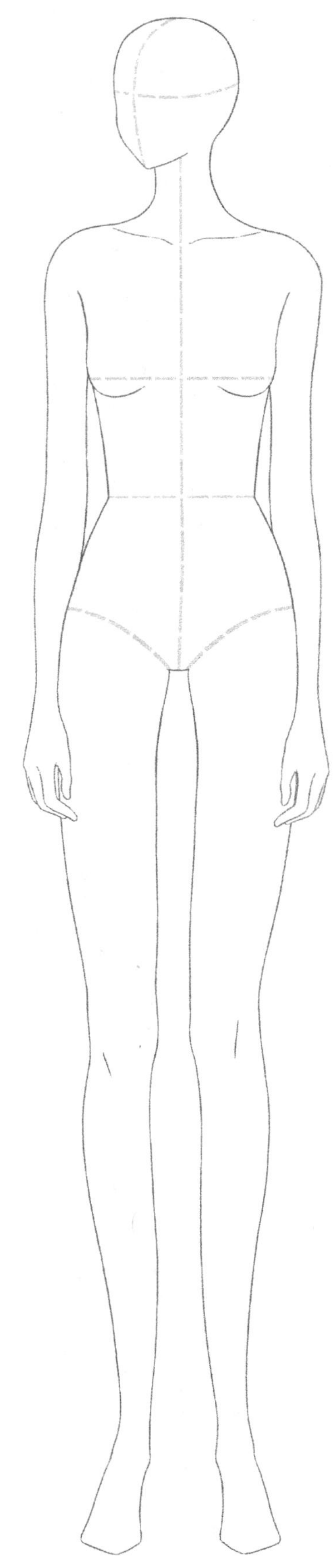

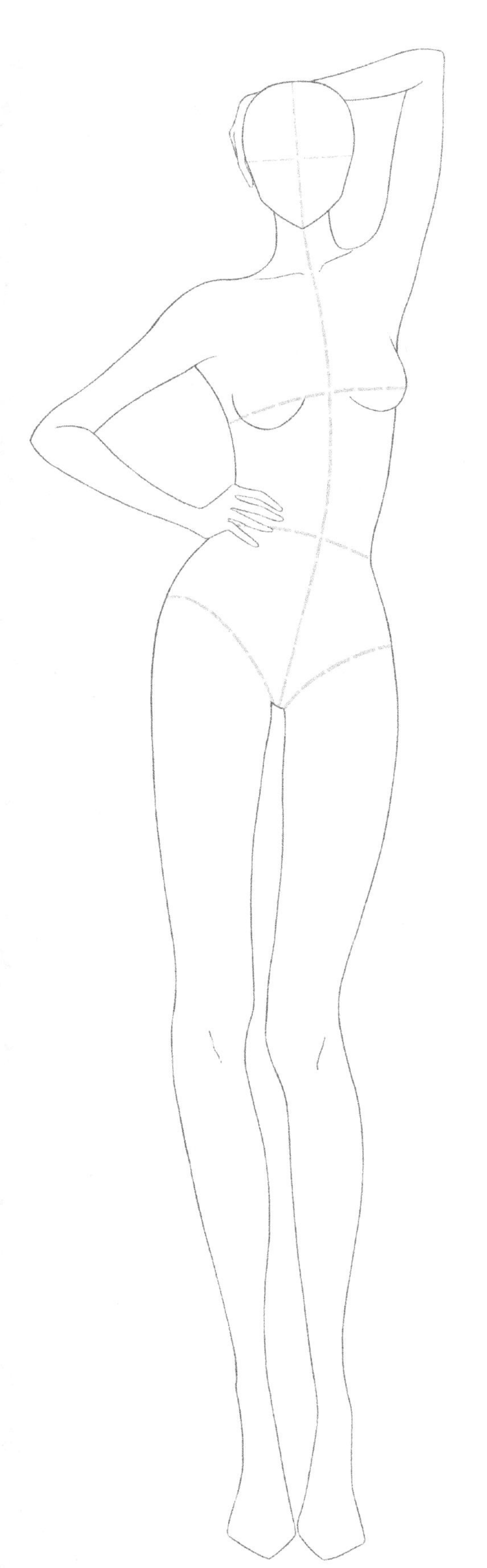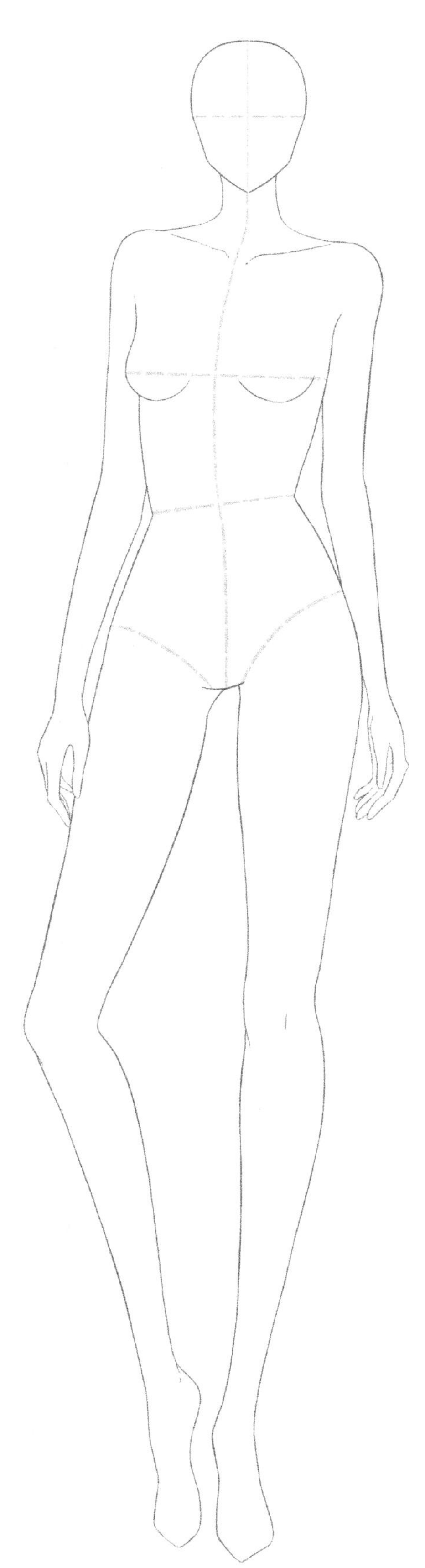

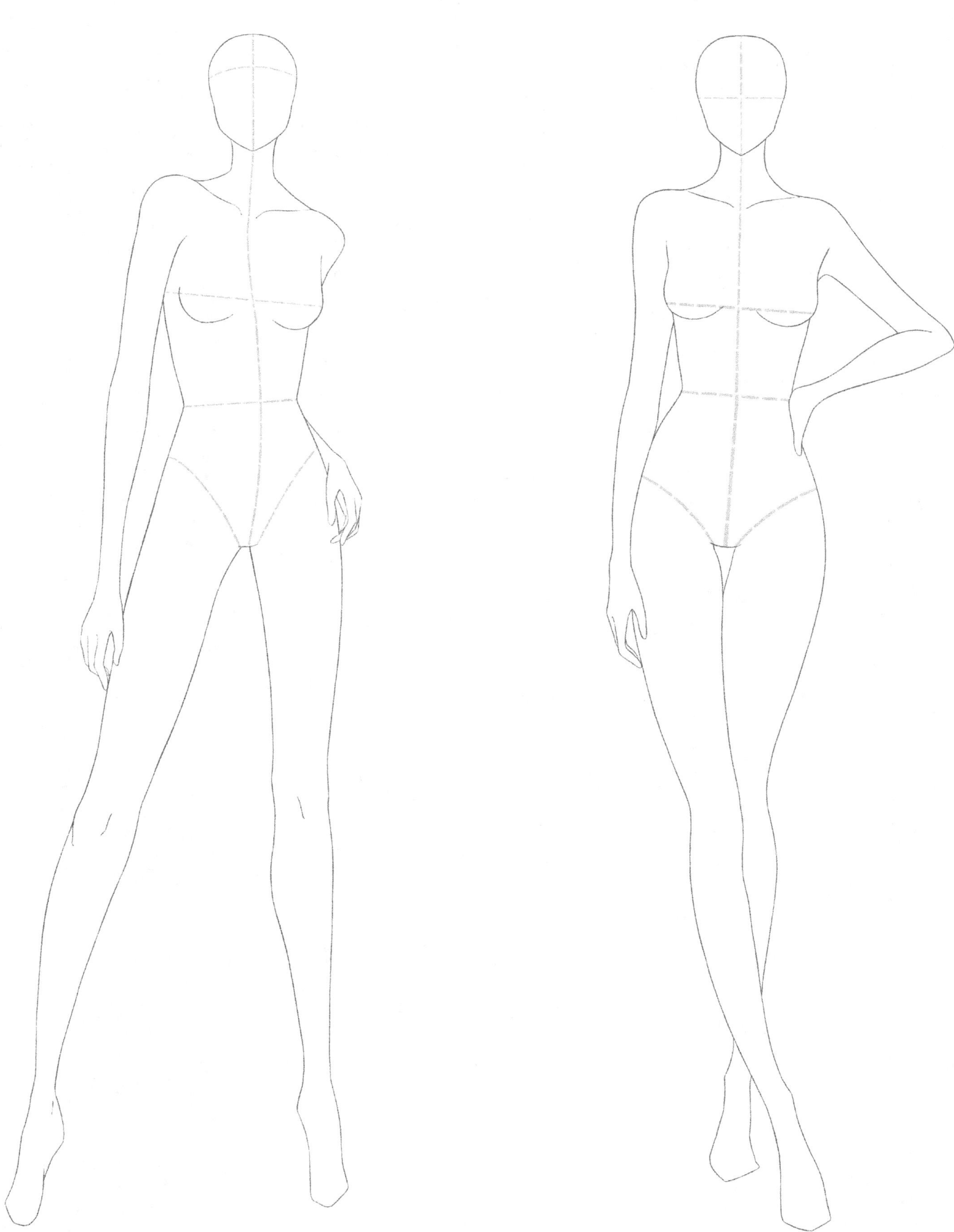

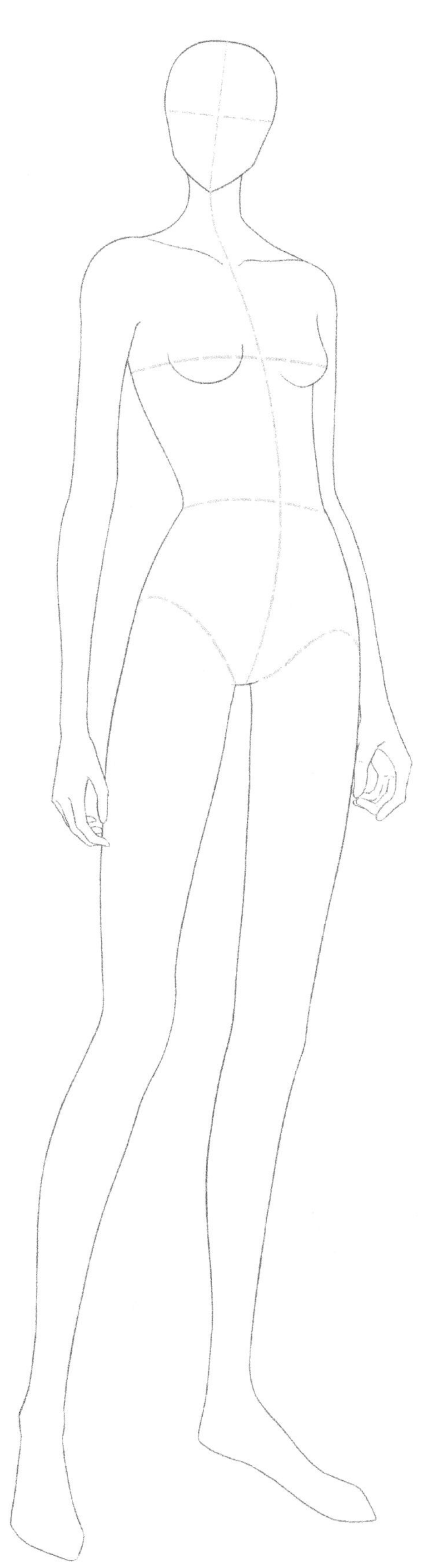
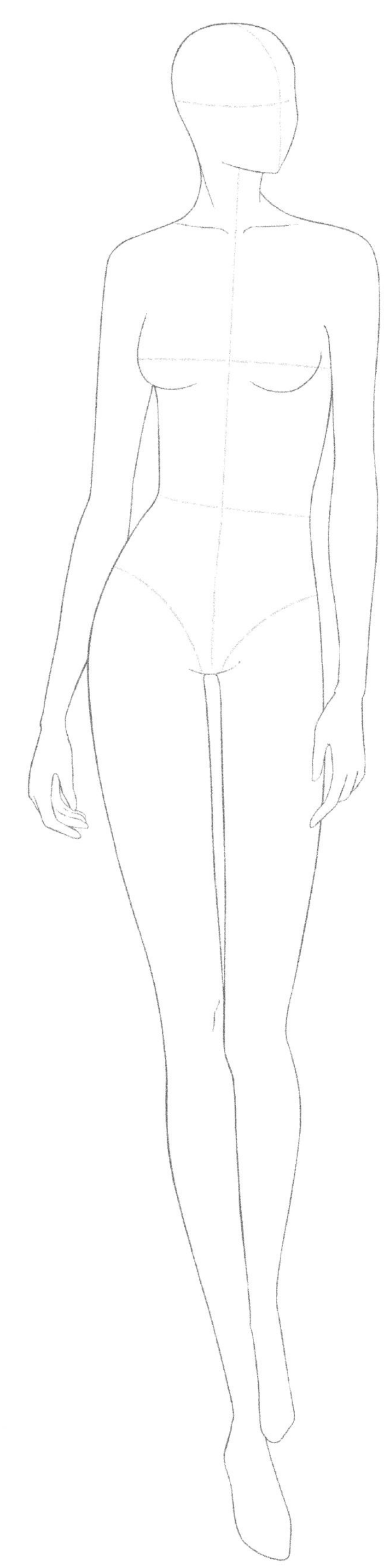

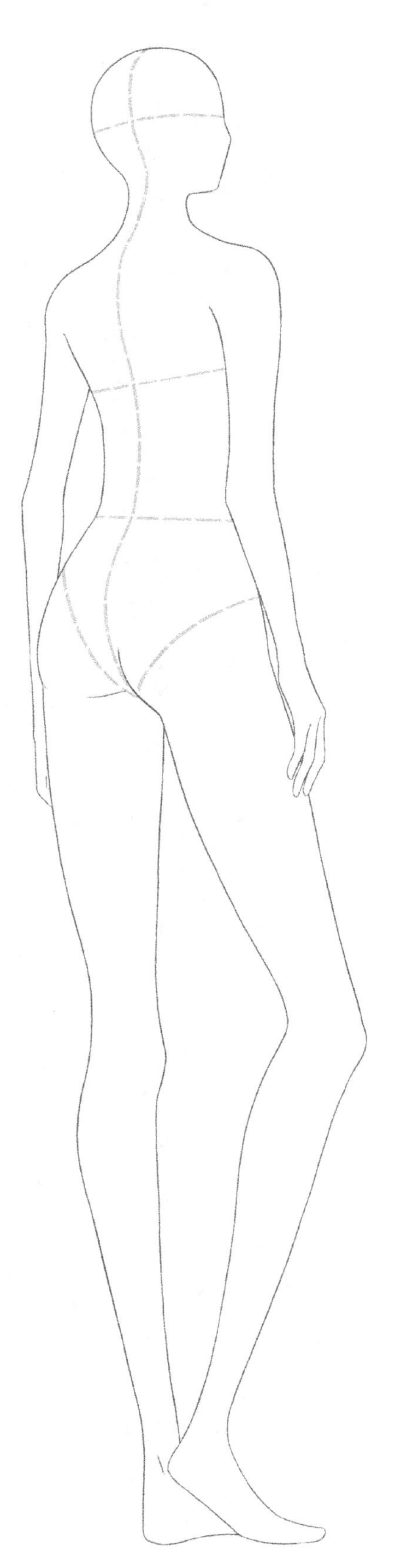
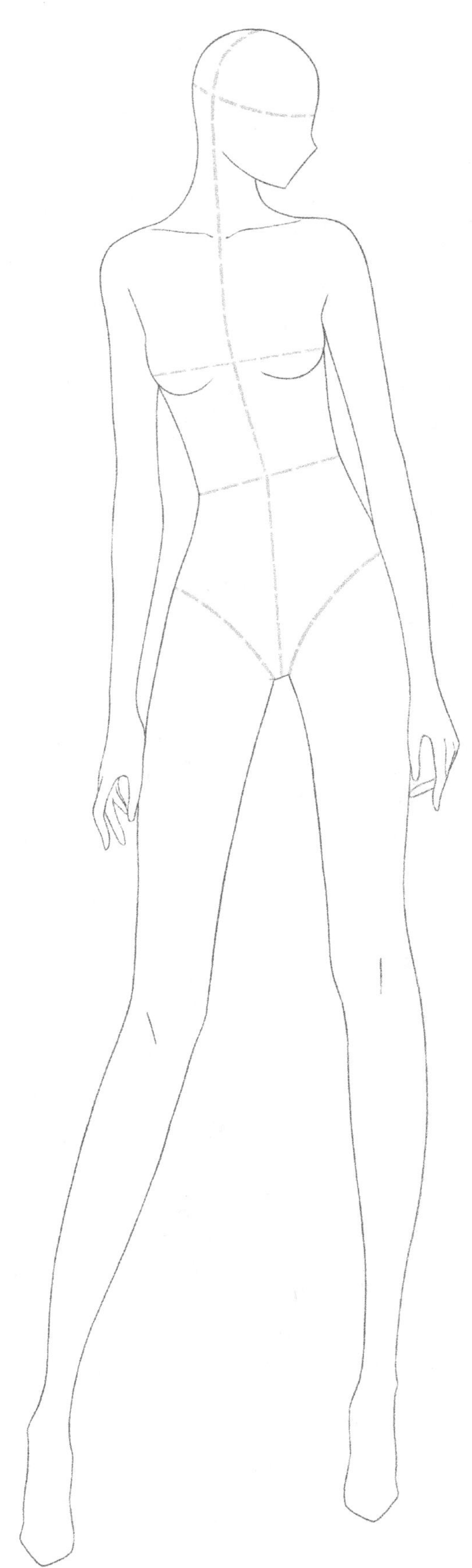

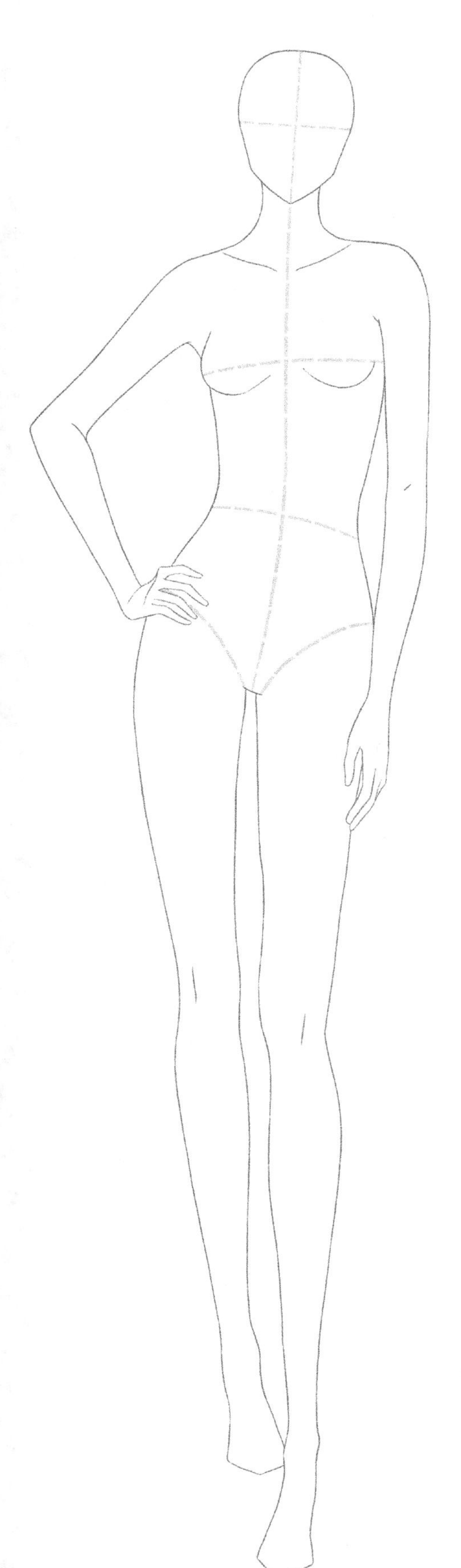
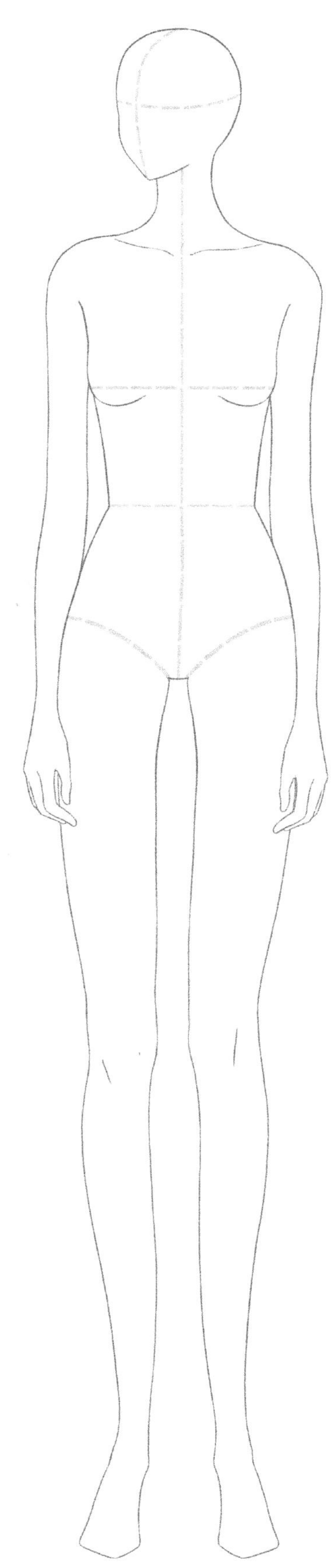

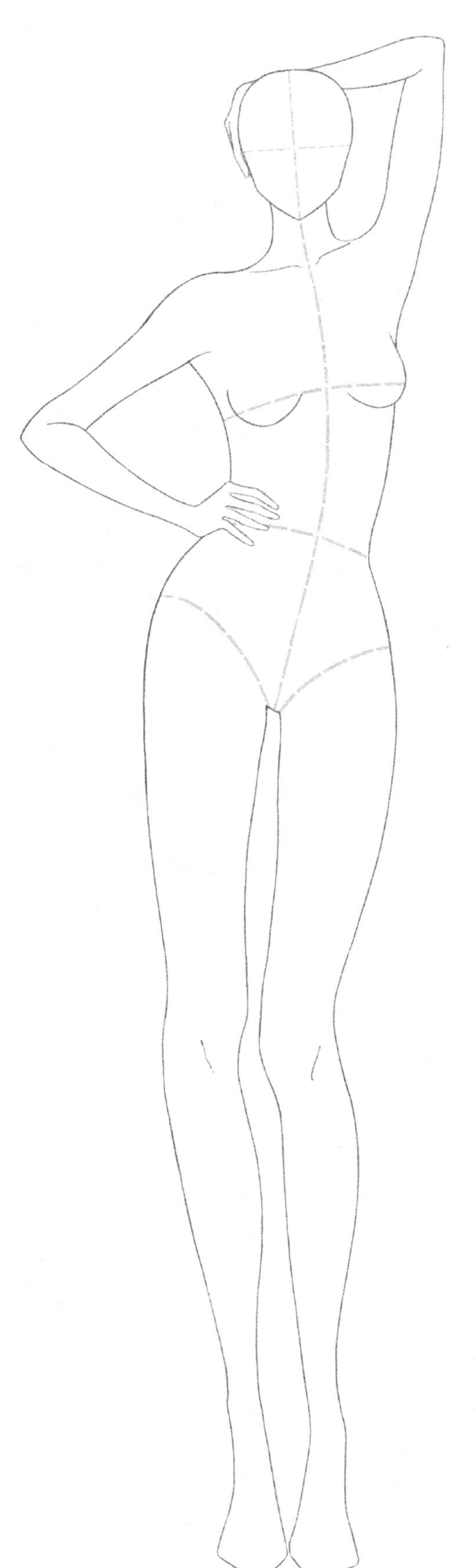
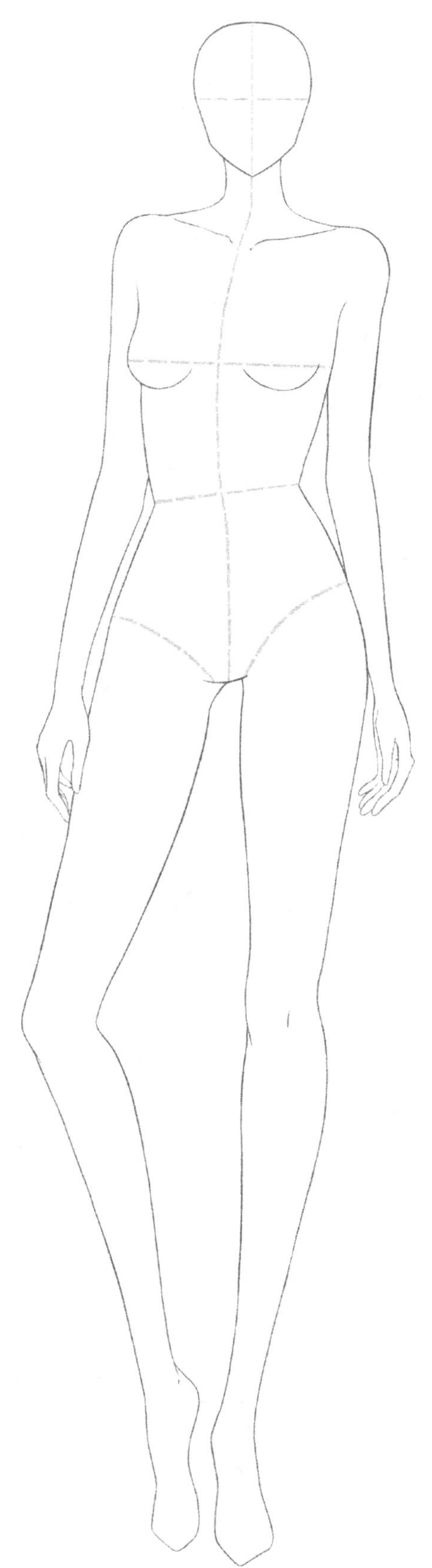

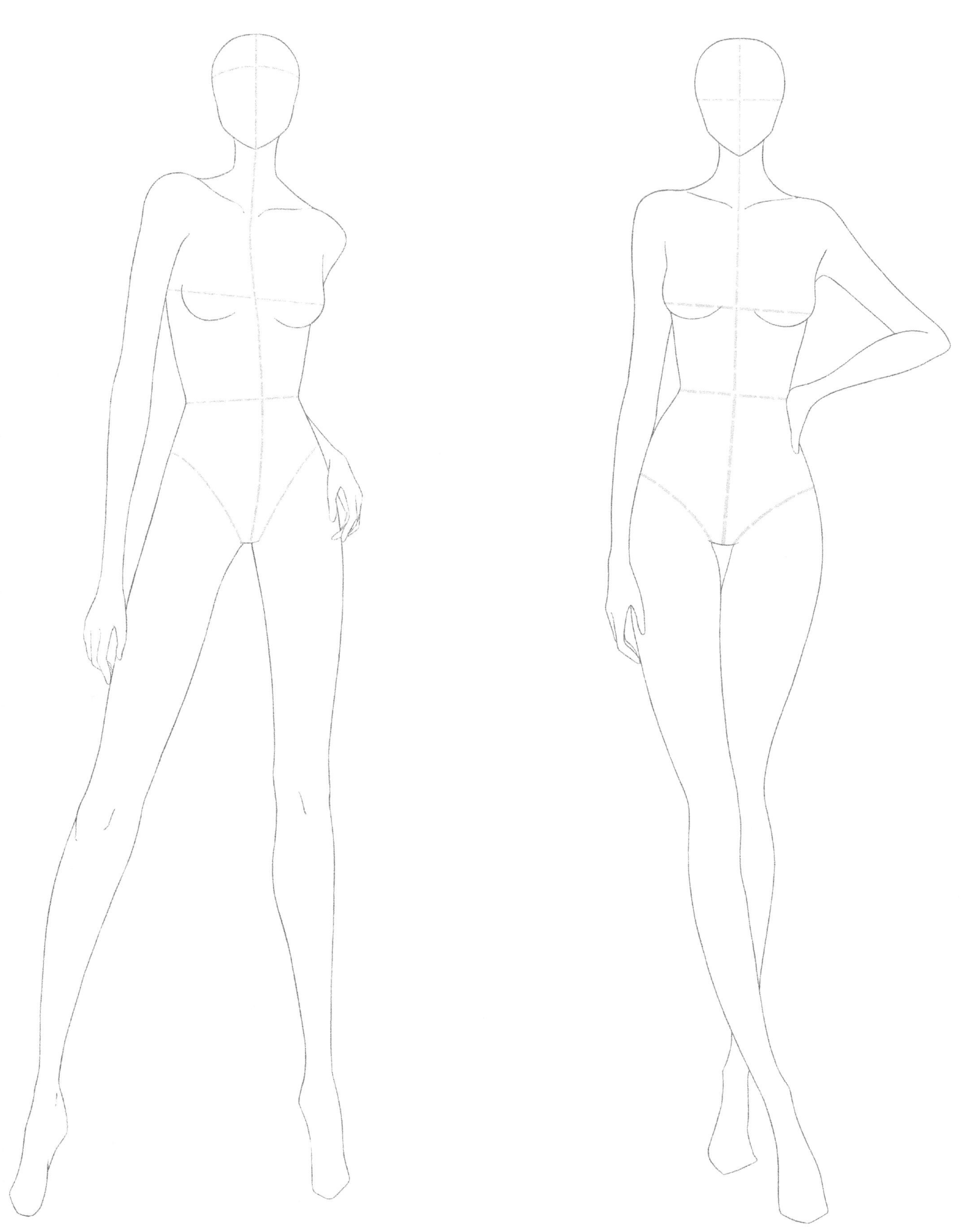

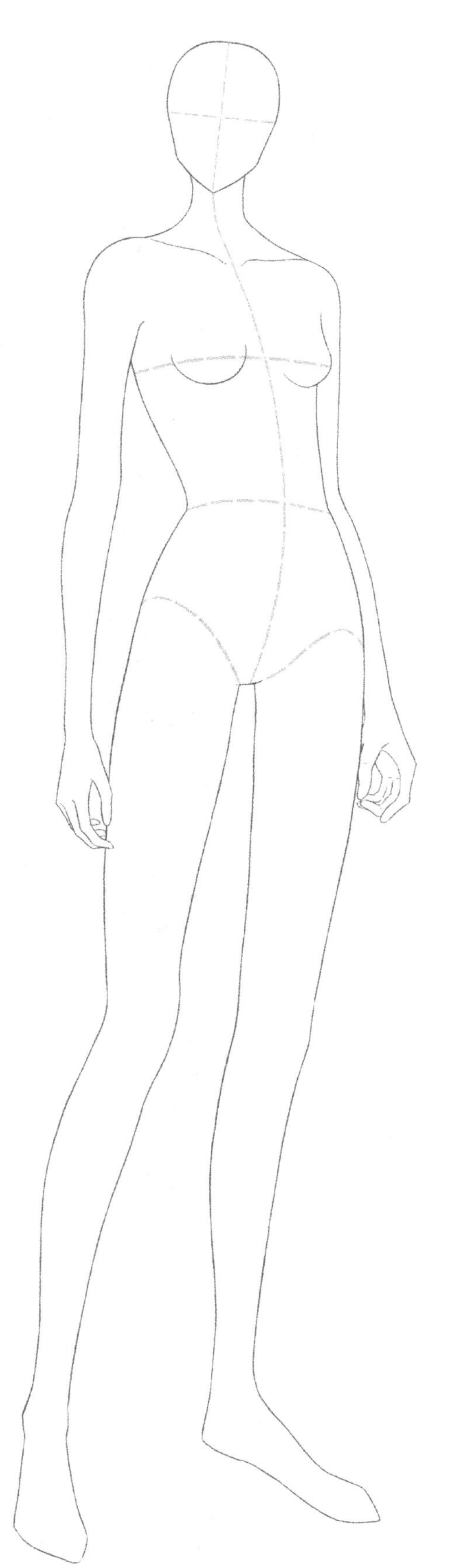
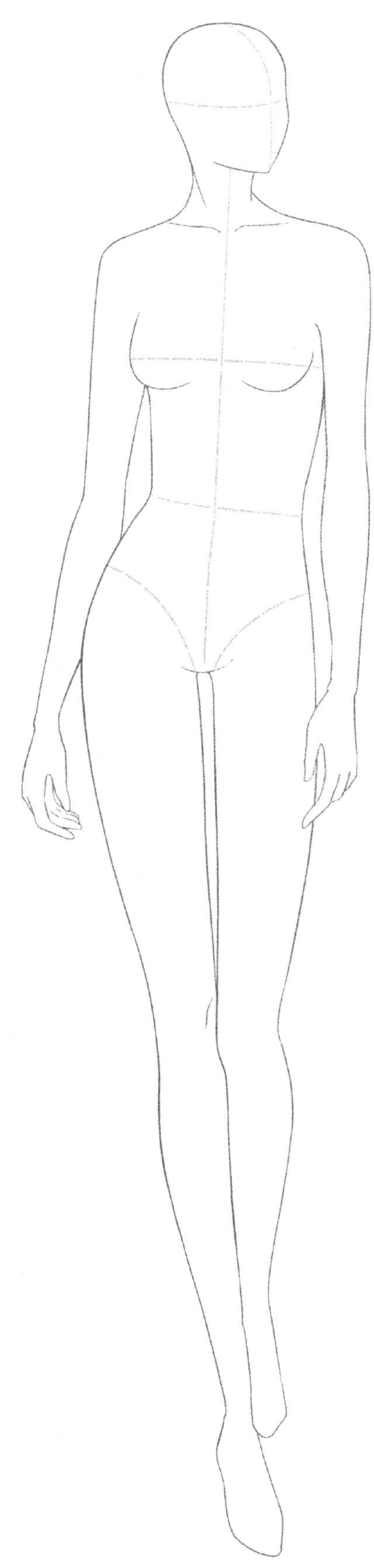

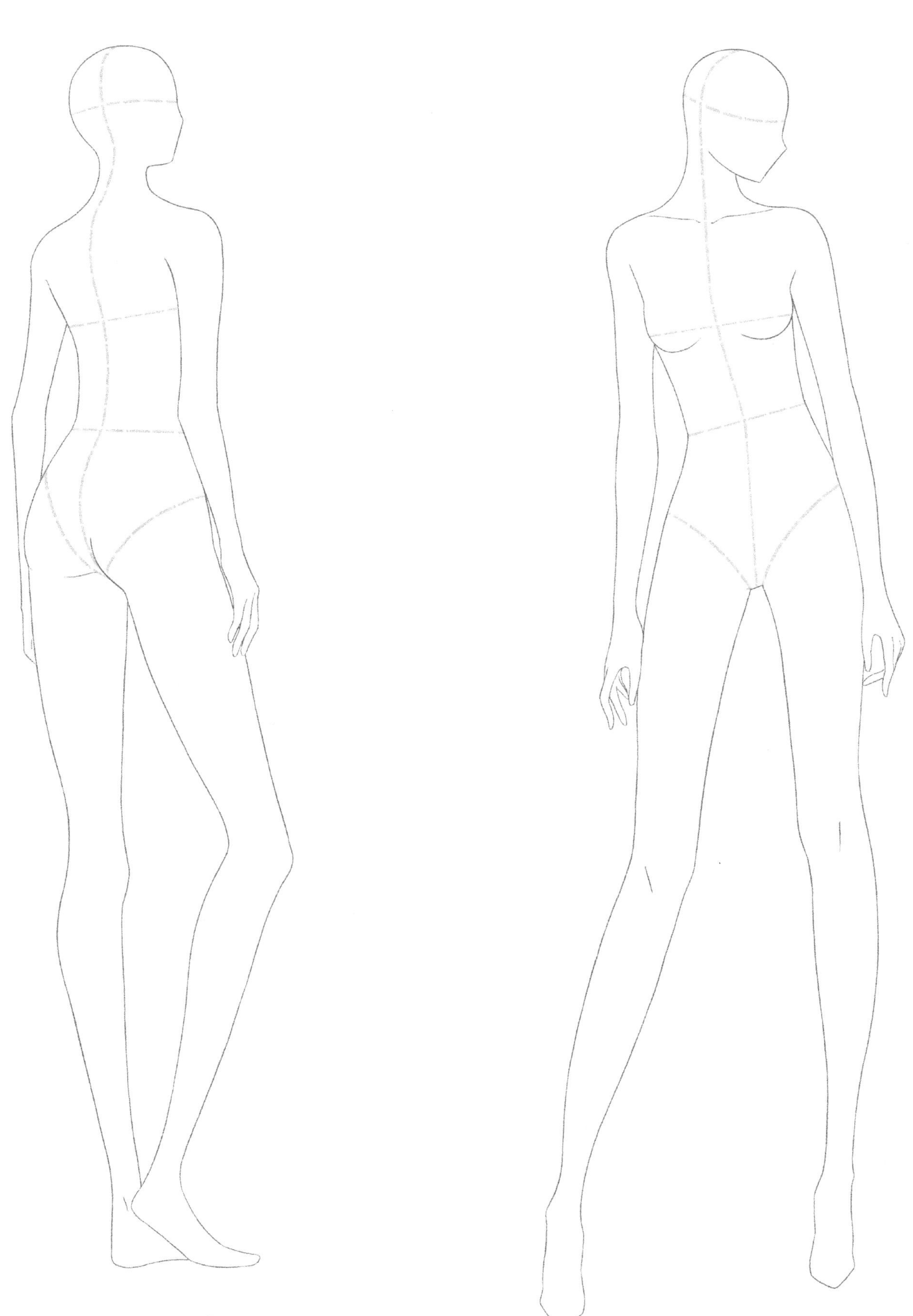

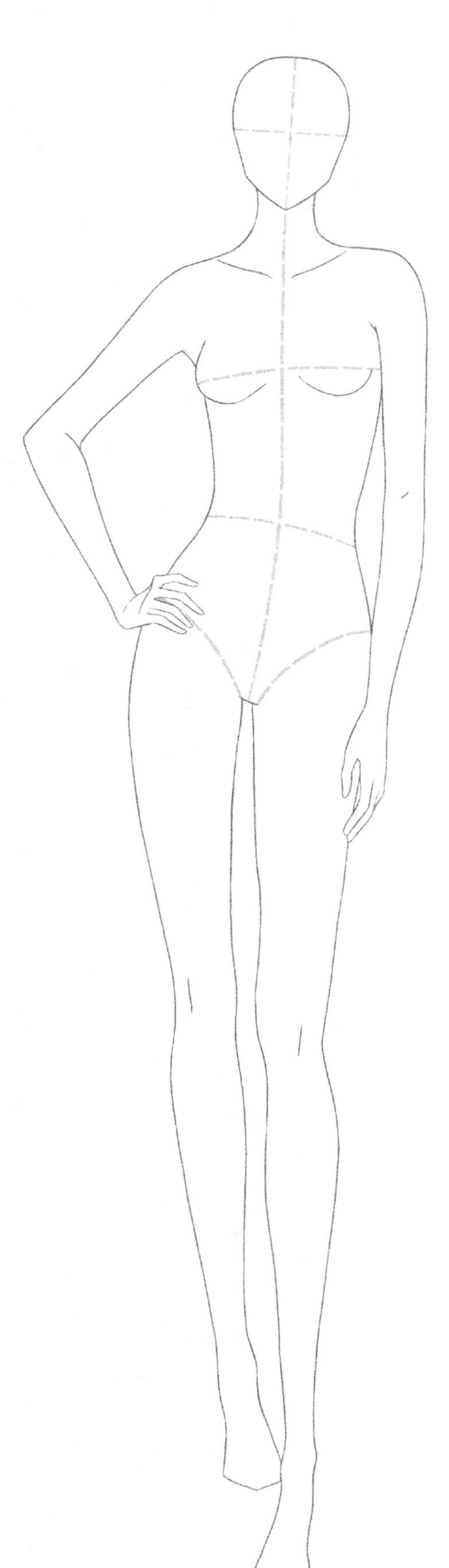
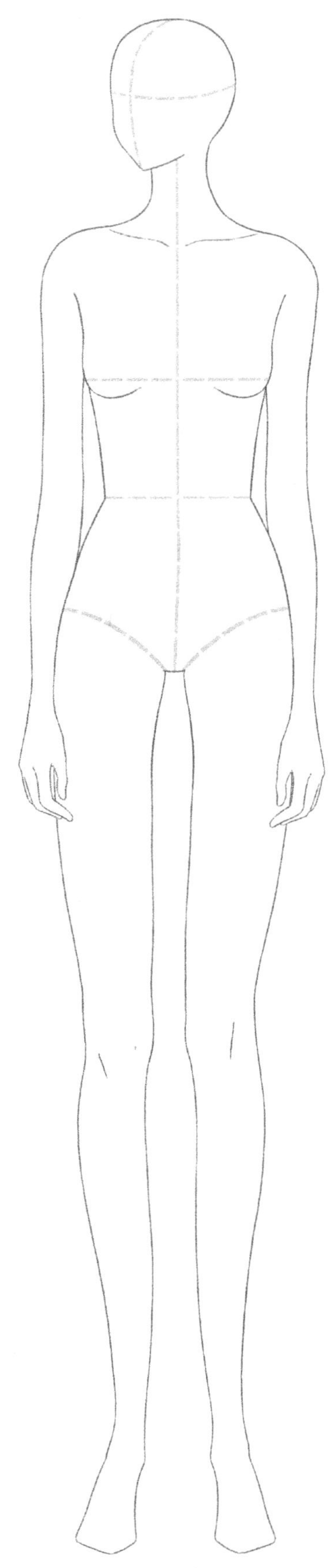

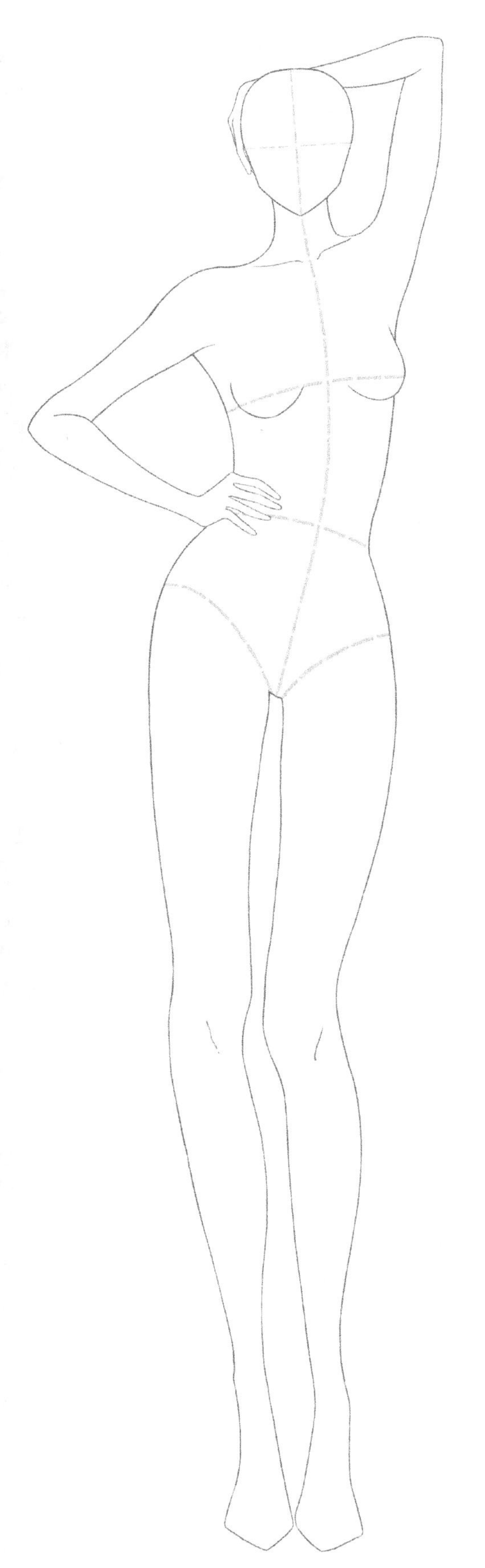
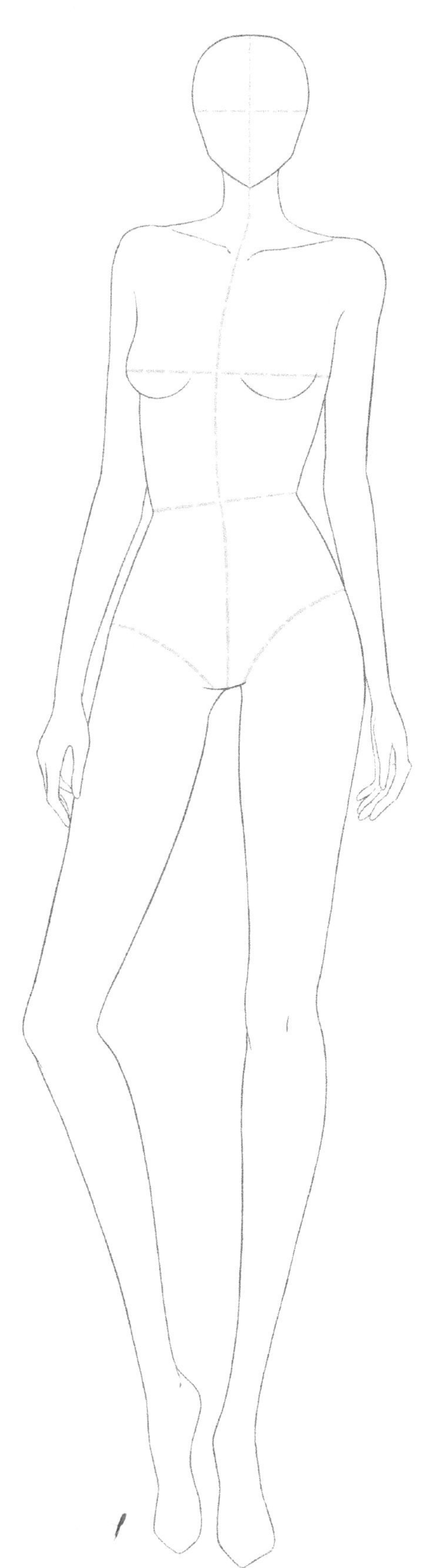

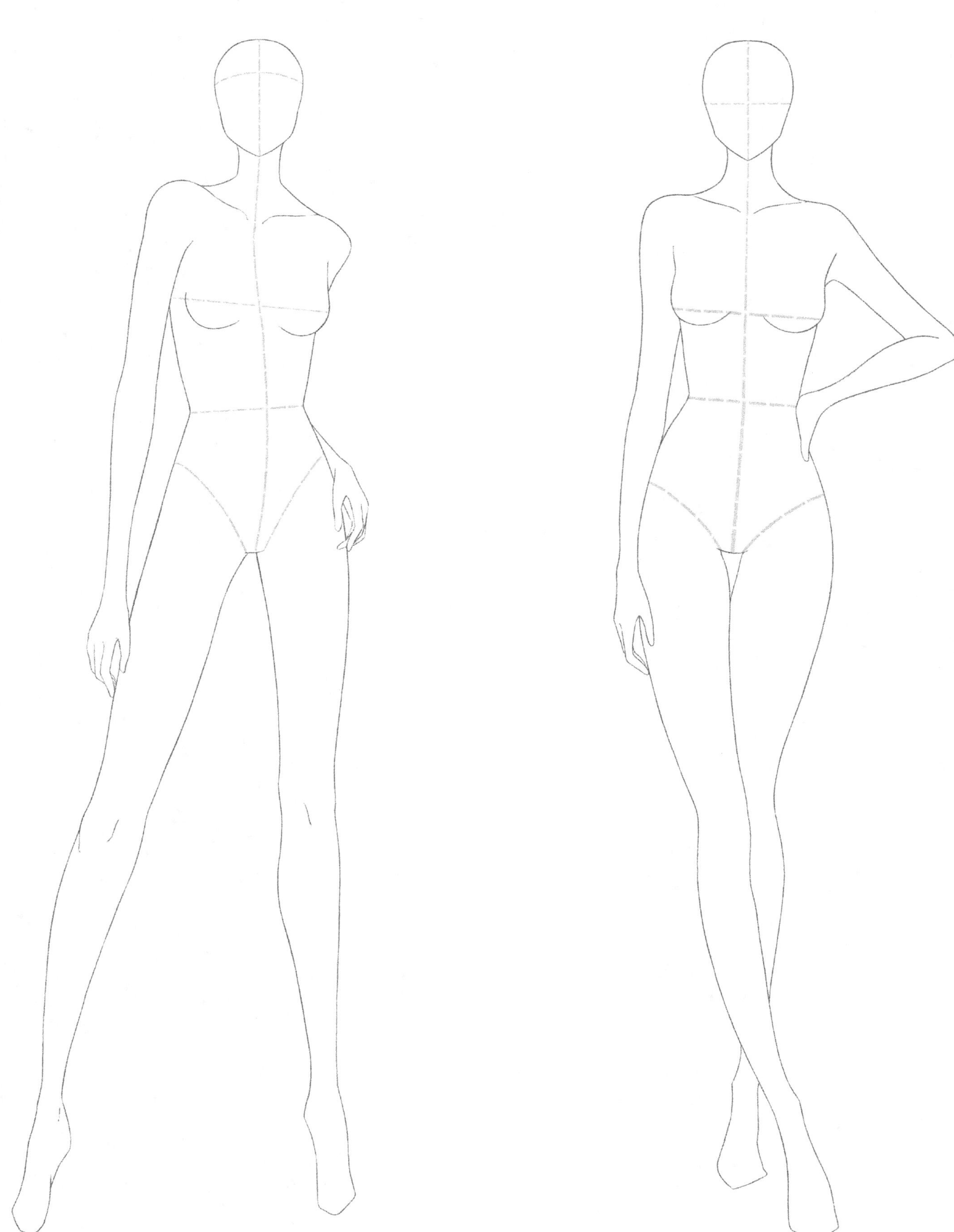

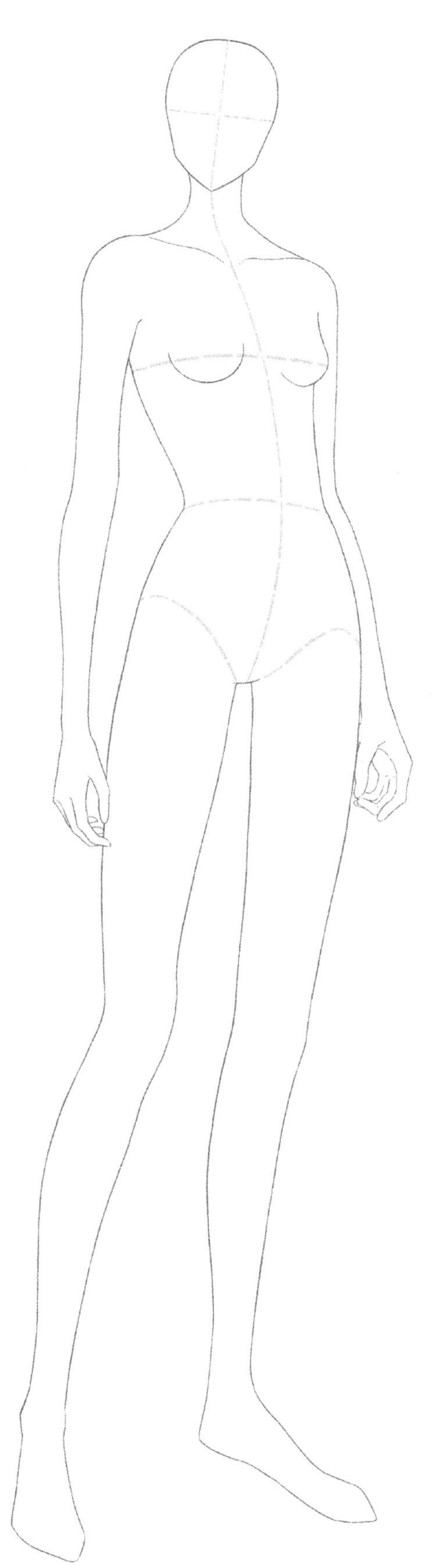
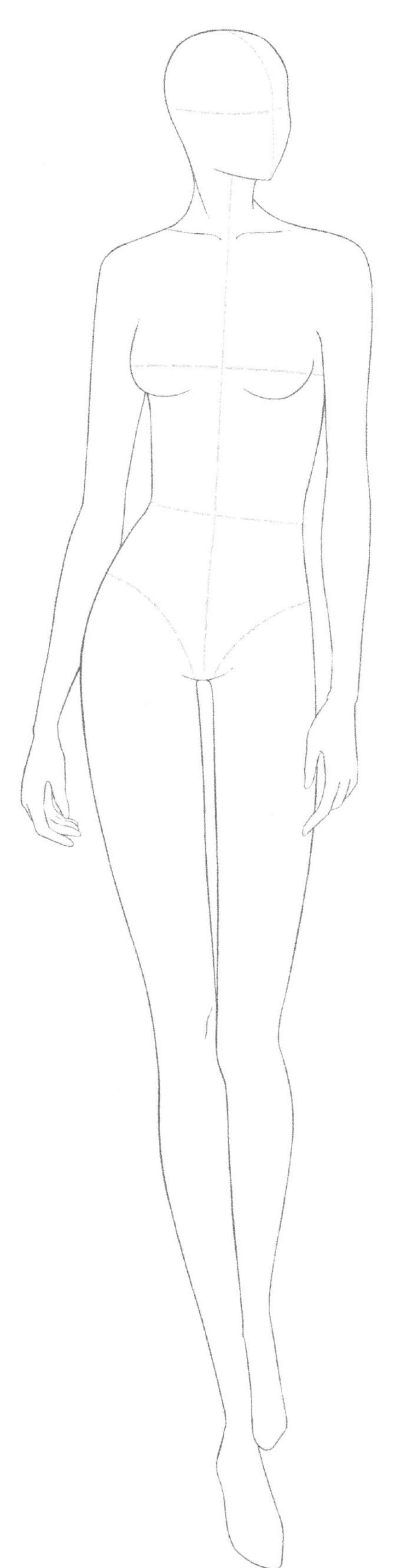

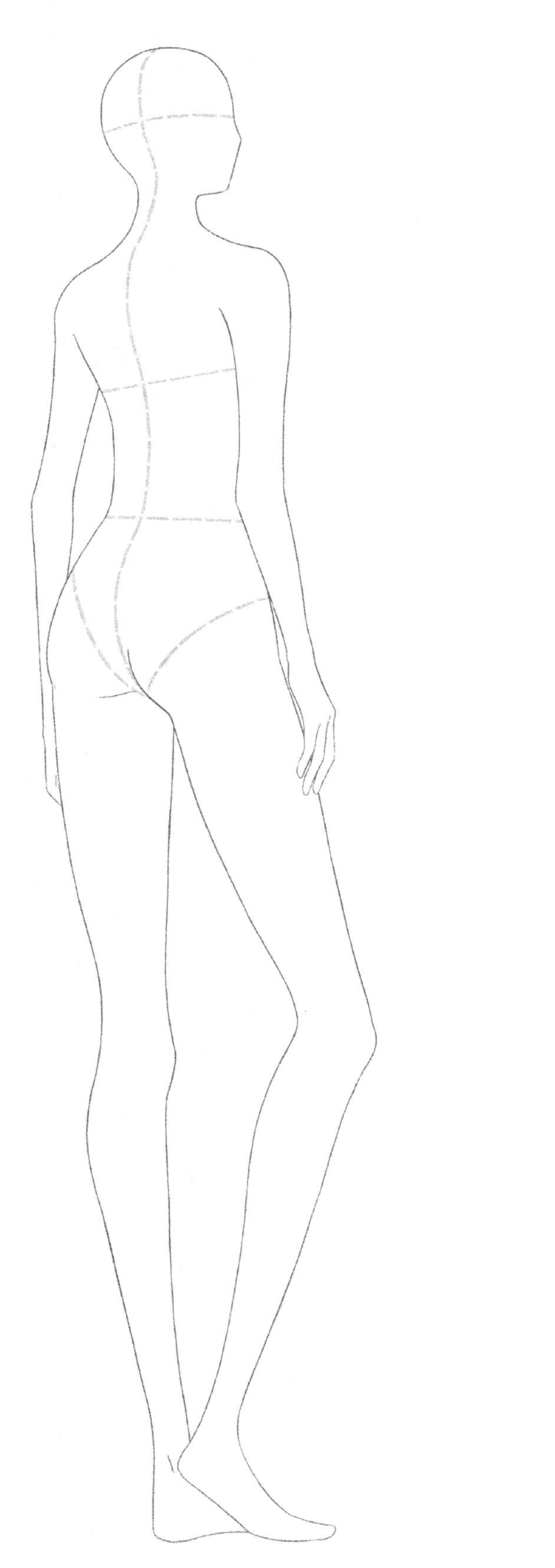
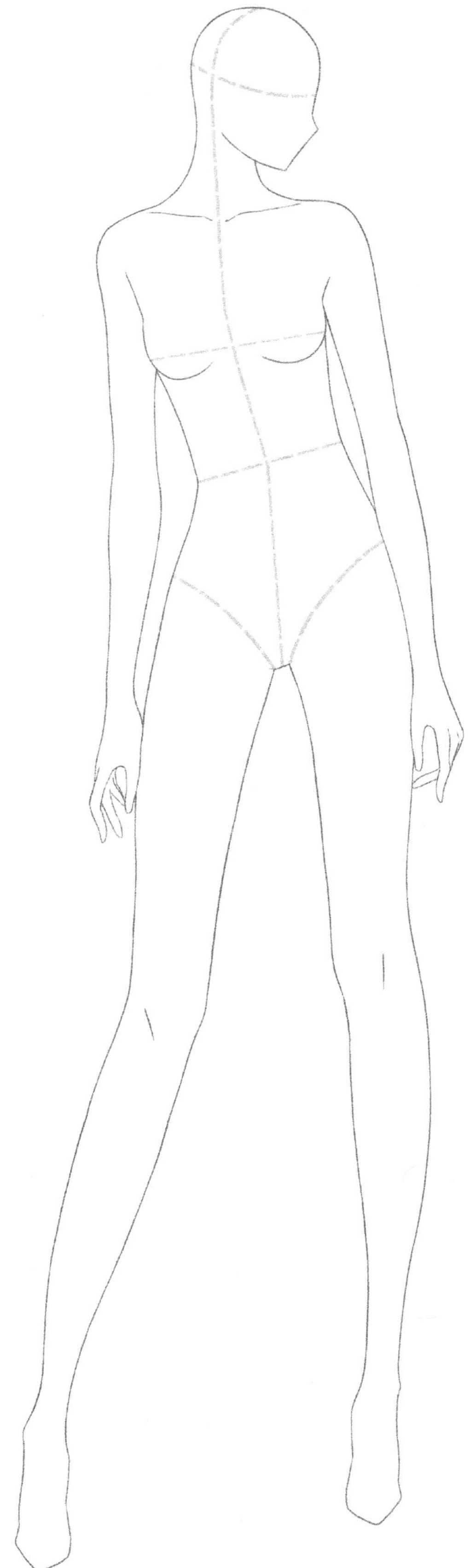

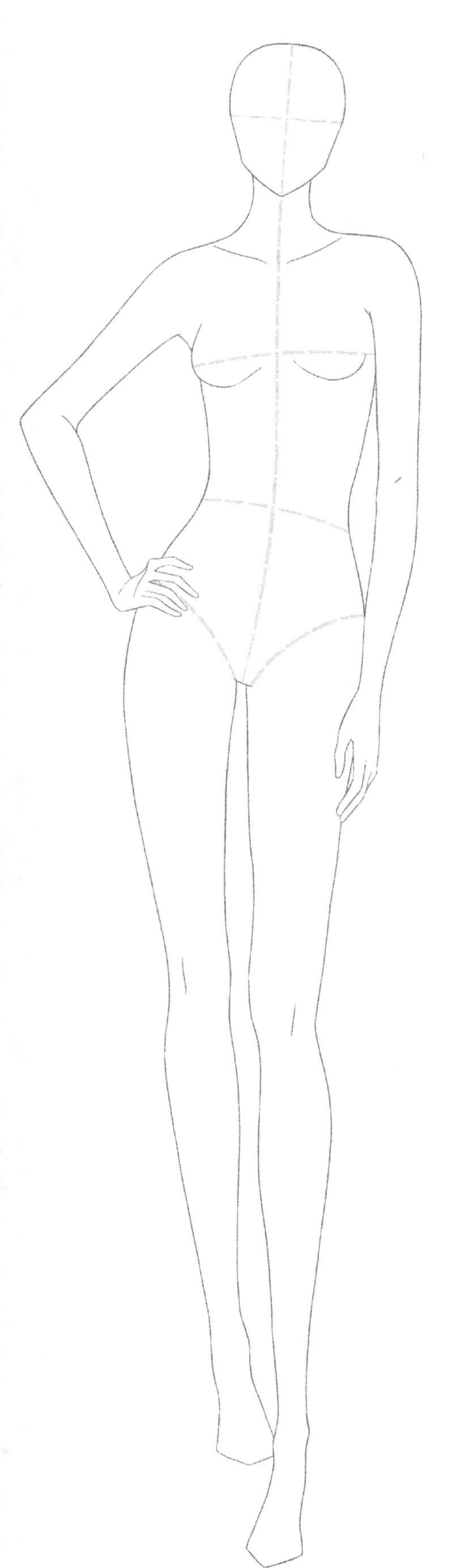
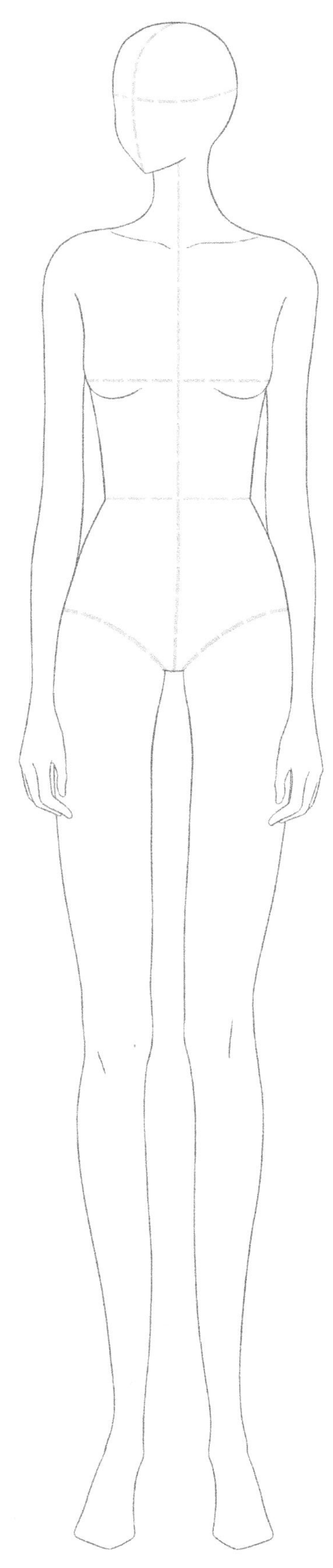

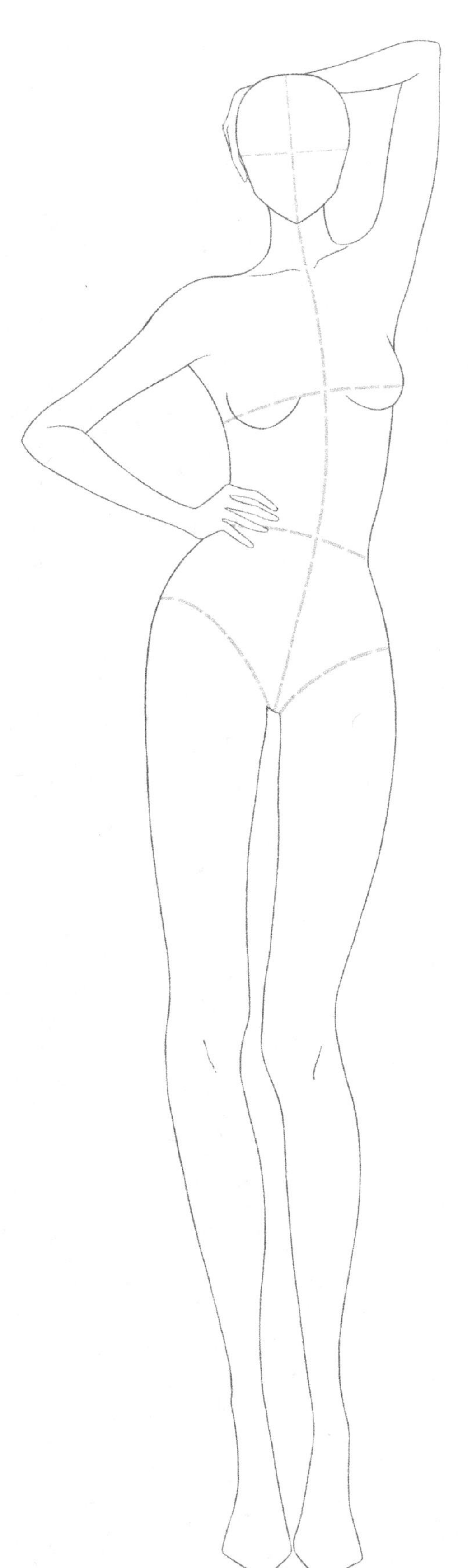
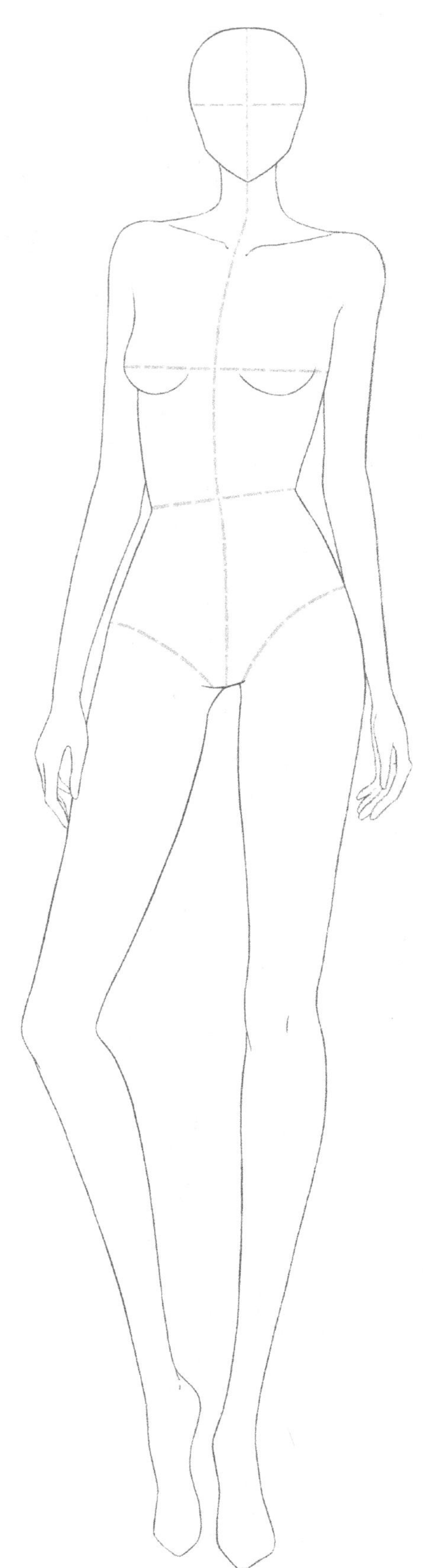

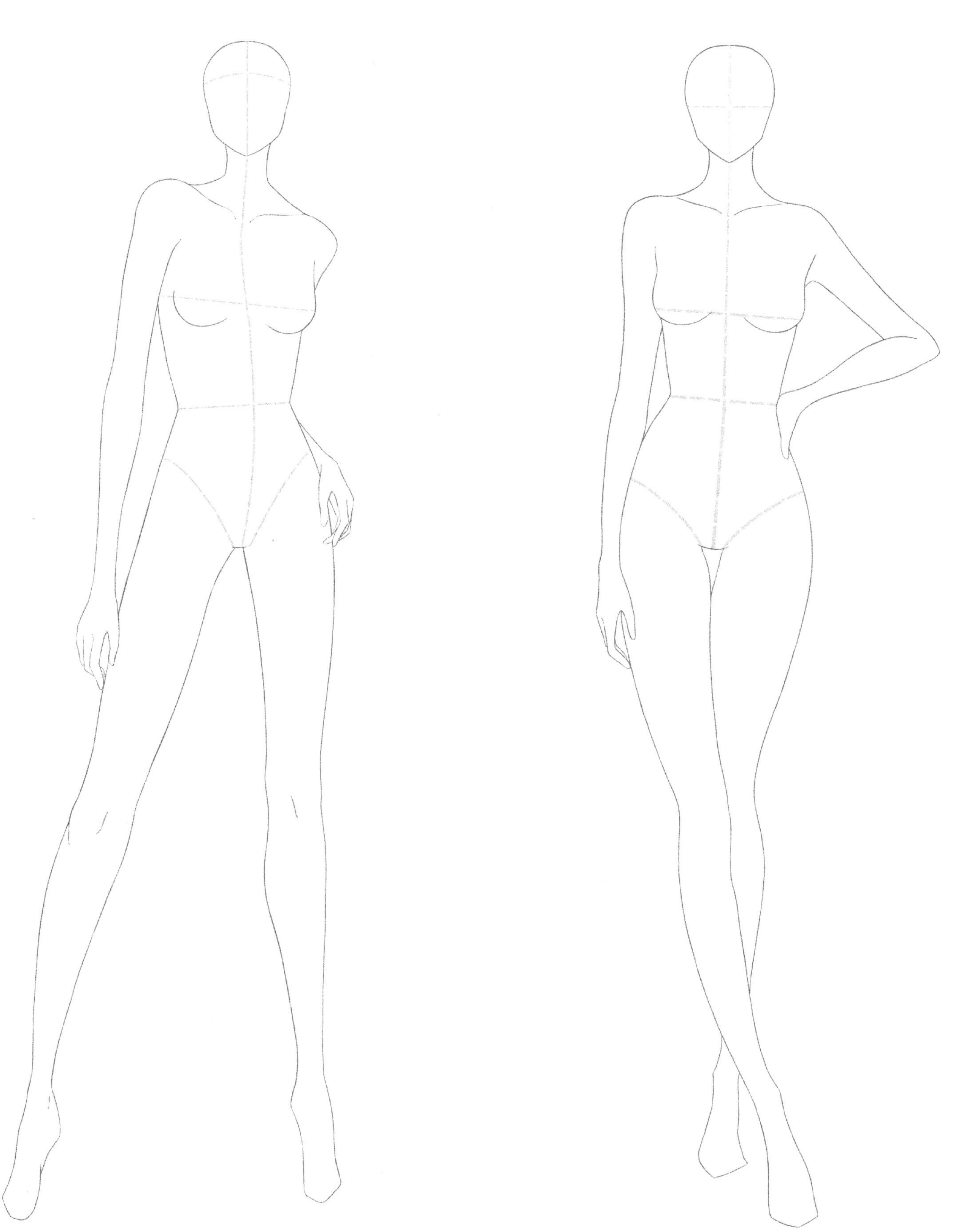

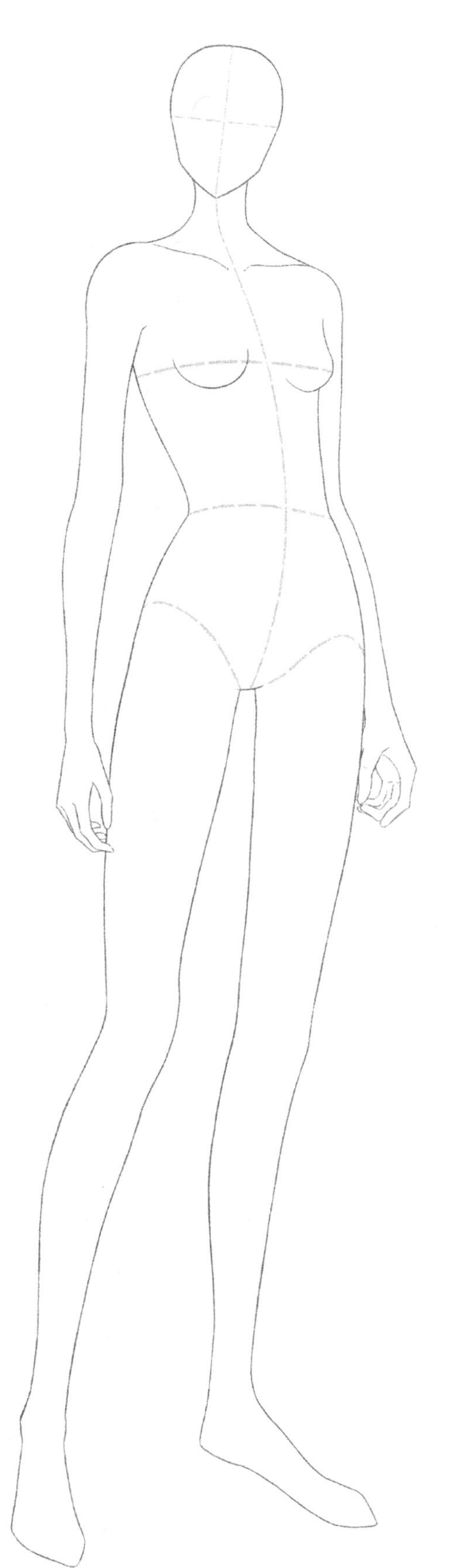
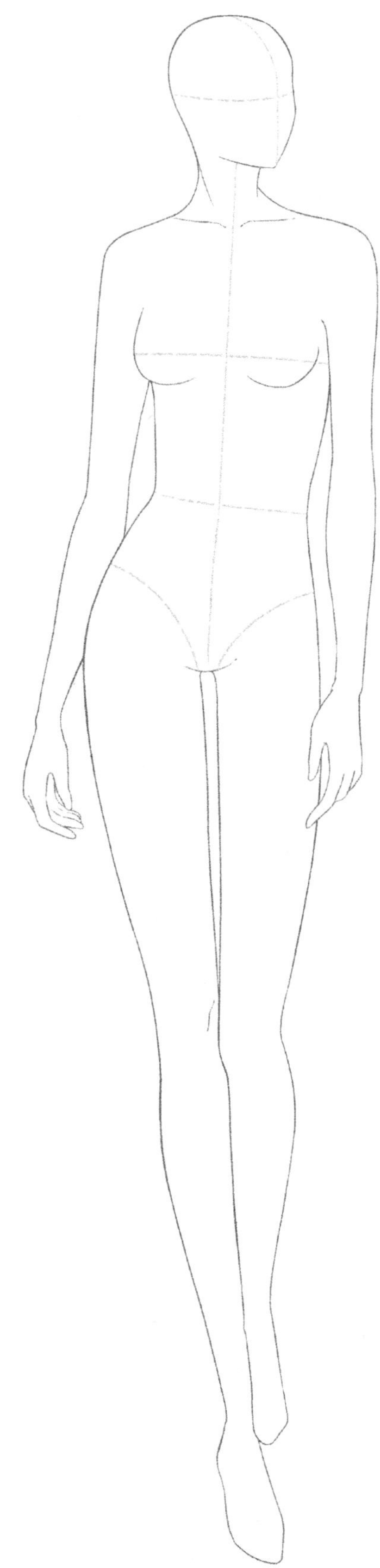

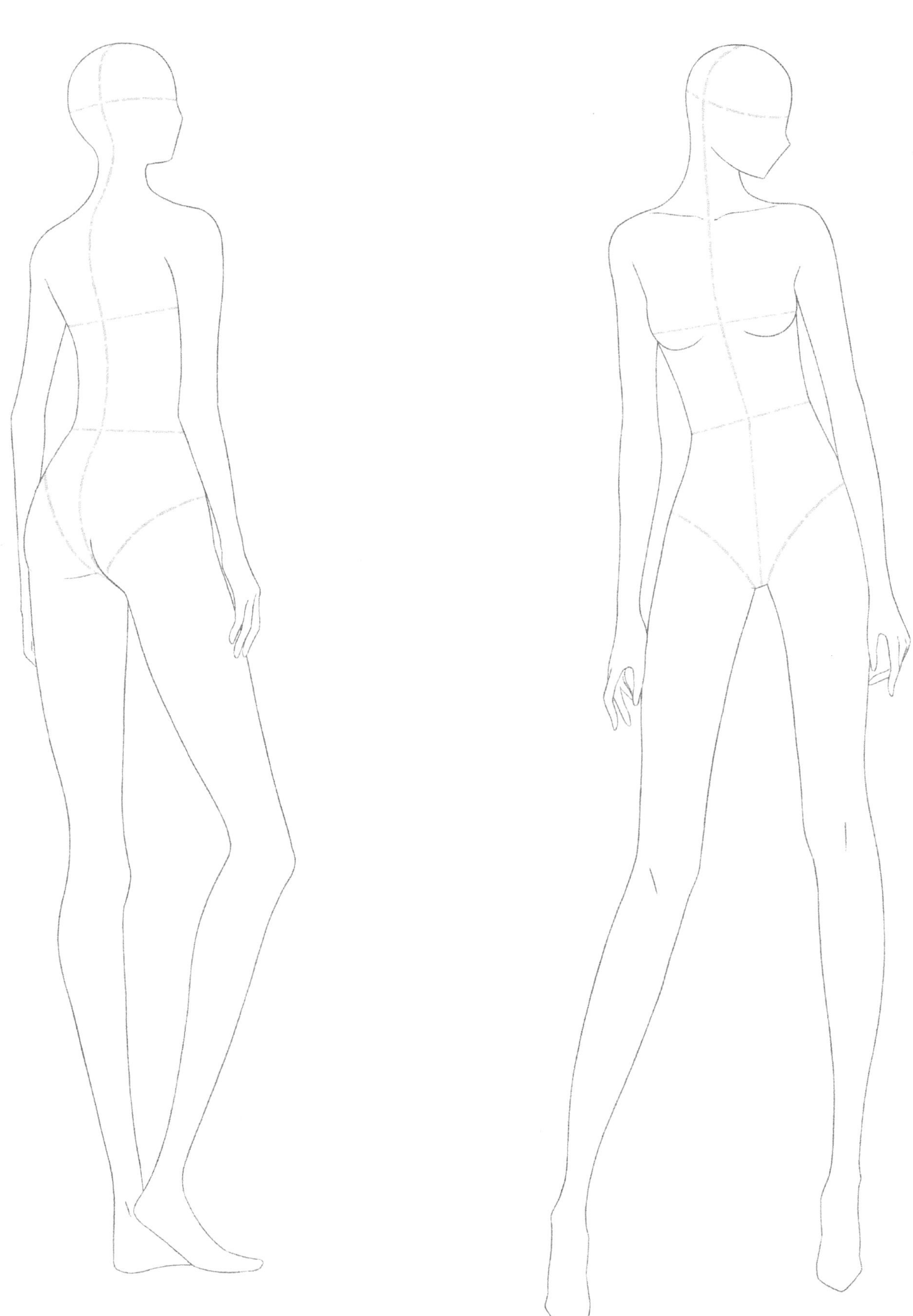

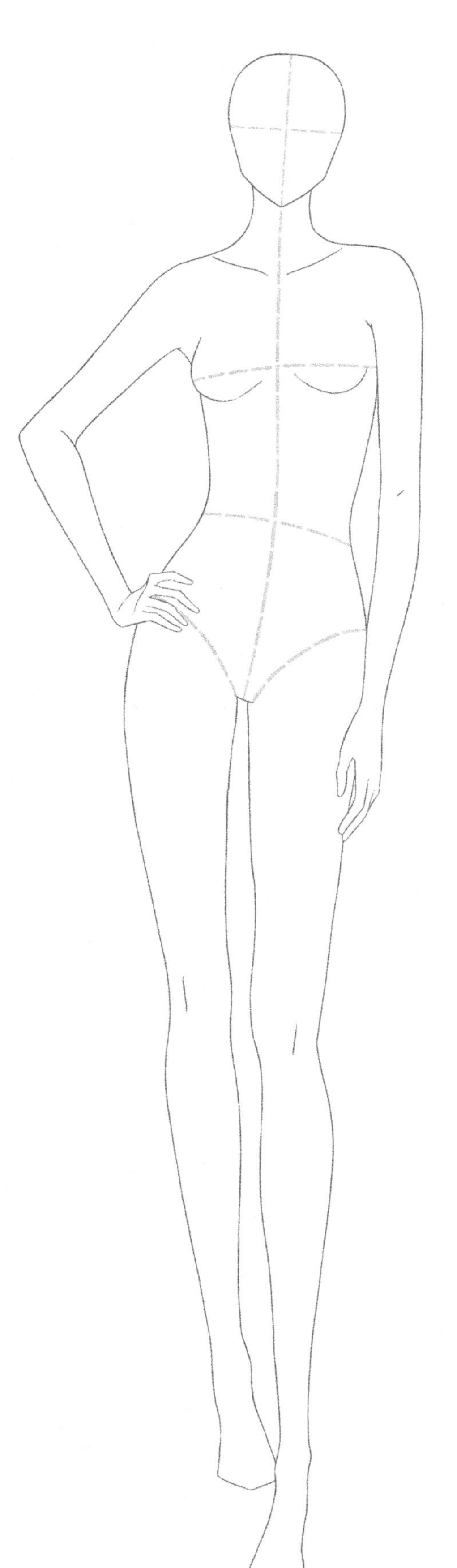
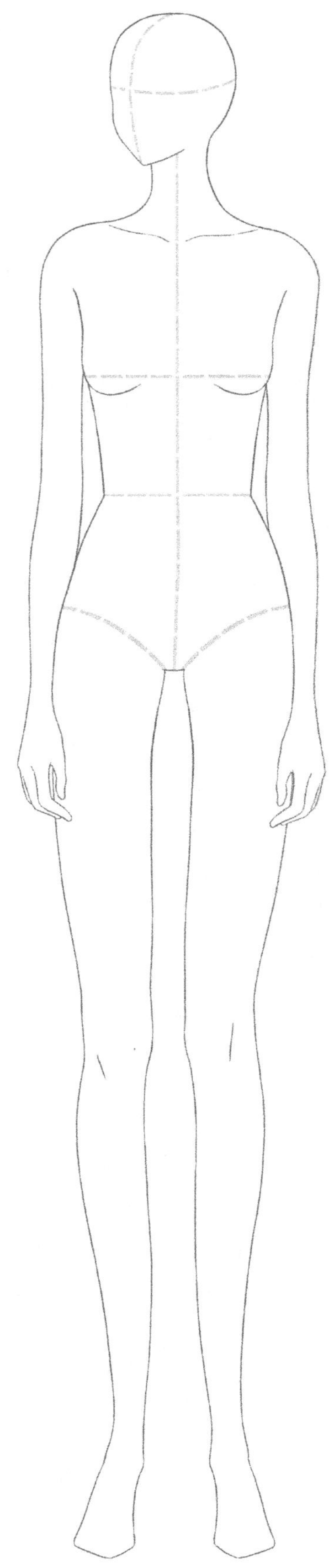

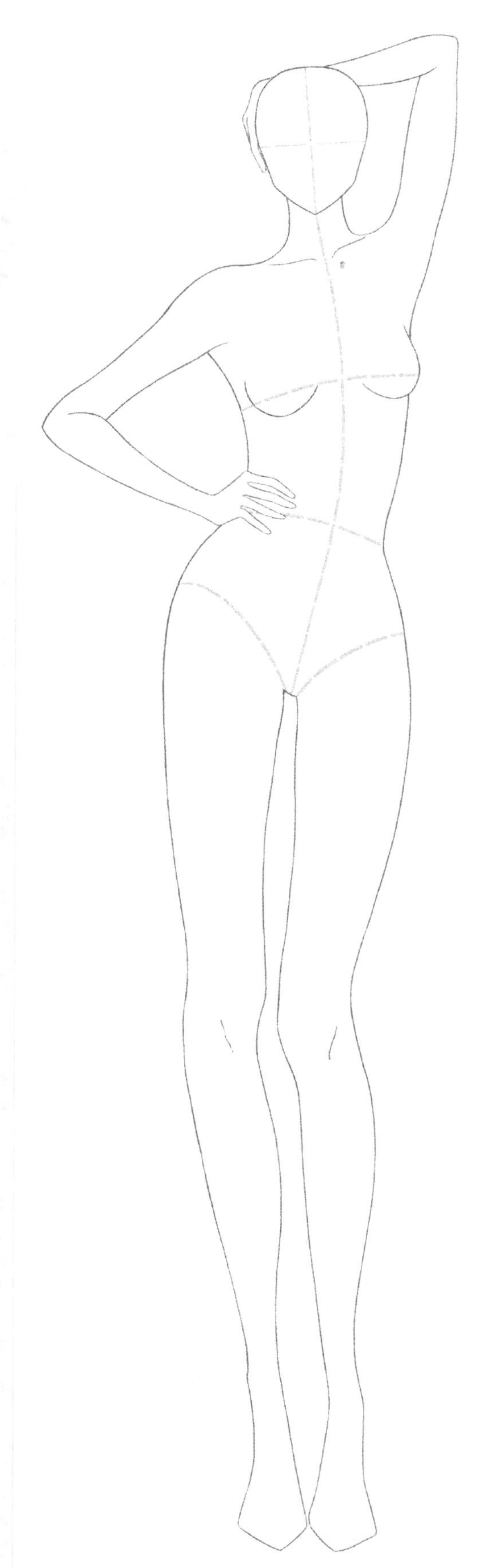
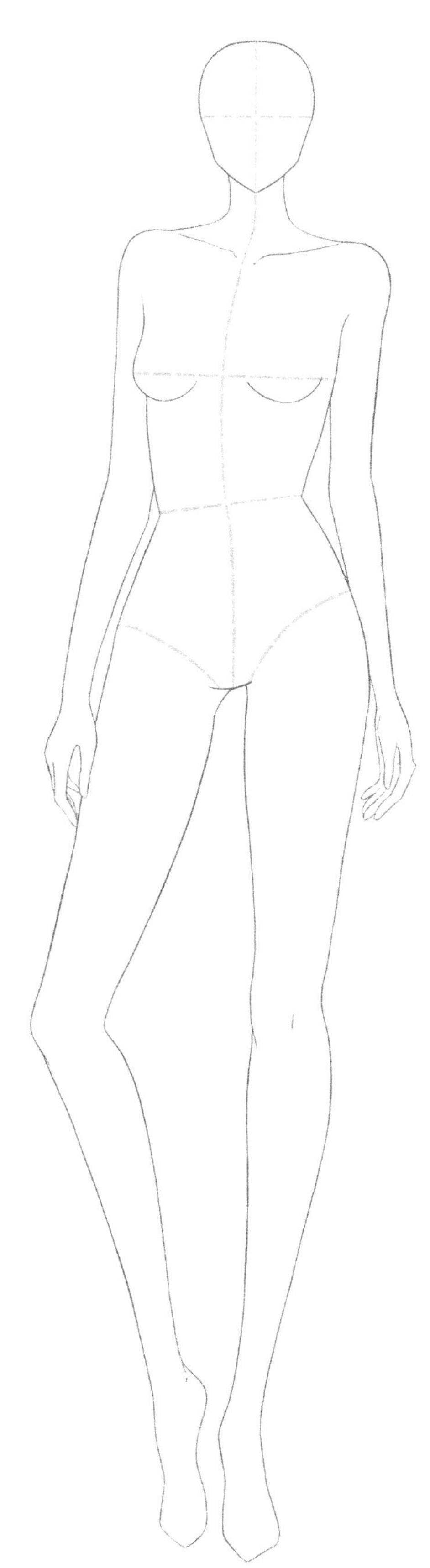

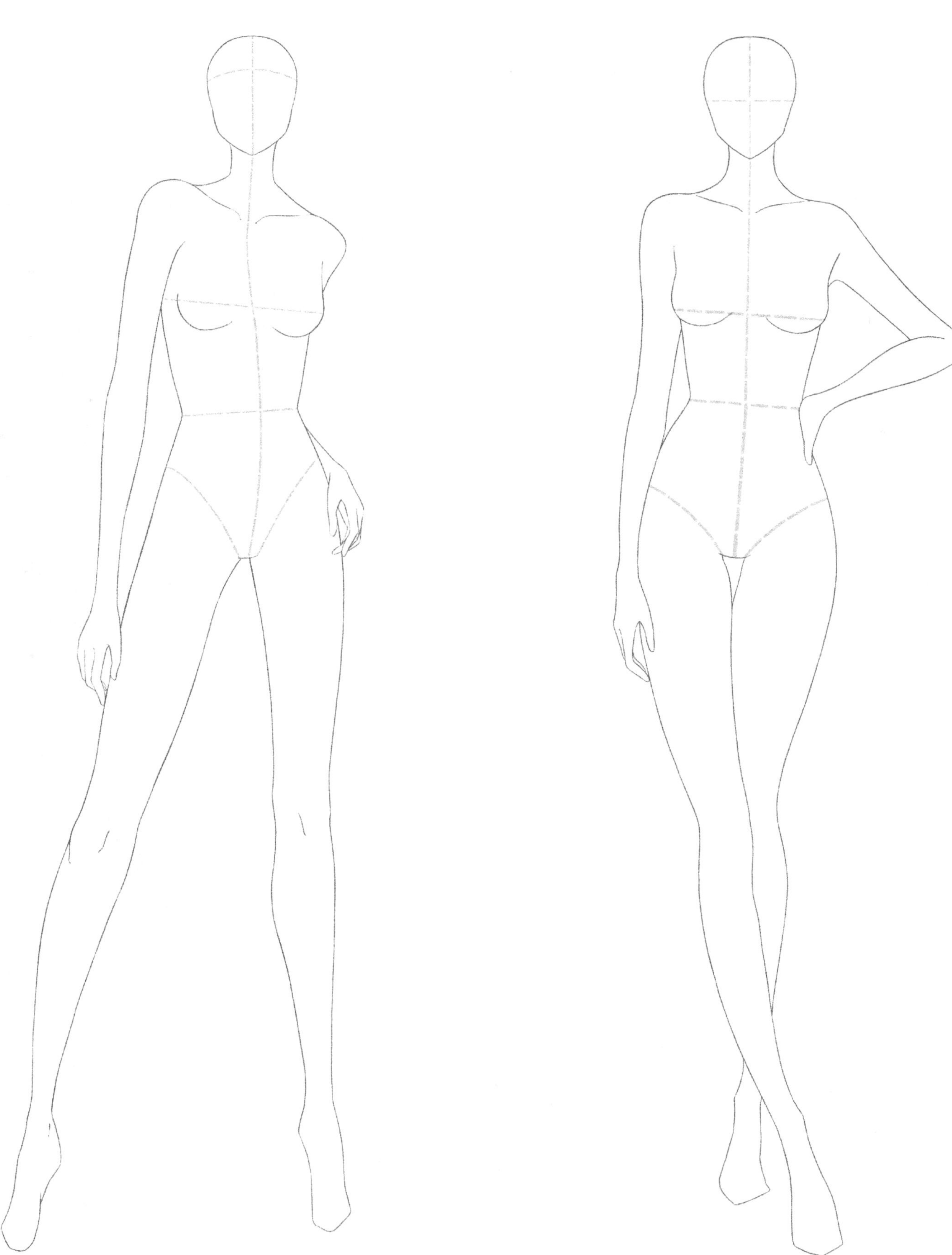

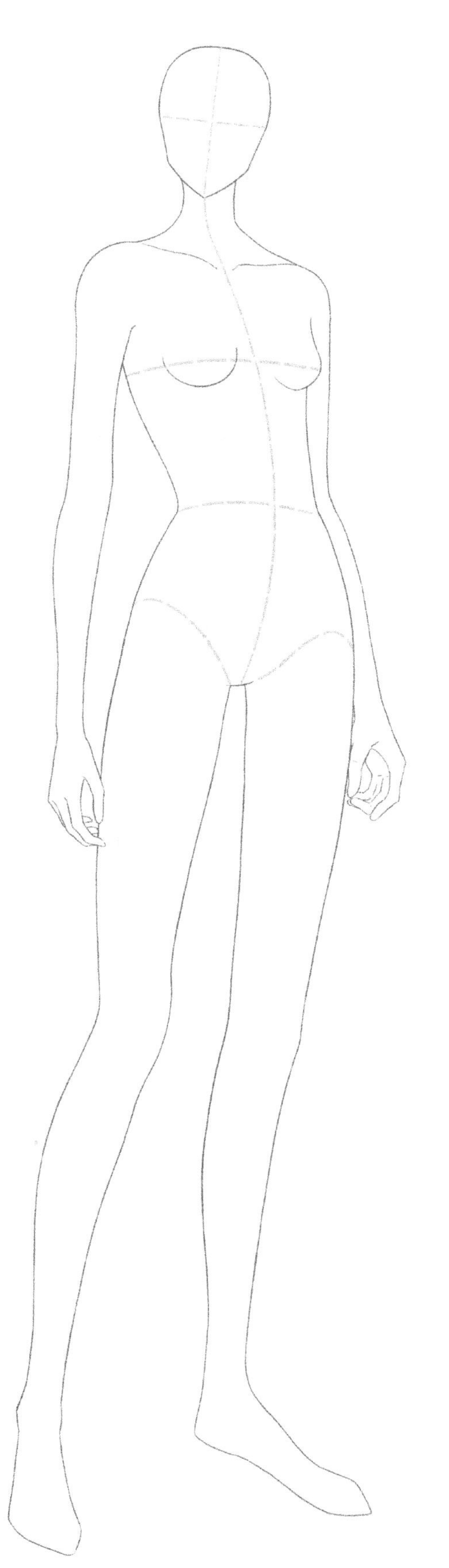
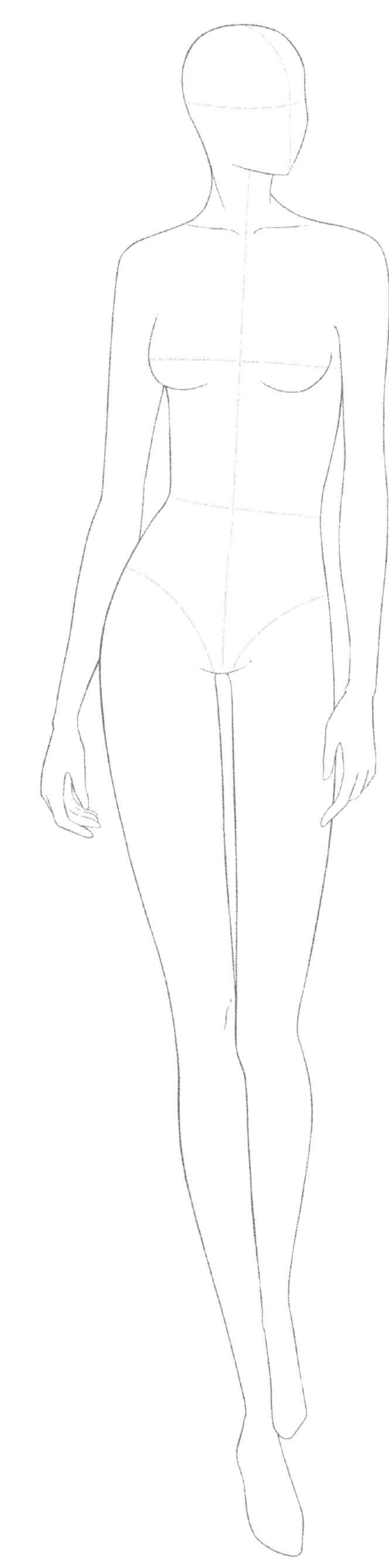

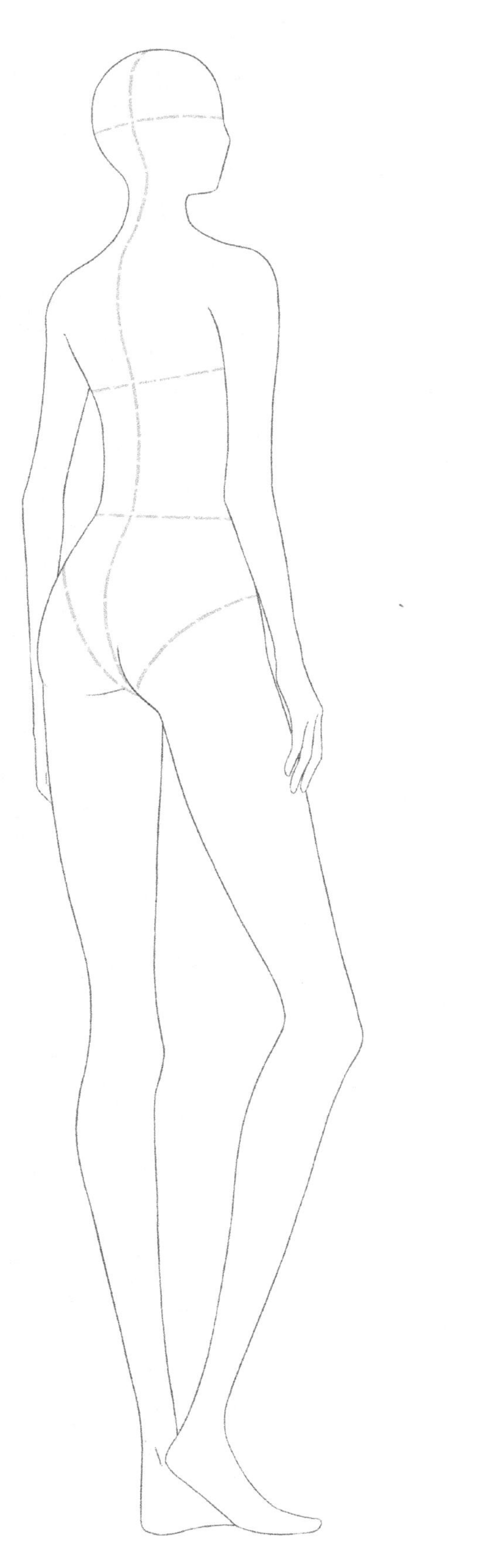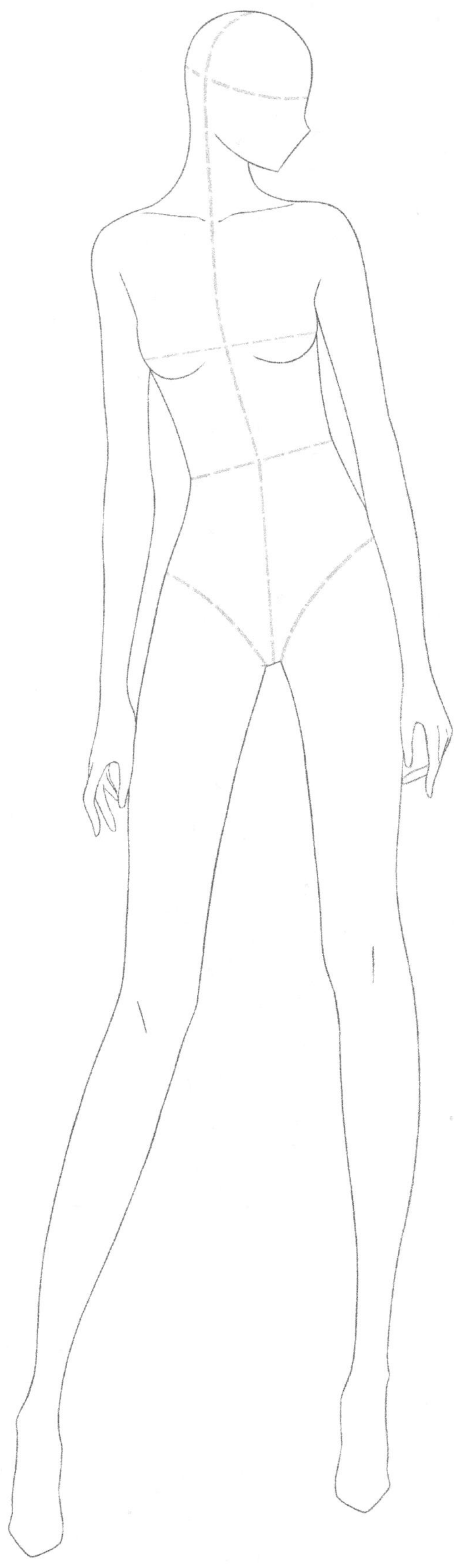

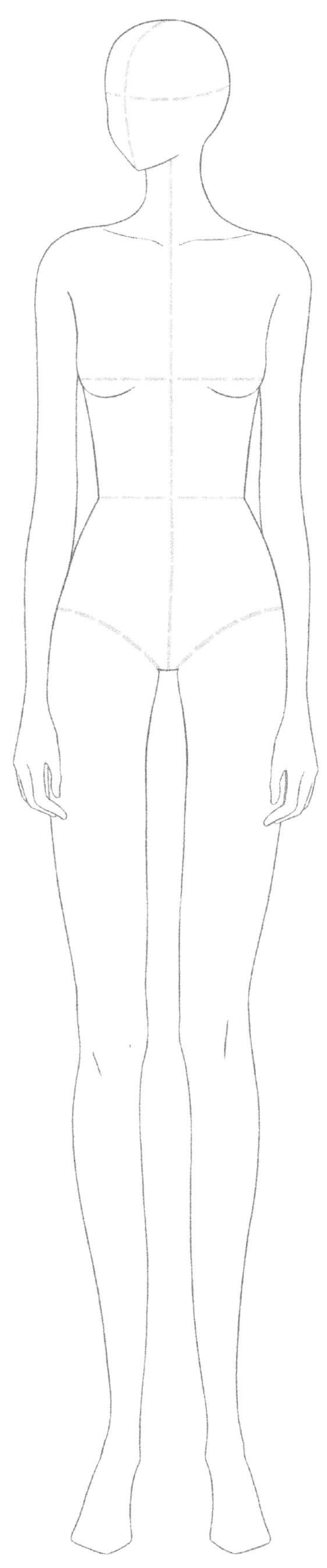

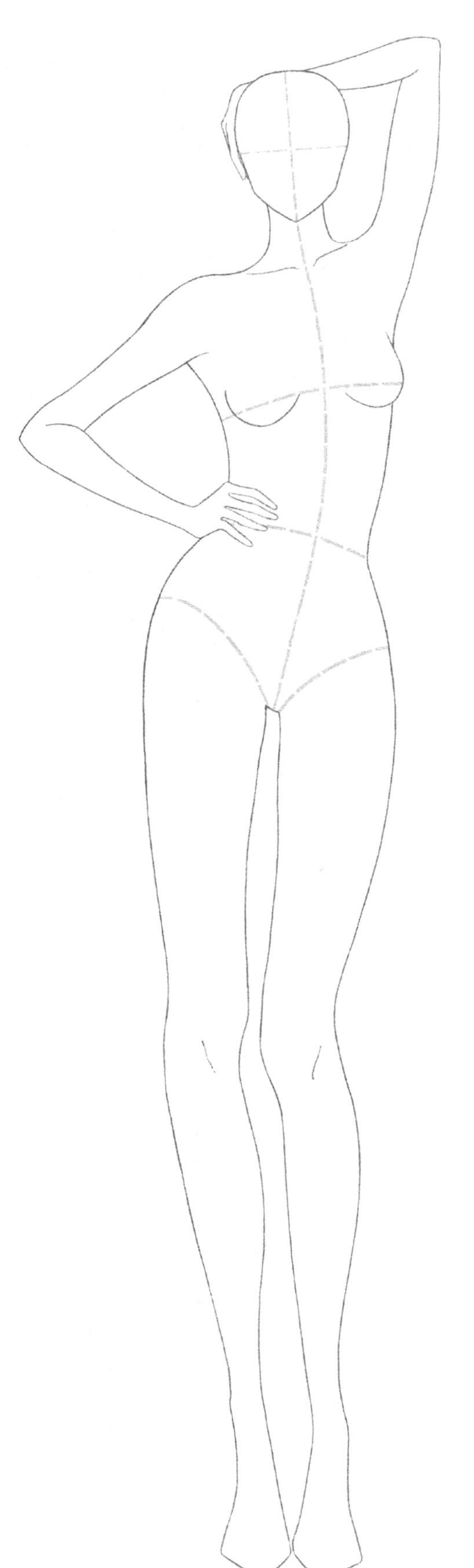
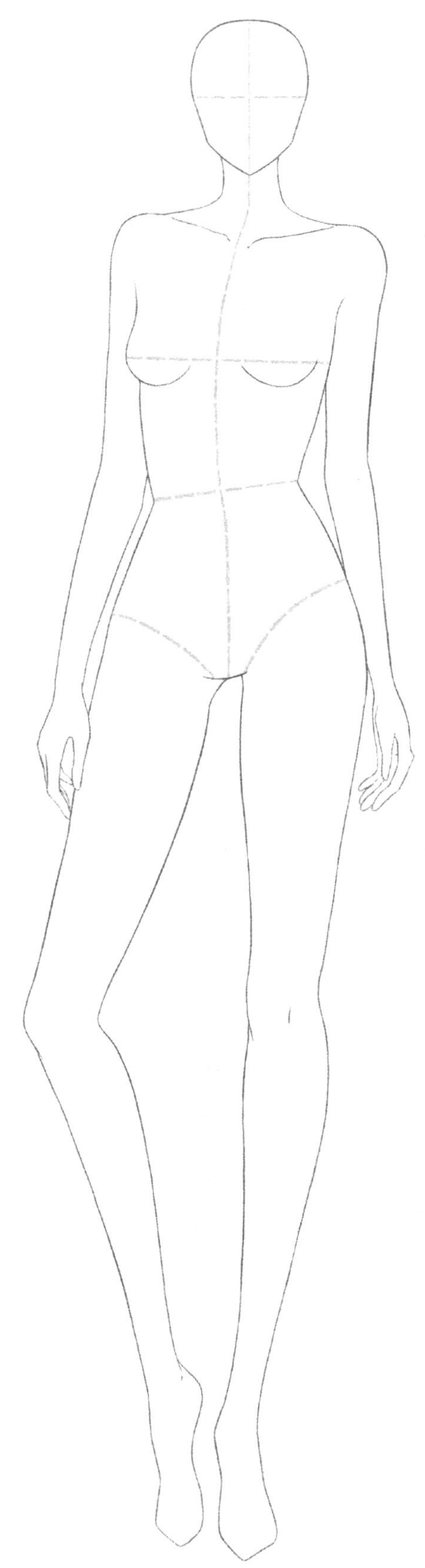

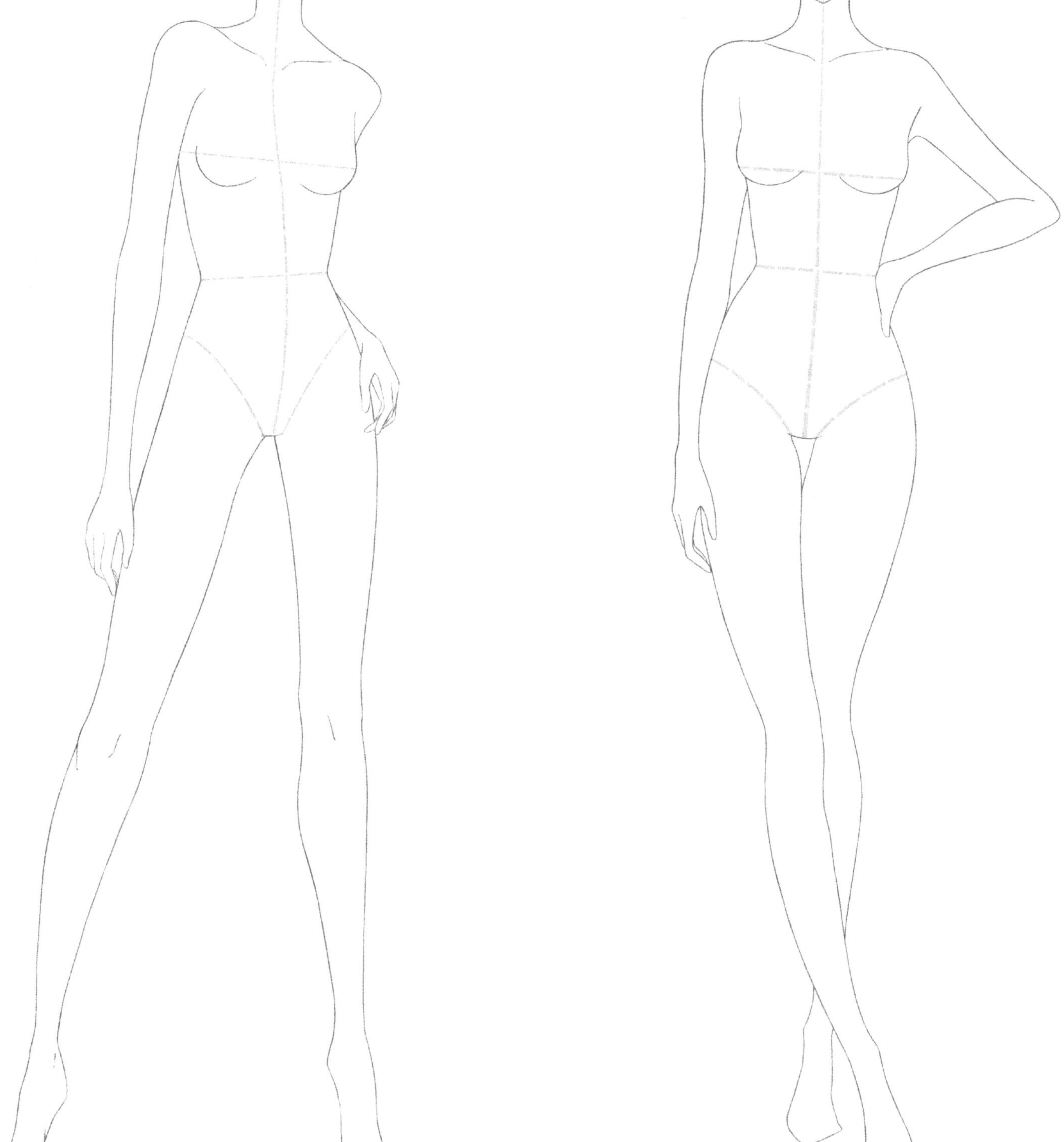

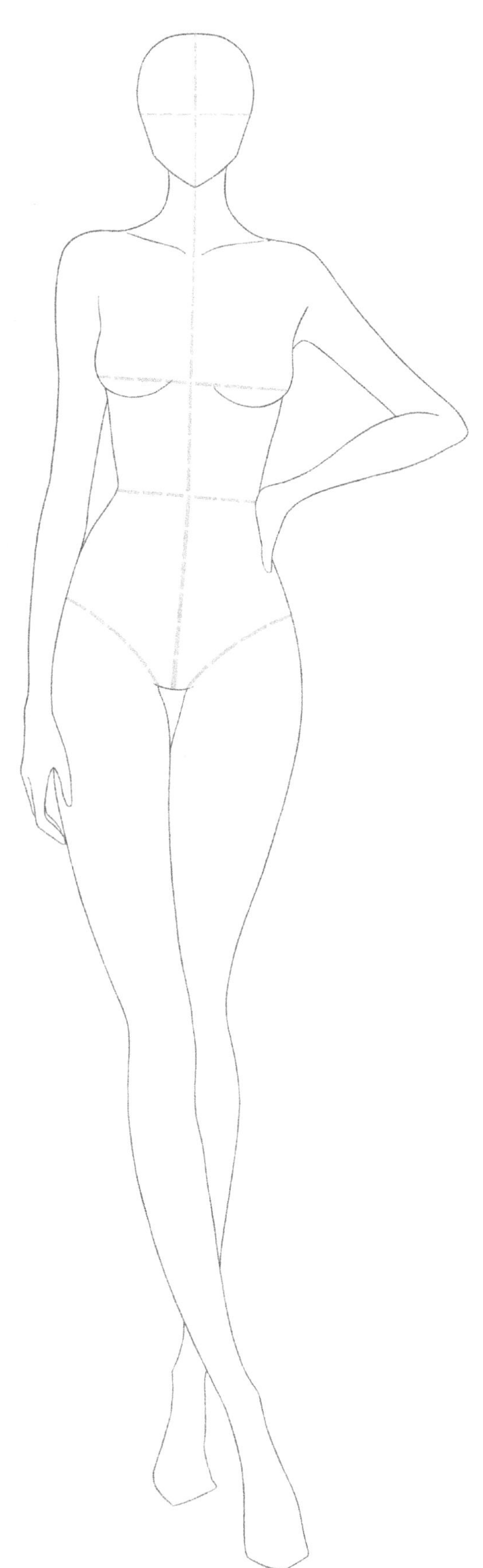

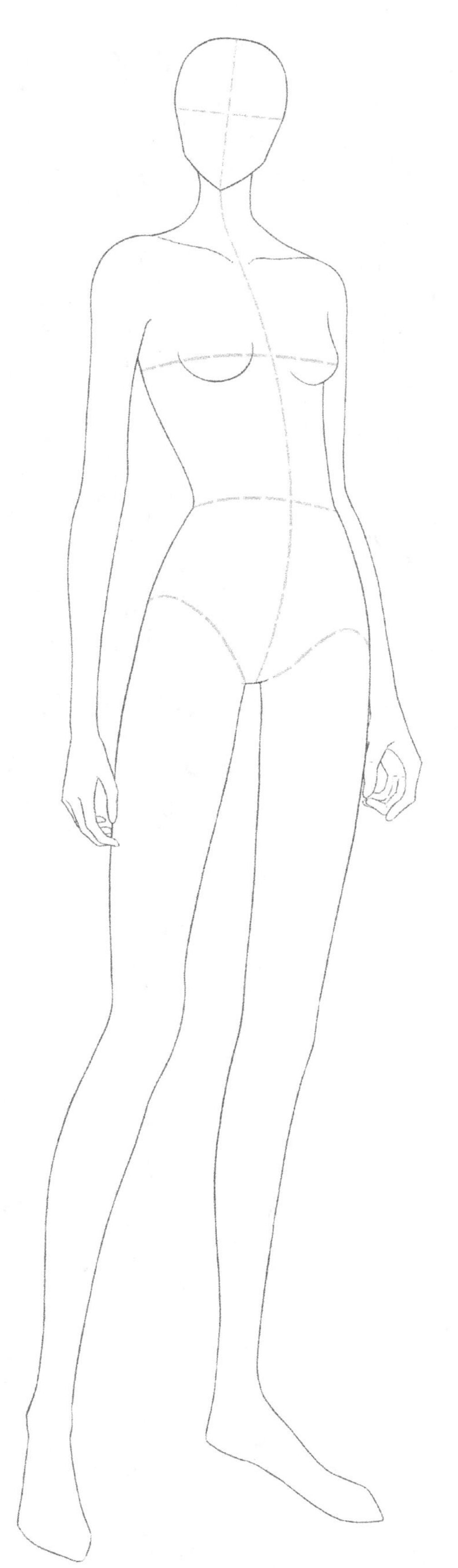
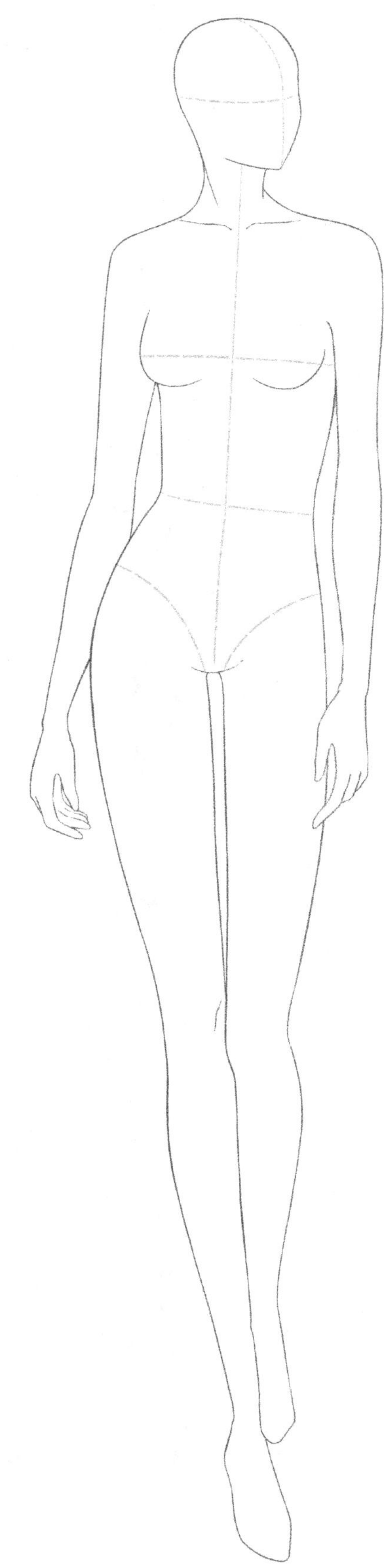

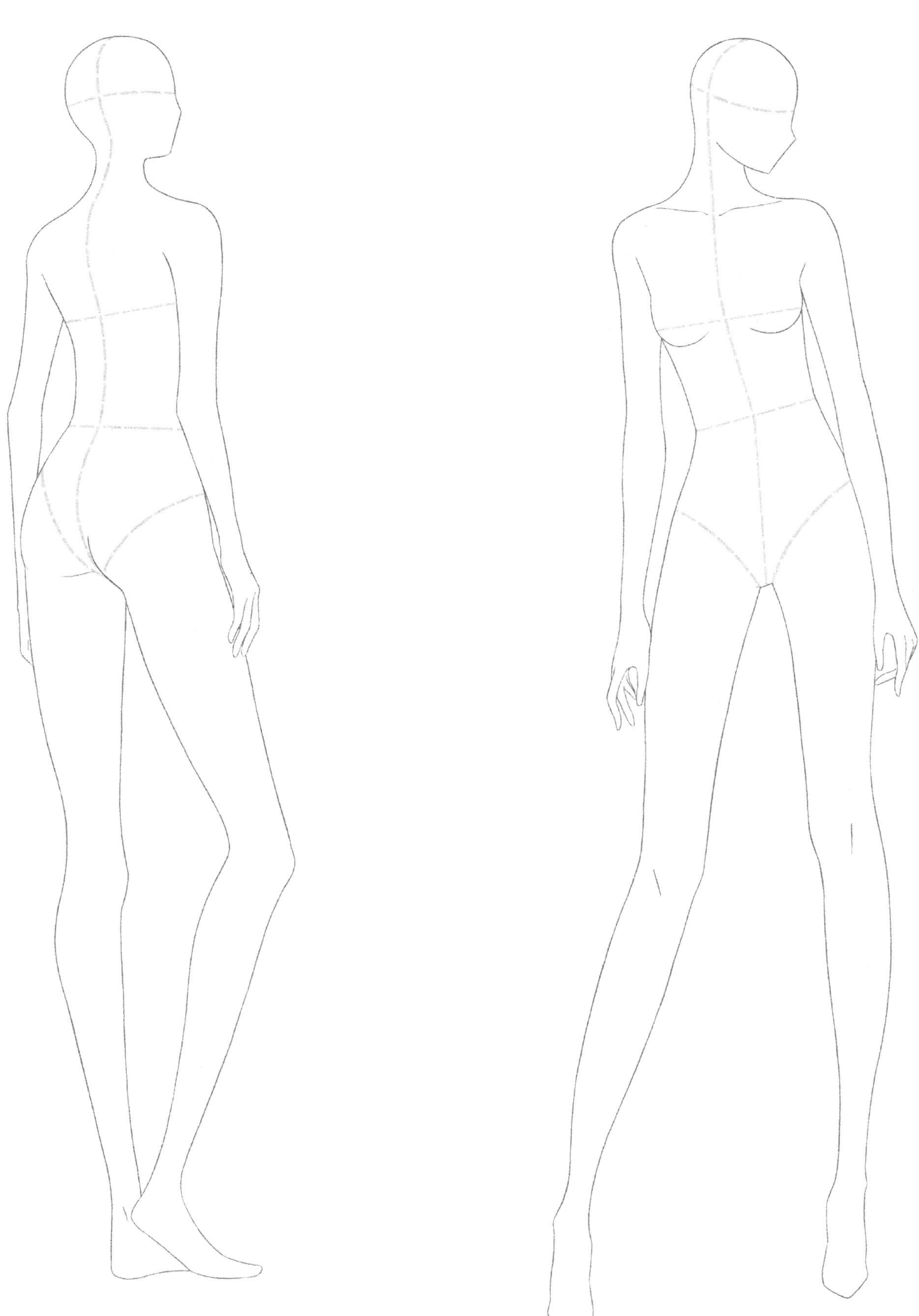

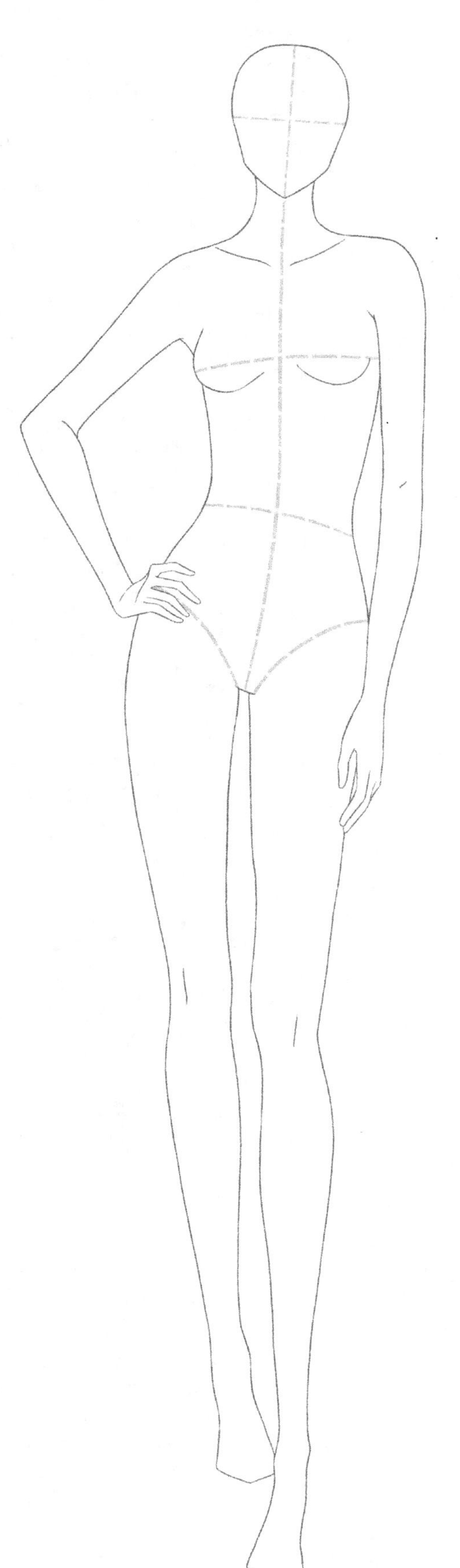
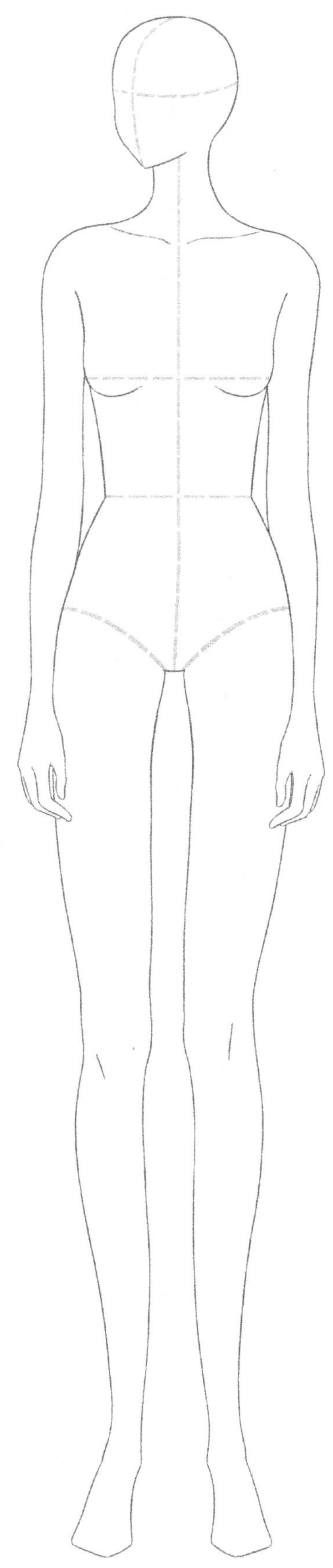

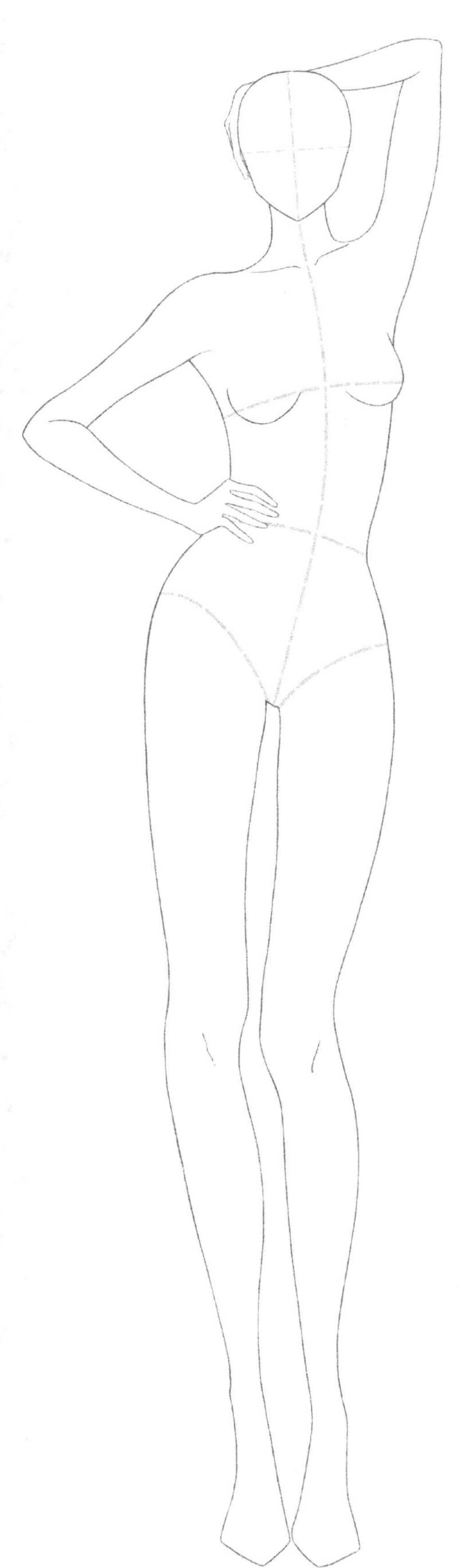
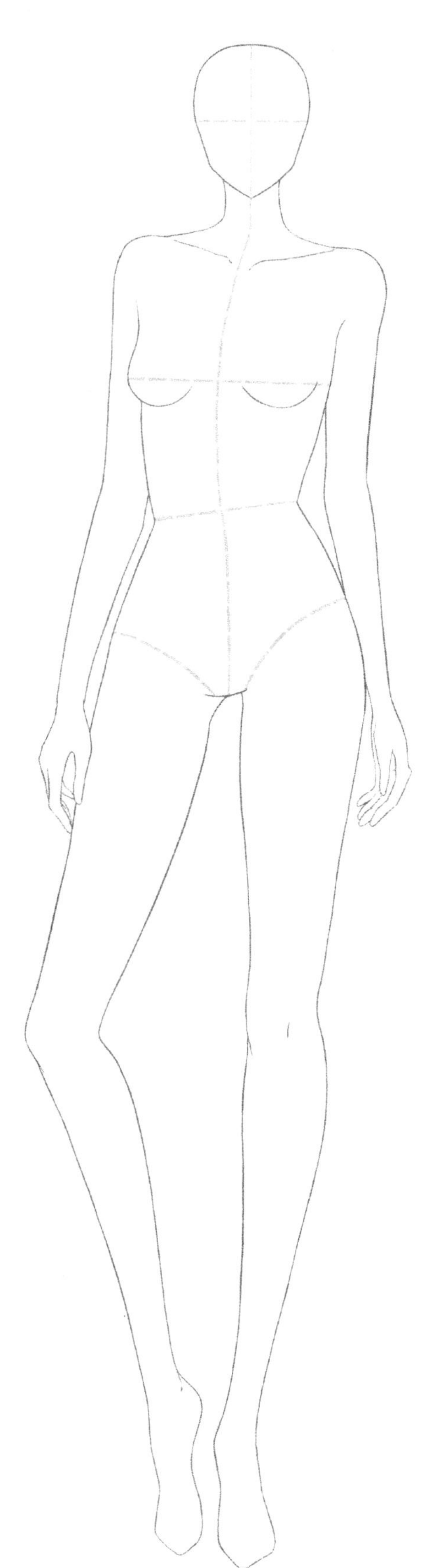

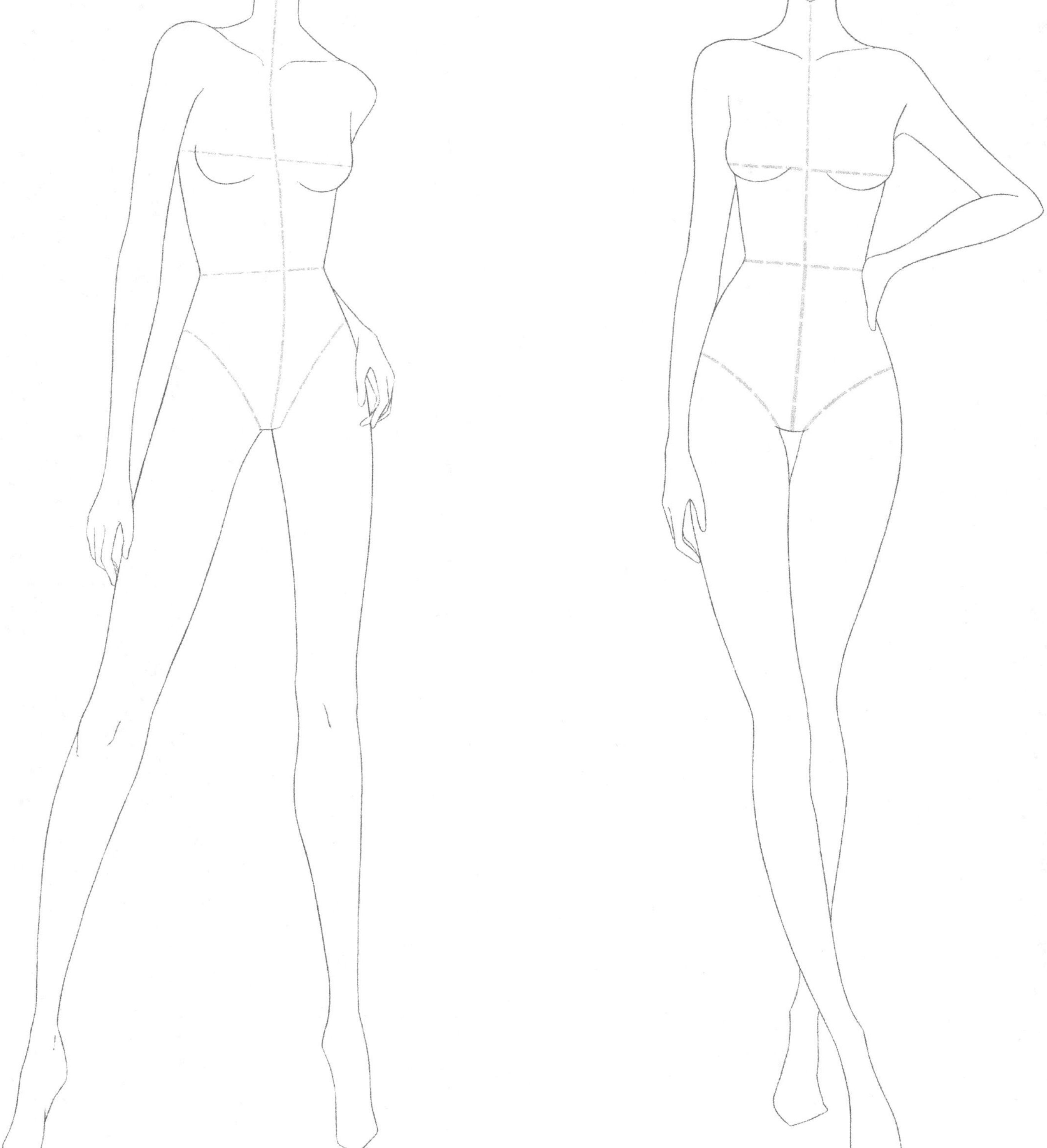

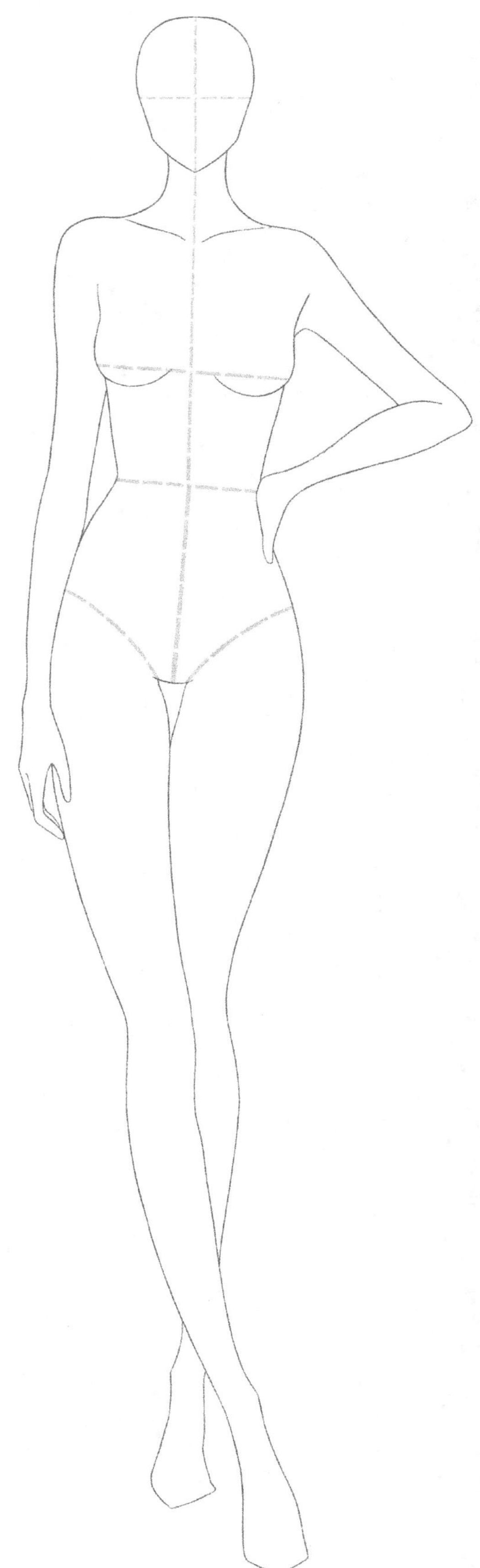

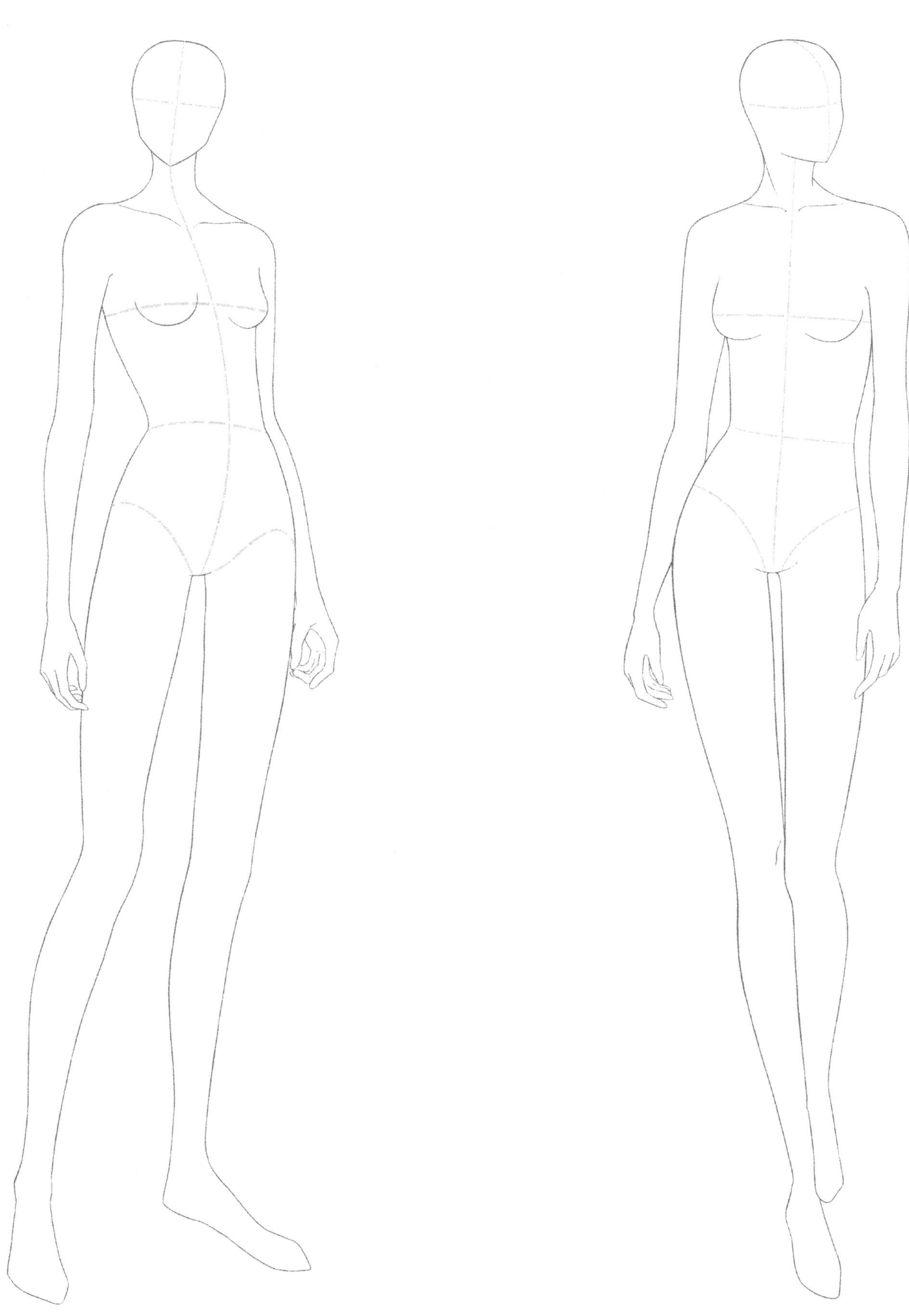

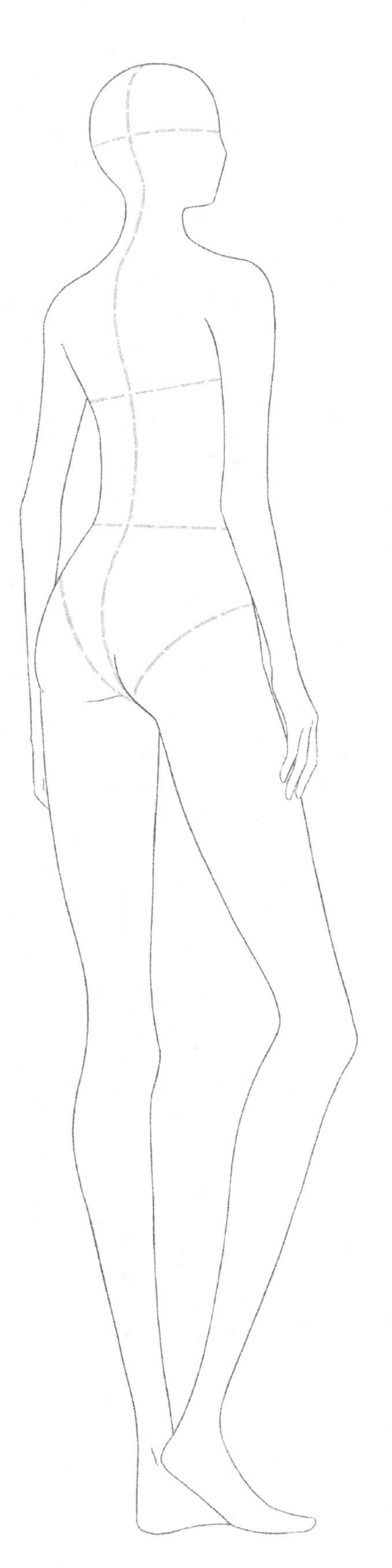
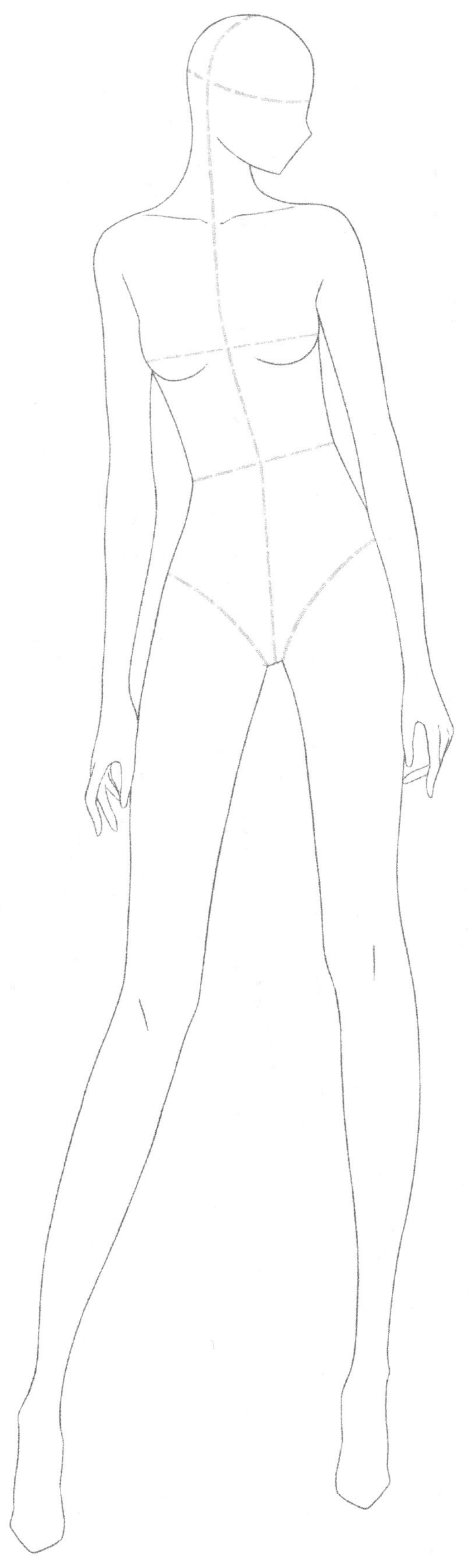

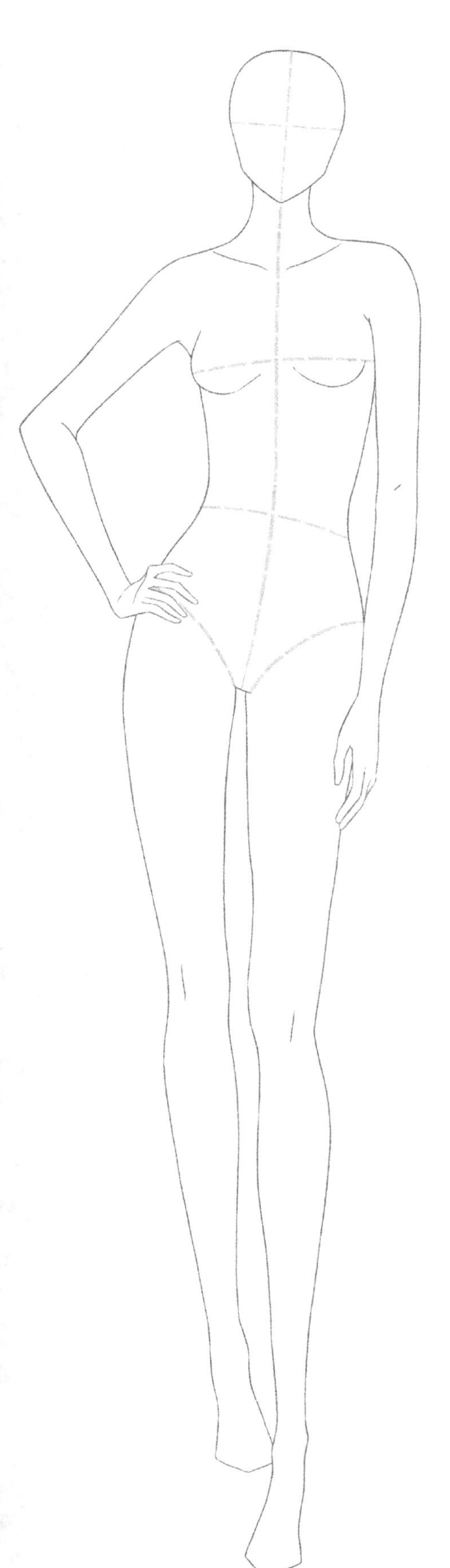
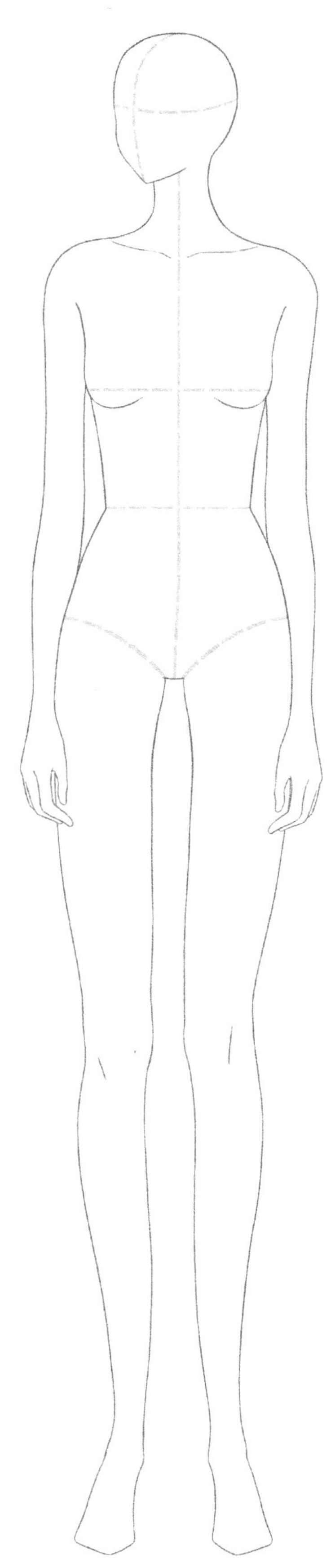

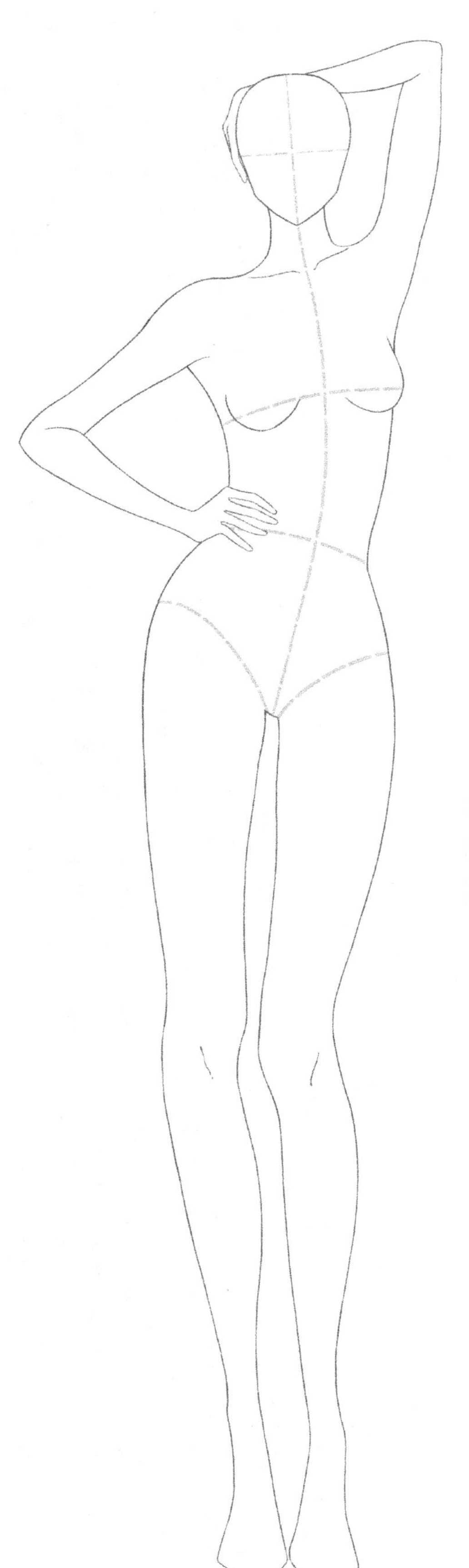
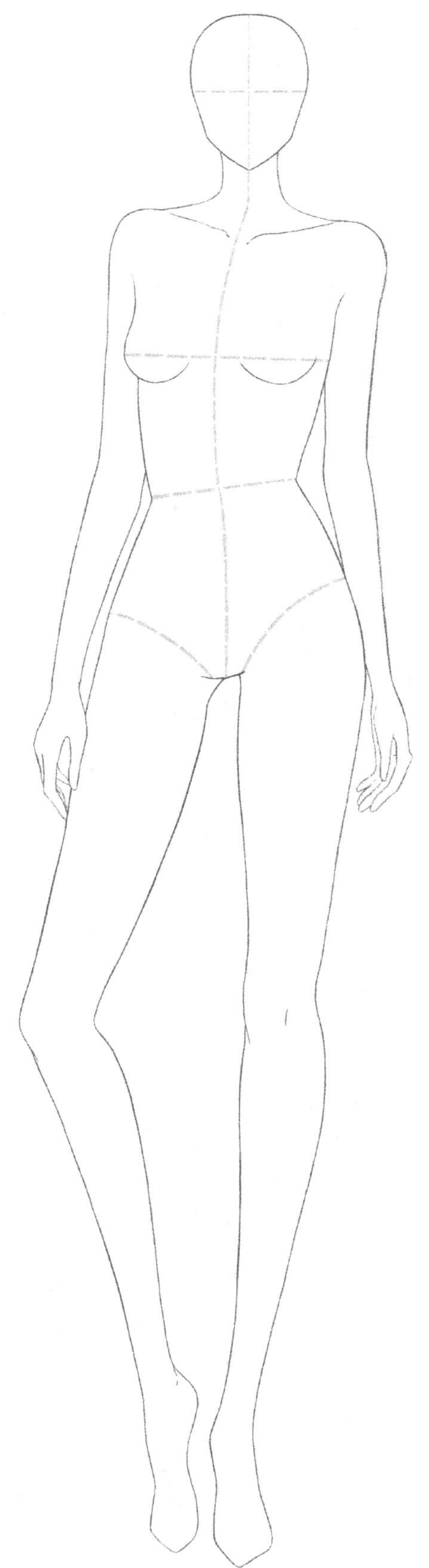

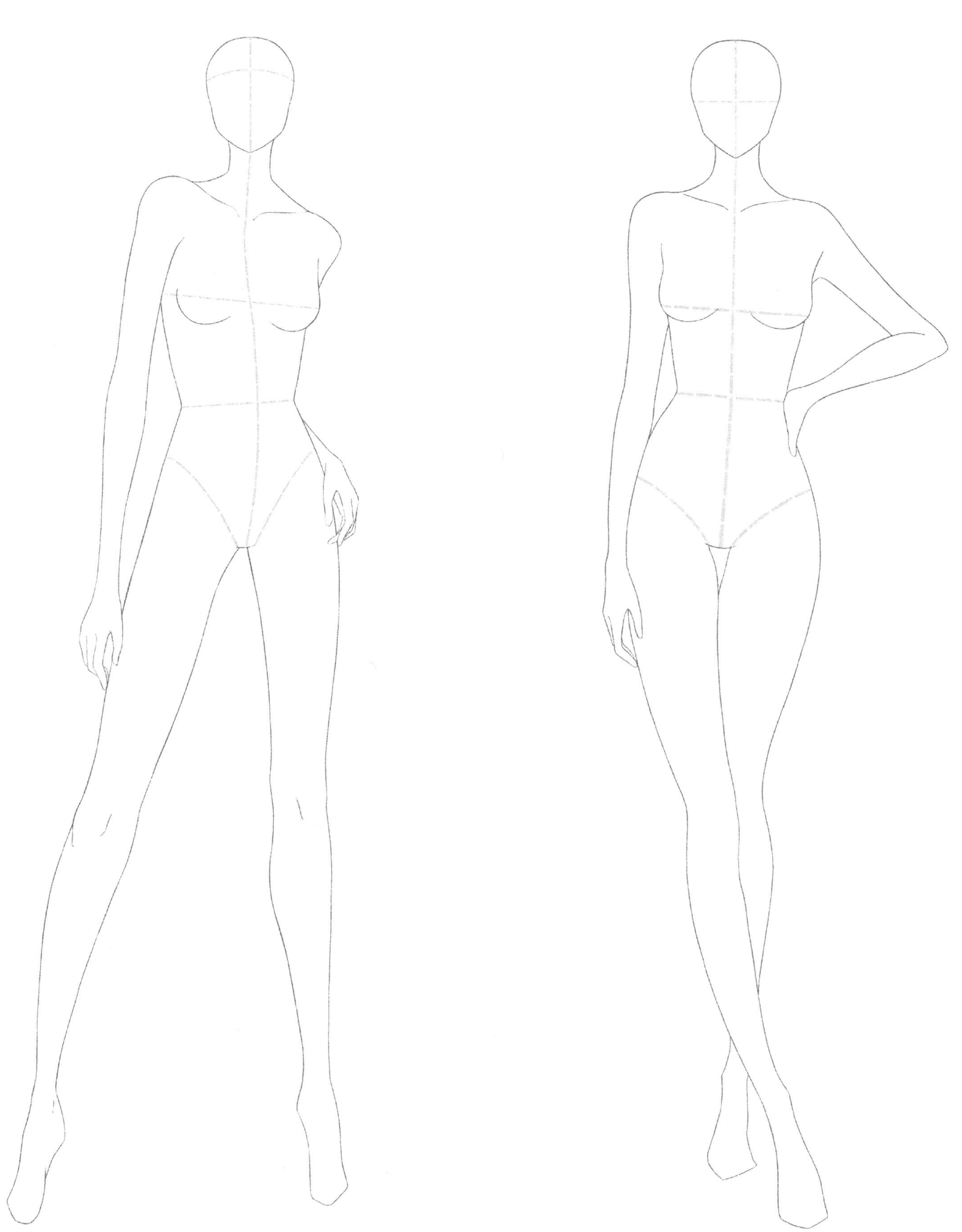

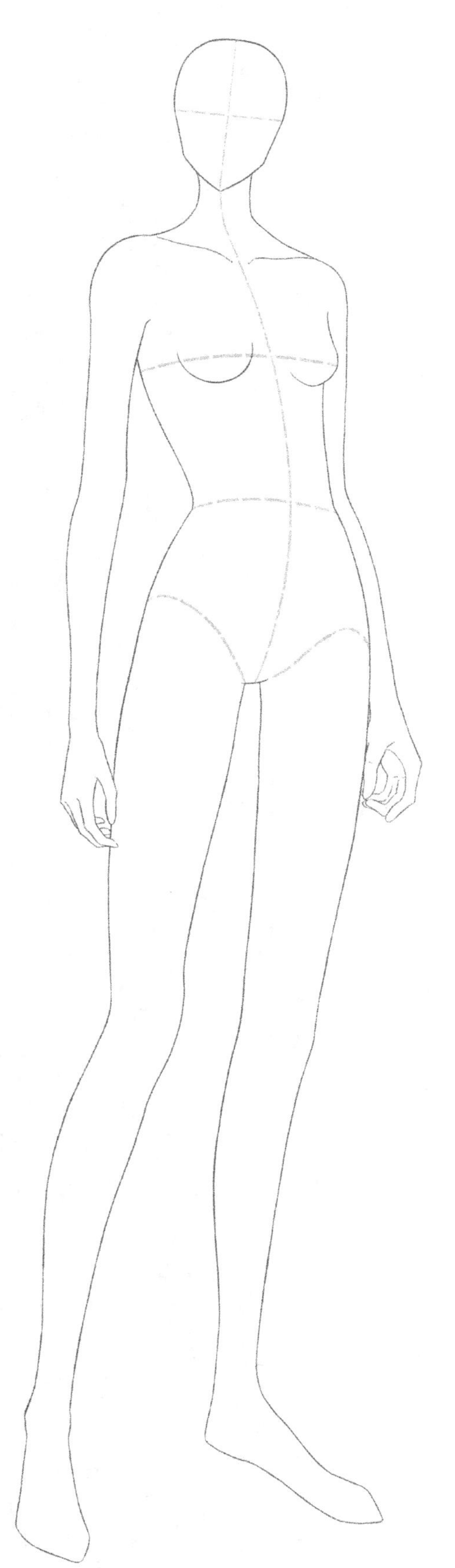
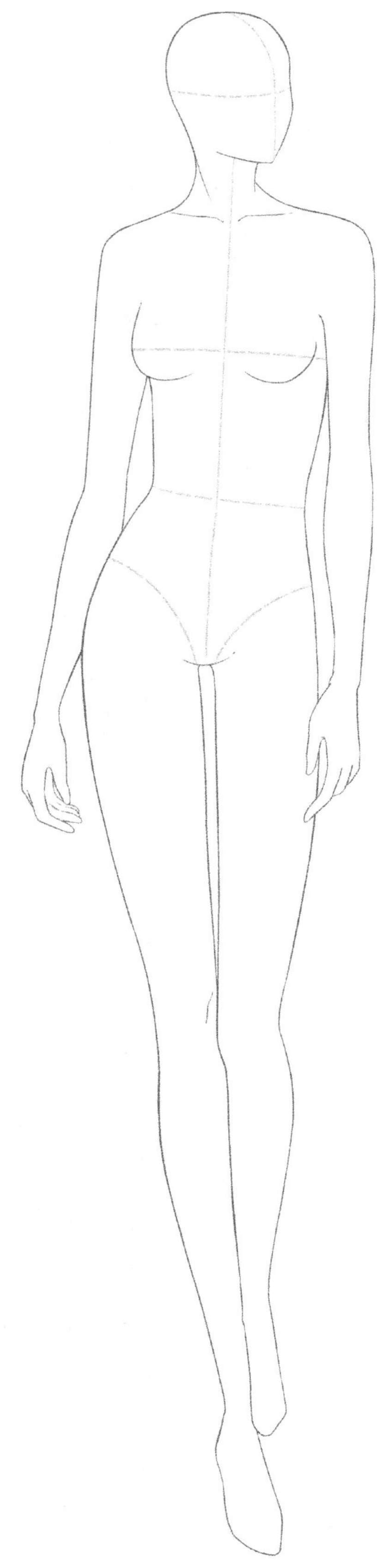

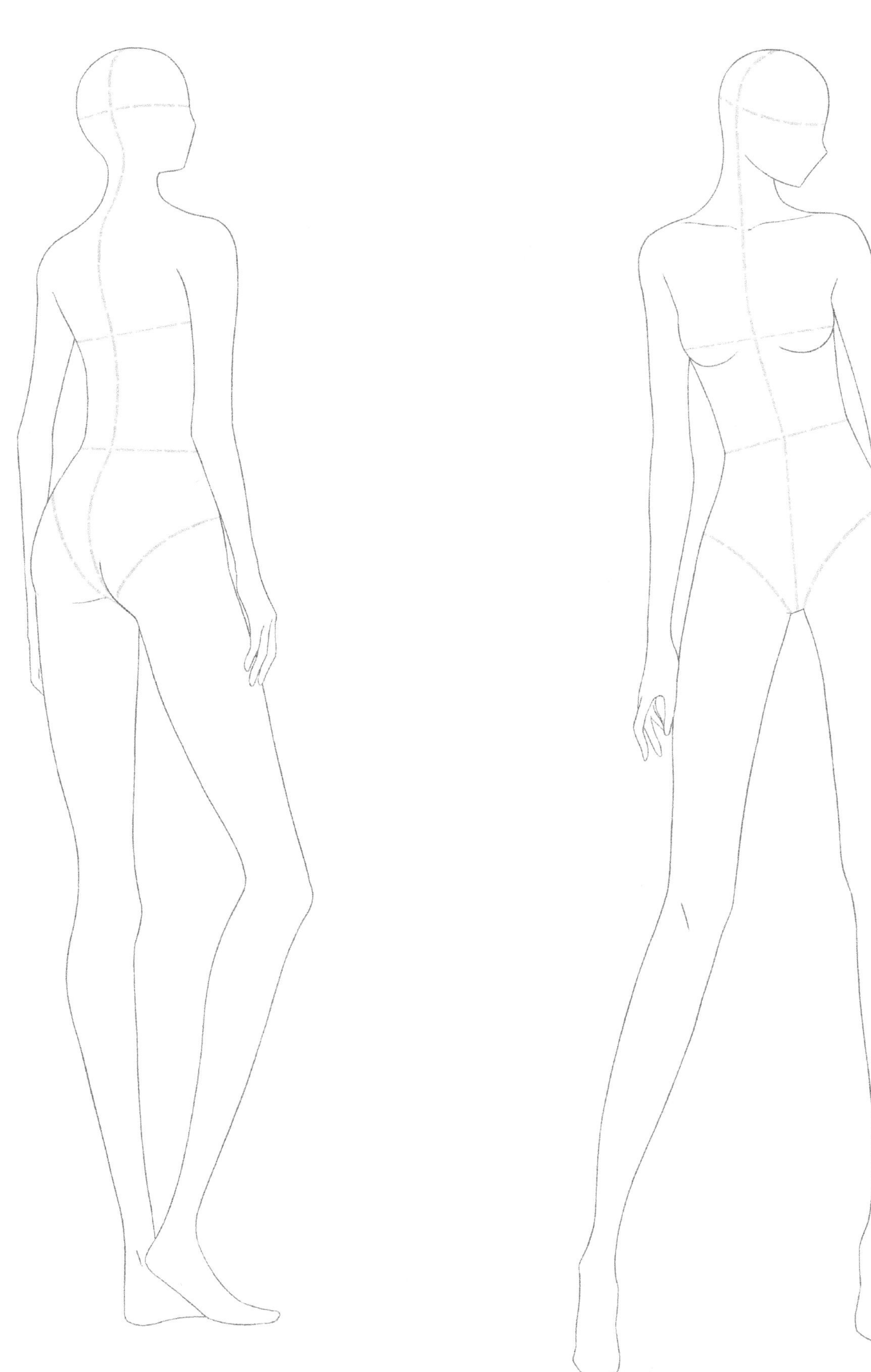

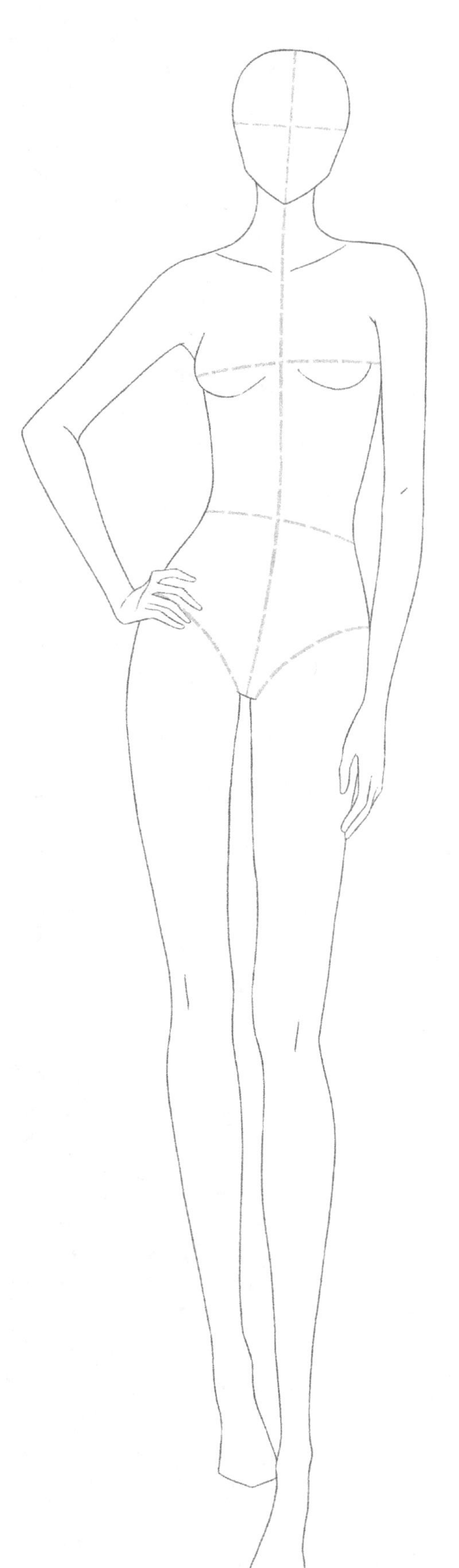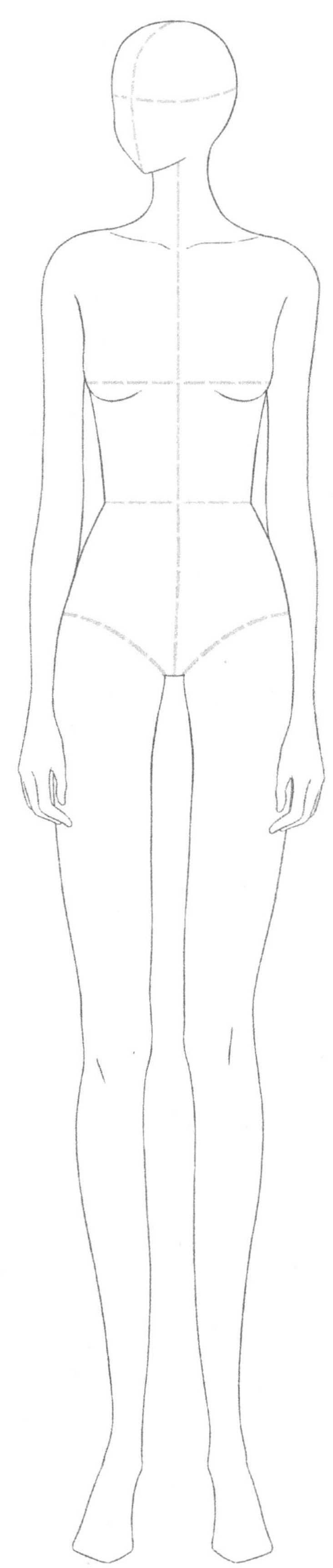

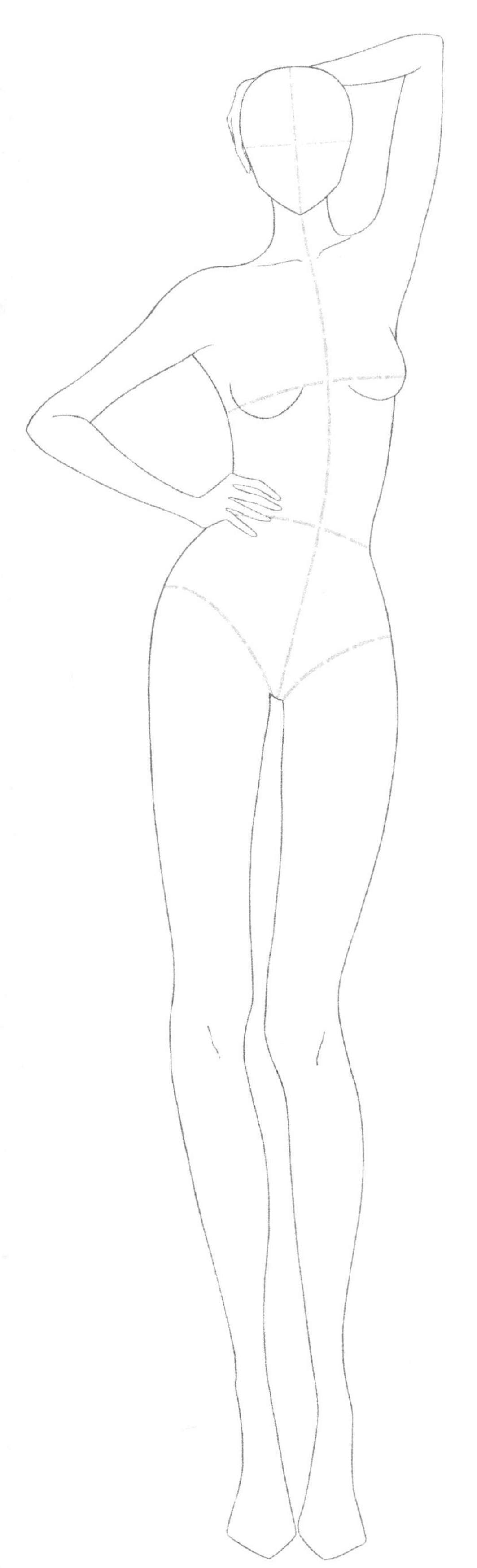
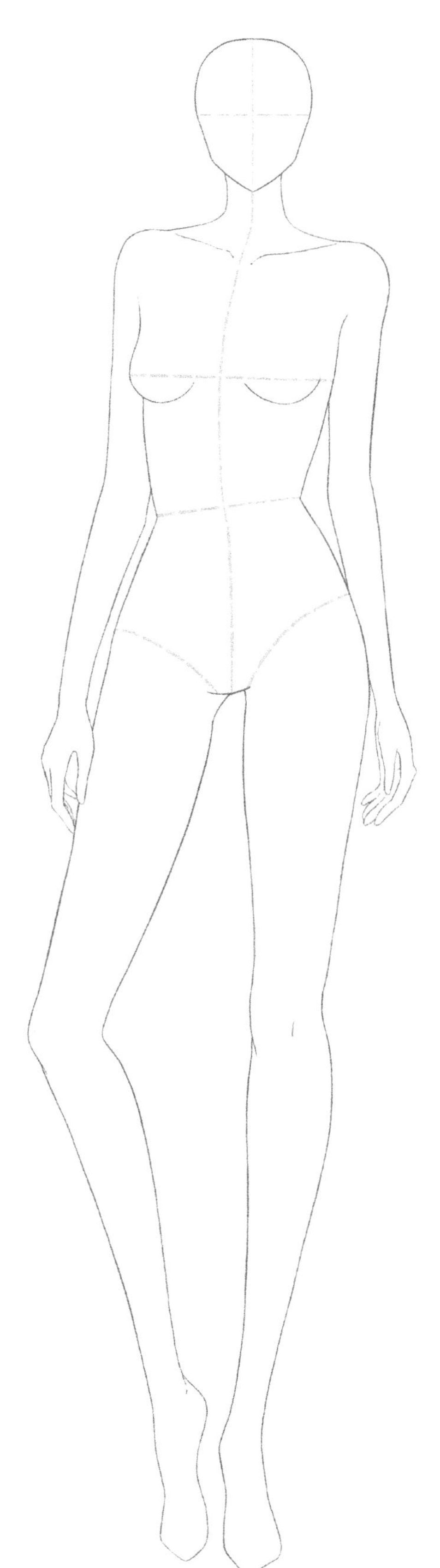

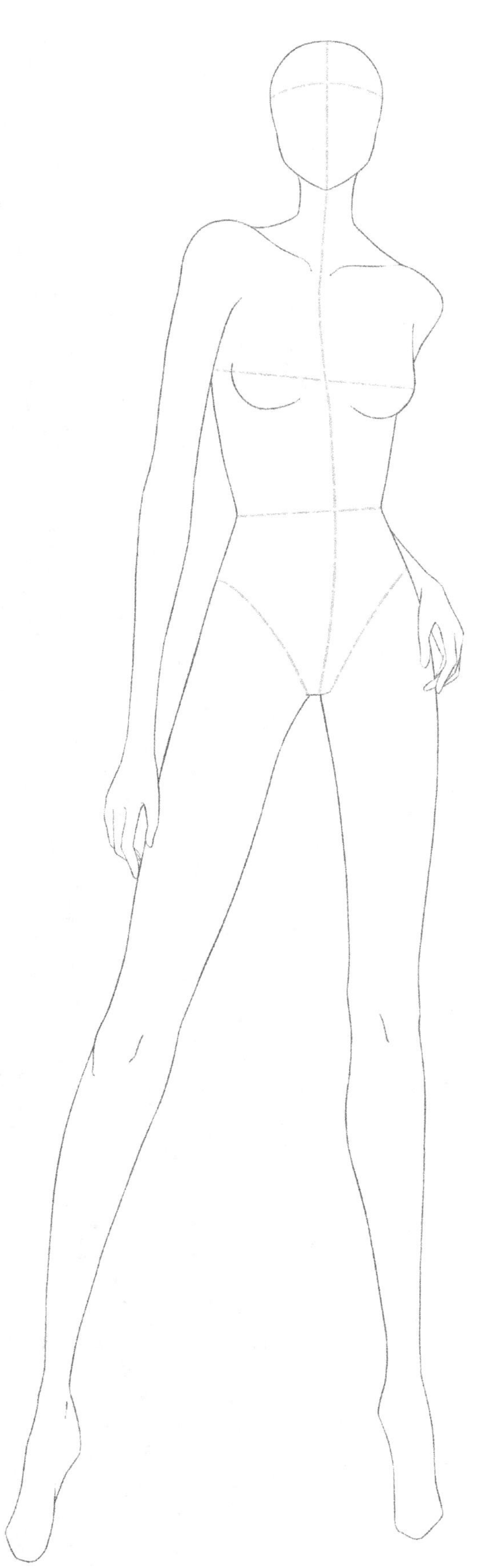
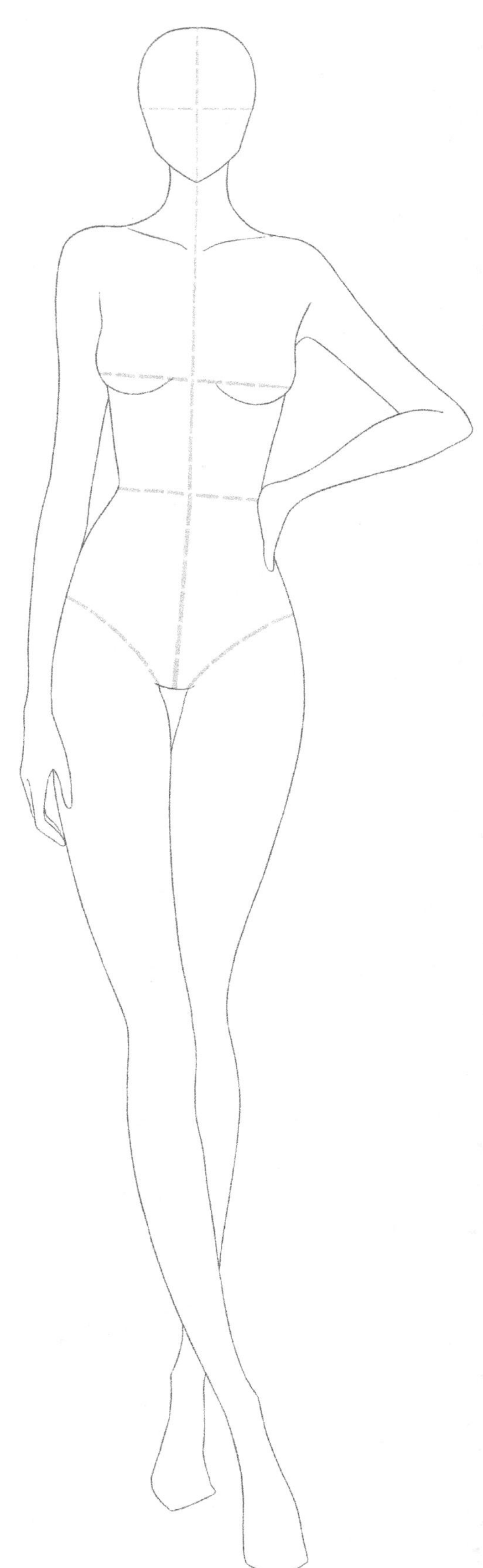

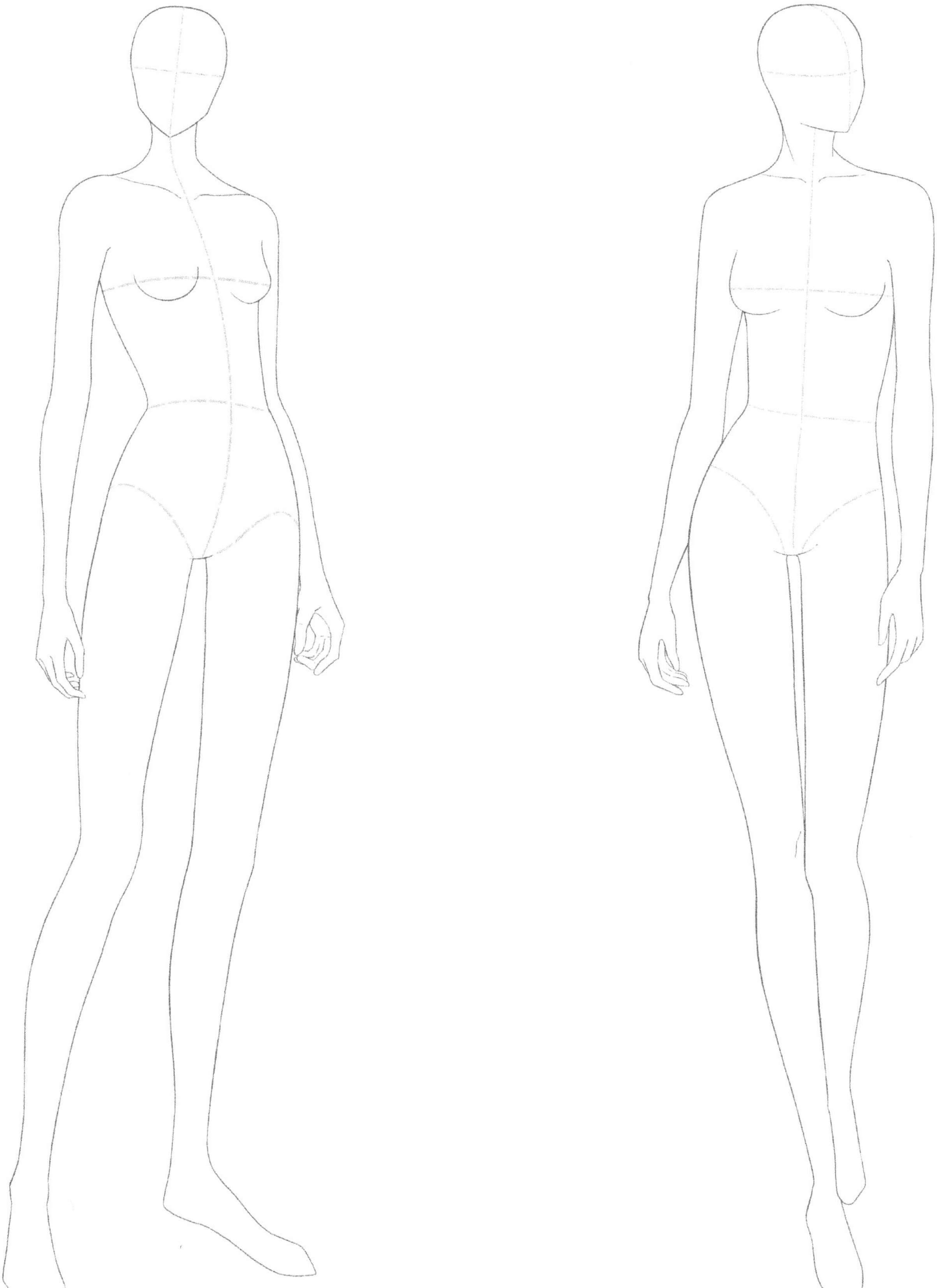

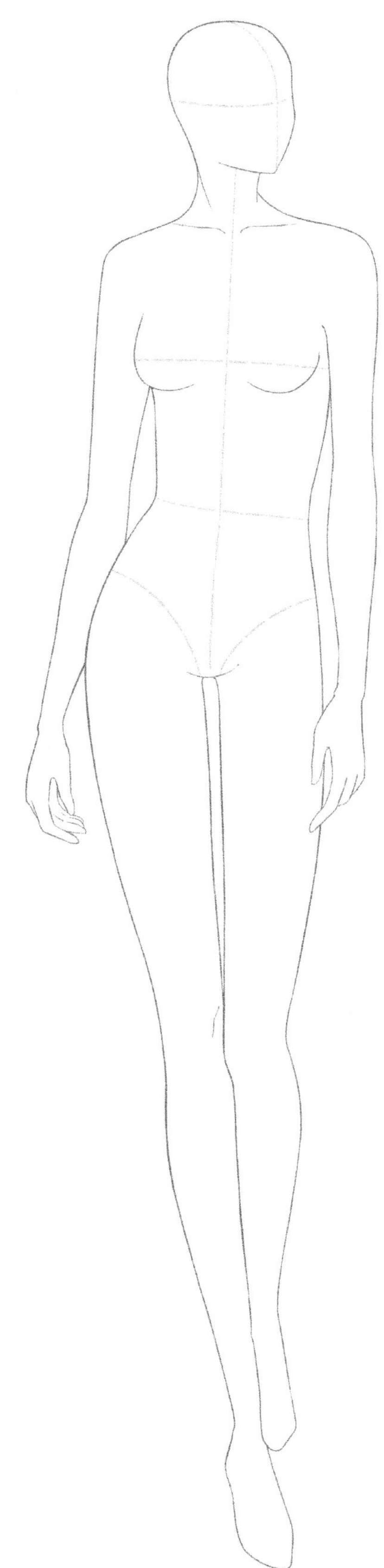

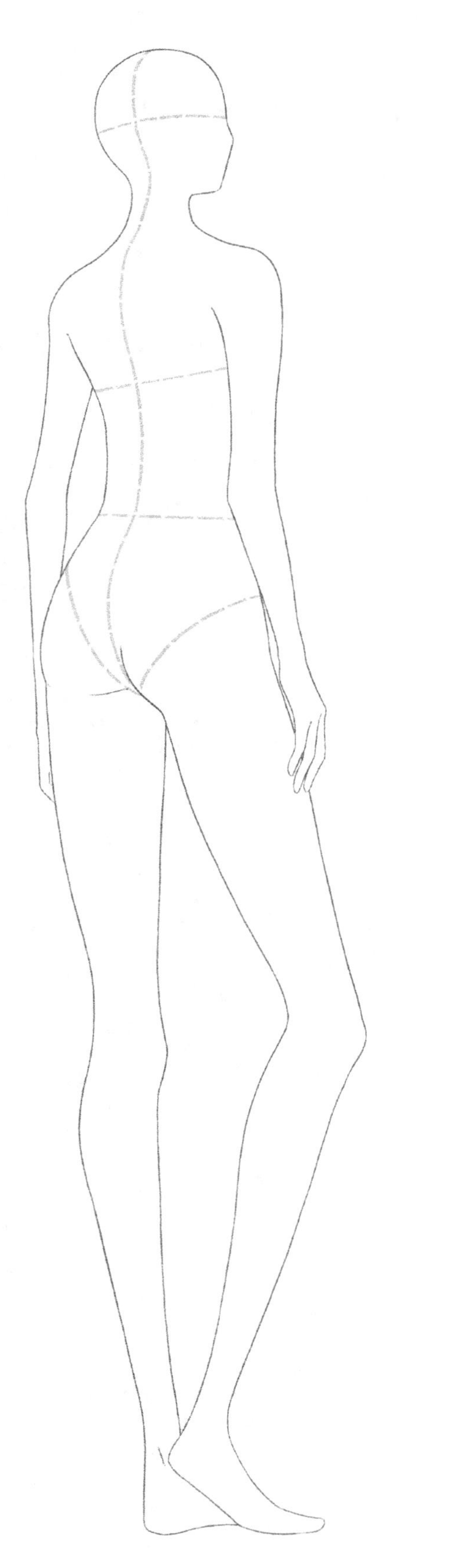
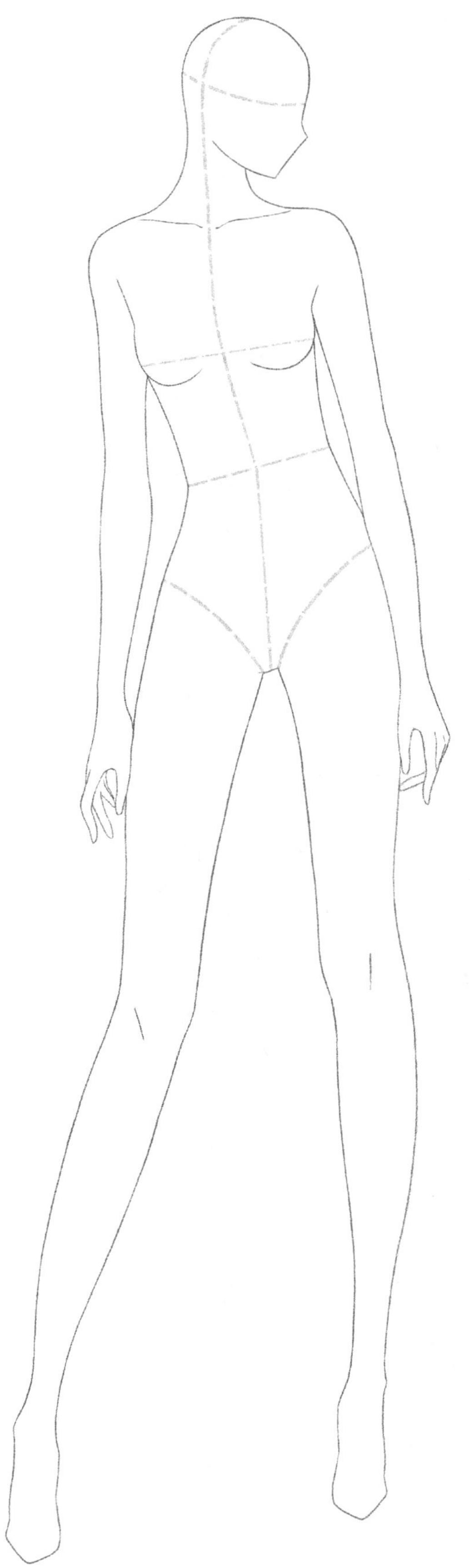

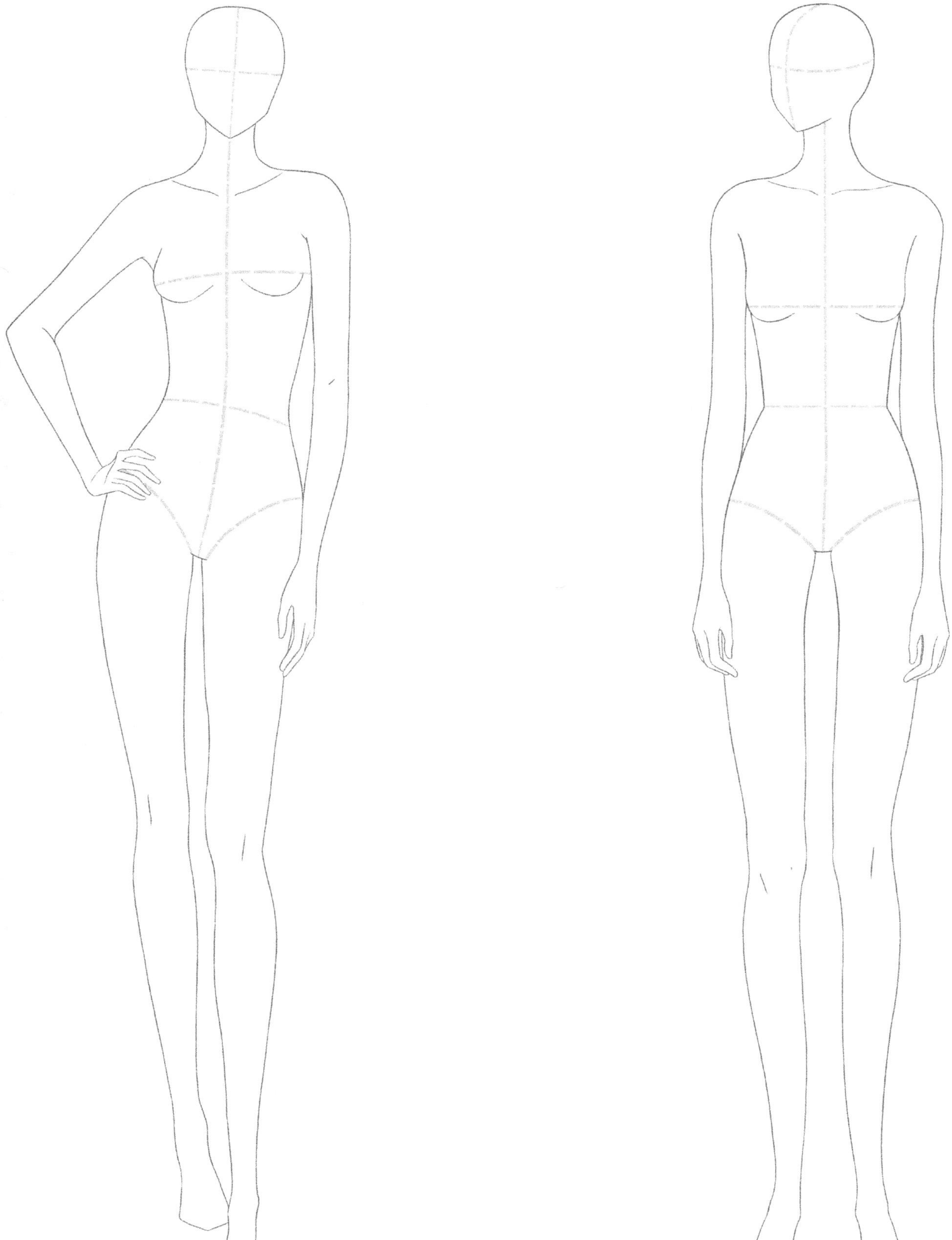

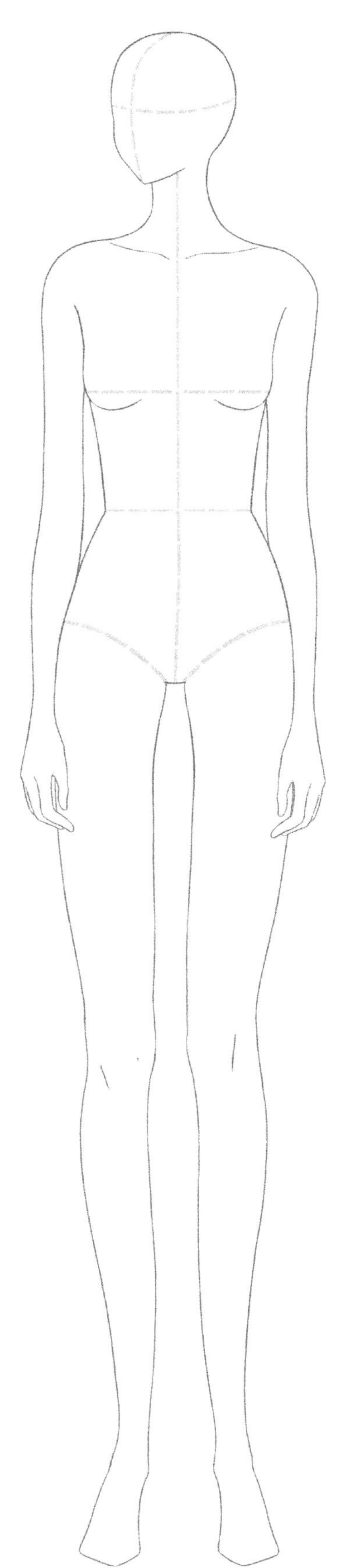

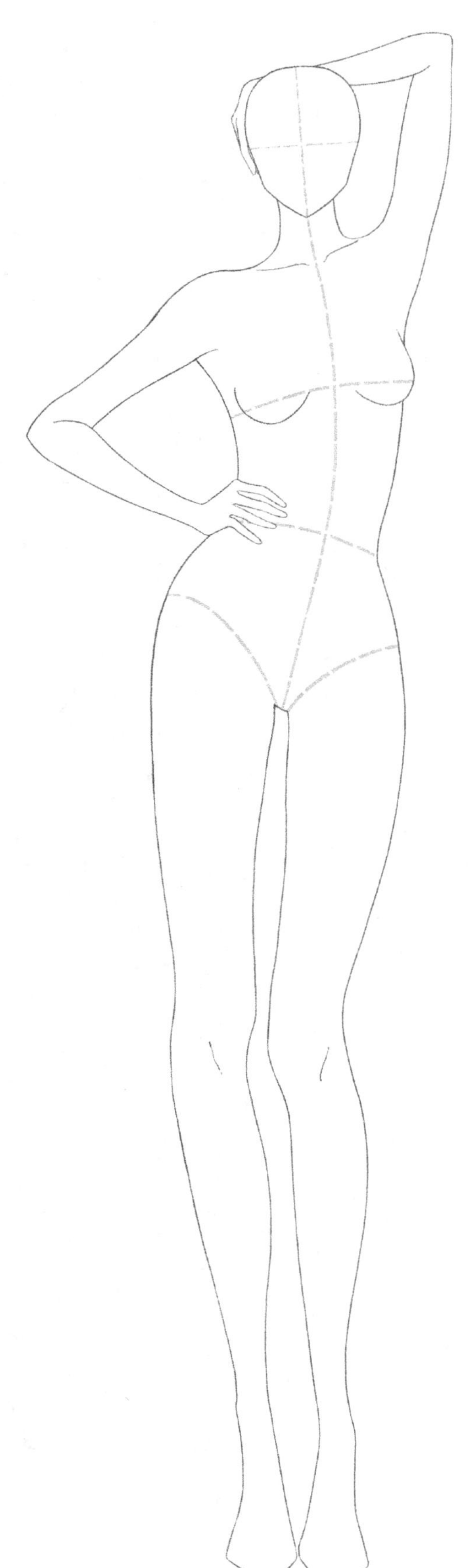
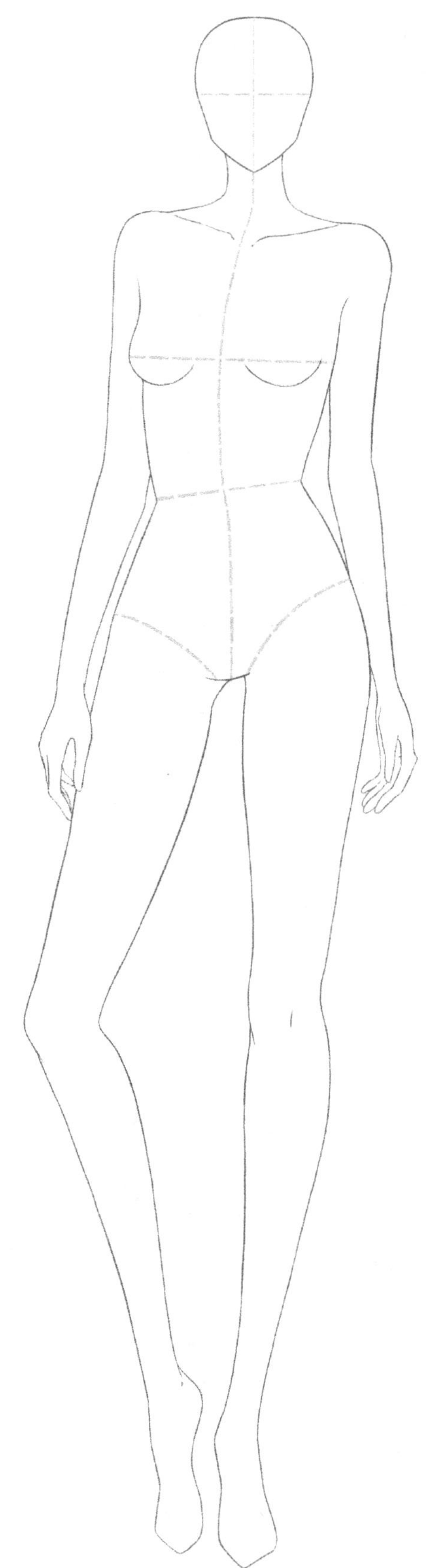

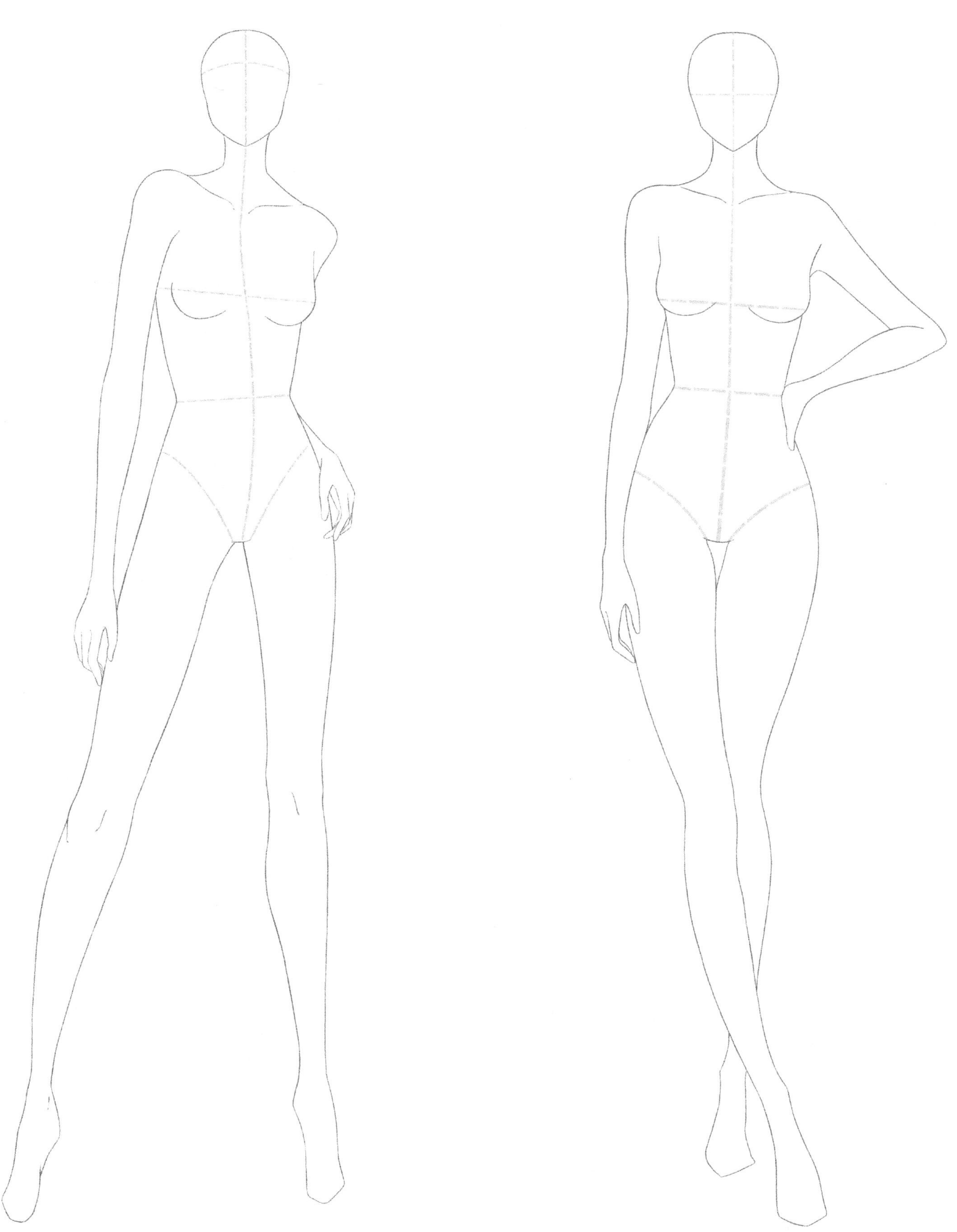

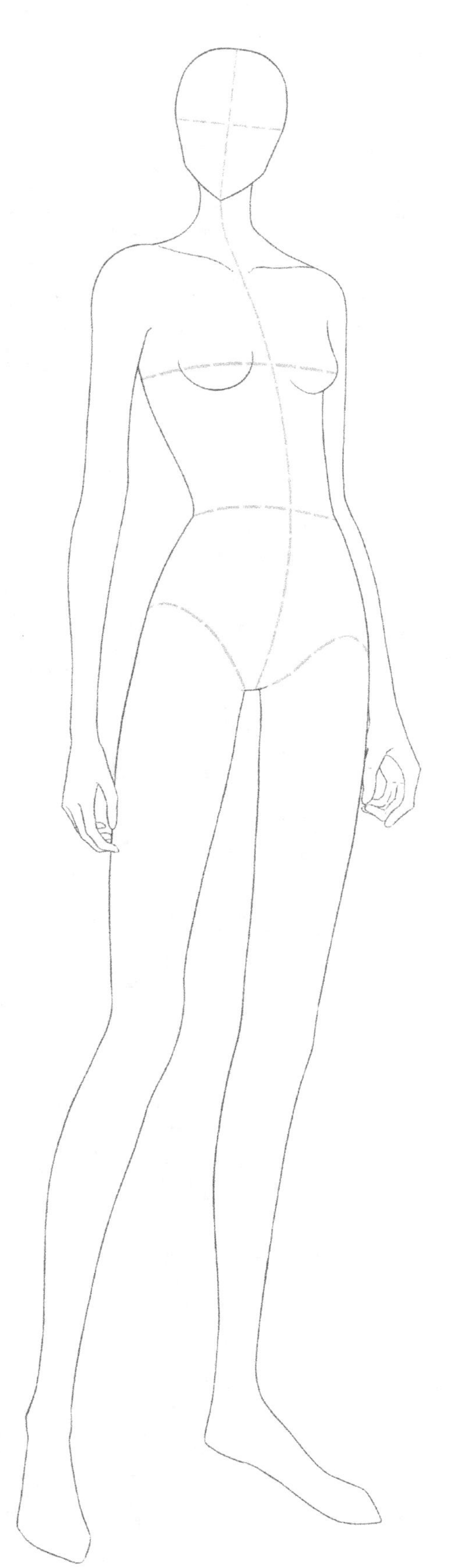
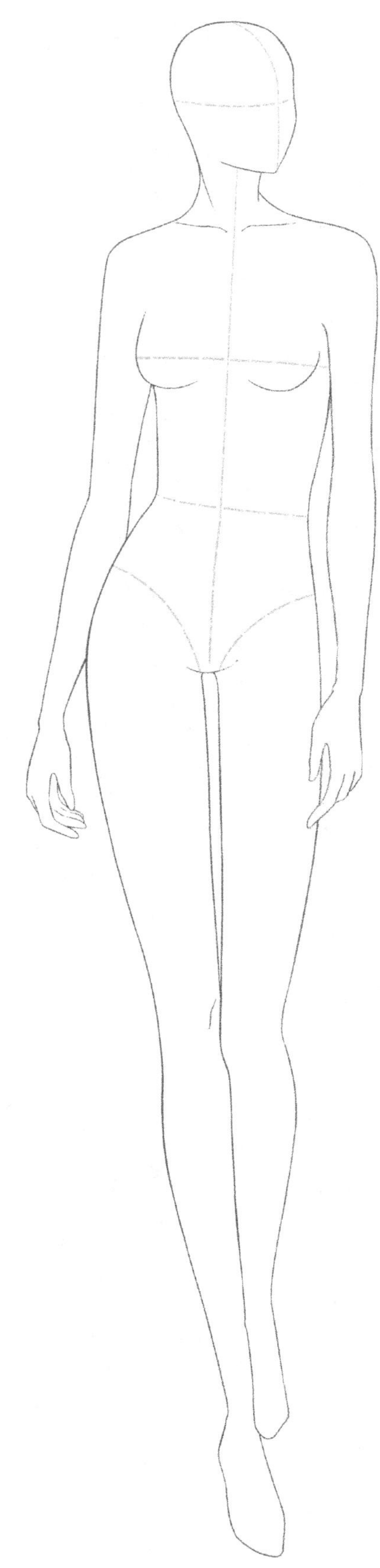

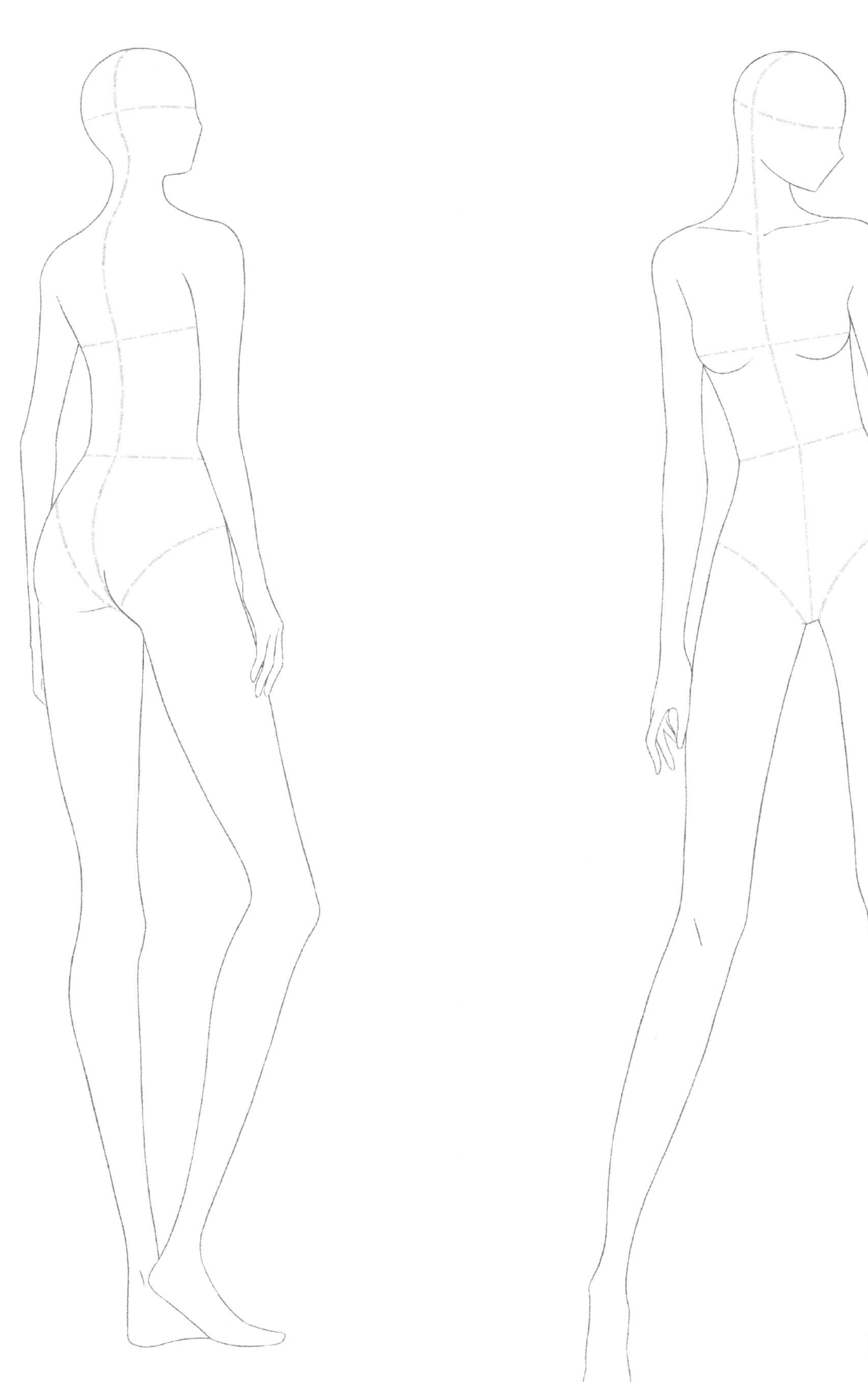

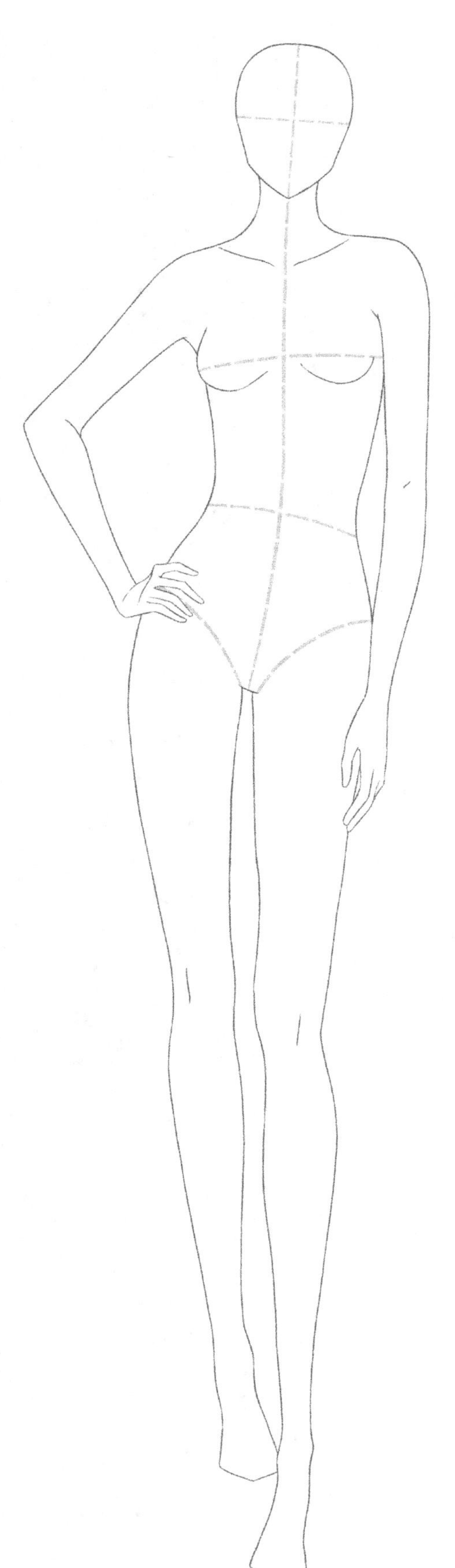
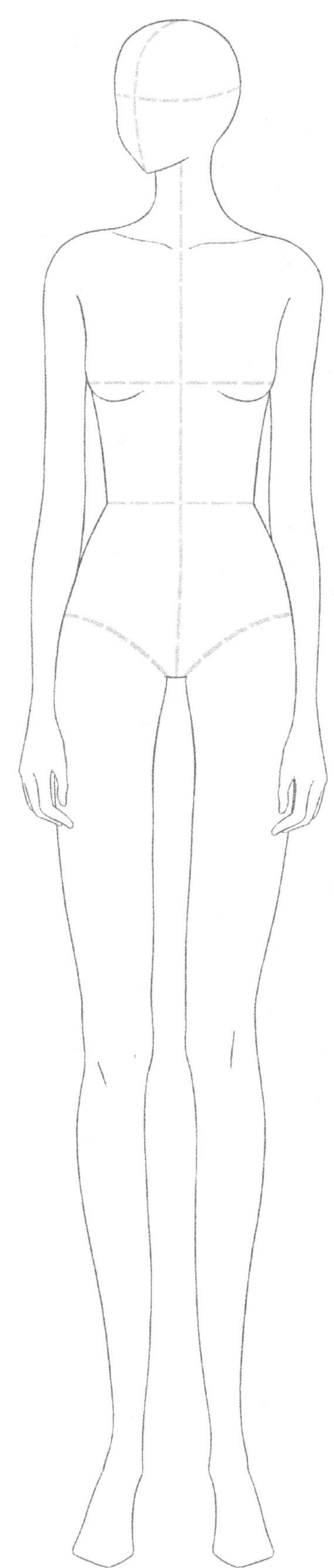

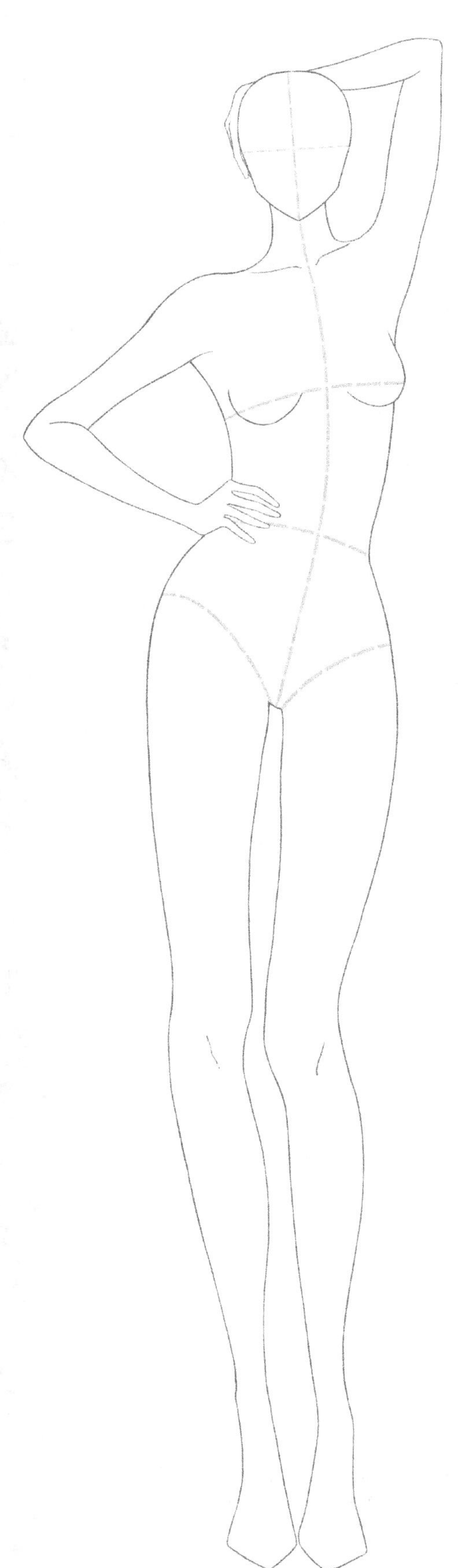
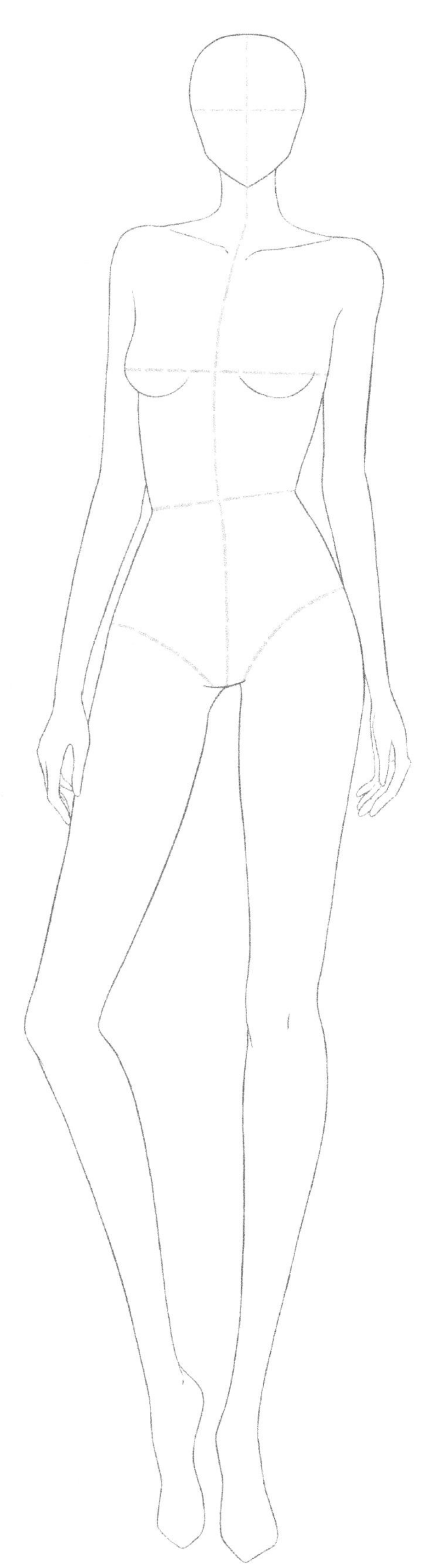

JOIN US AND GET 2 FASHION FIGURE TEMPLATES FOR FREE!

https://content.byebye.studio/designersupplynews

@_byebye_studio_

/byebyestudio

BYE
BYE
PAPER

www.ingramcontent.com/pod-product-compliance
Lightning Source LLC
LaVergne TN
LVHW080102160726
843469LV00047B/1879